THE FAILURE
OF SUCCESS

BOOKS BY ALFRED J. MARROW

edited by
ALFRED J. MARROW

THE FAILURE
OF SUCCESS

A DIVISION OF AMERICAN MANAGEMENT ASSOCIATION

Once again to Monette,
and now to Paul and Naomi

DESIGNED BY SCOTT CHELIUS

International standard book number: 0-8144-5305-8
Library of Congress catalog card number: 72-78300
Second Printing

For the Puzzled Executive

A BRIEFING

Every citizen is aware of the failure of public and private institutions alike to meet the needs of the people they deal with—employees, customers, clients, the public. The complaints voiced are constant, pervasive, and increasingly strident:

Cars, tires, TV sets, and other products are shoddy and often defective when delivered; workmanship is sloppy; repairmen are rude; managers are arrogant; workers are apathetic; service is poor. Similar deterioration of quality is reported in medical care, education, transportation, and public utilities.

These criticisms hit home. Puzzled policy makers know that quality is declining and costs are mounting. The present level of production in American organizations, particularly among the forty million workers in the service industries, is estimated by authorities as only 50 percent of the potential available from existing human skills, initiative, and energy. If just a part of the missing potential could be recovered, the effect on costs and profits would be enormous. But how can it be done?

Executives are now considering whether there are better ways to enlist the energies of employees so that each man works for the success of the organization and does not merely aim to do as little as necessary to hold his job. What kind of management system will help establish a climate in which performance of all employees is high; where costs, absences, and turnover are low; where quality is everyone's concern; and where all people in the organization respect and trust each other?

Thoughtful administrators recognize that their management methods are essentially the same as they were generations back. Now they are inquiring about the brand-new concepts and methods the behavioral scientists have been advocating. They are asking: How dependable is the new knowledge? Does it really help us understand what makes us act the way we do? Where has it been applied? How do we proceed? Where do we look for guidance?

Discovery by discovery, new scientific research provides promising answers. But little of this new knowledge is being applied. The problem is the twenty-five-year lag between discovery of new evidence and its general application. This gap has occurred because the present generation of executives has been unwilling to replace dying managerial traditions and to start learning a new system. They still prefer to play it safe by asking for more data and for further corroboration. Even when the evidence from additional research confirms the earlier findings, general acceptance continues to be reluctant and slow.

But rapidly changing conditions and expanding scientific research are now compelling them to get under way. There are now enough case studies, gathered together here for the first time, to provide empirical evidence of how the use of these new methods can improve performance, increase satisfaction, and narrow the gap between an organization's potential and its performance. The individual subjects treated range from how to pick the right man for the right job to new strategies for motivating employees; from the practice of organization development to the effects of organizational stress on coronary heart disease.

The data is here. It has been tested in leading organizations. If other companies will make use of this new knowledge, it will ease many of the painful stresses and strains created by the unprecedented complexity of our changing society.

Ideally readers will be interested equally in all the subjects; realistically they are likely to find some chapters more relevant than others to their immediate problems. It will serve the reader best if he dips into this book a couple of chapters at a time, not necessarily in the printed order.

ALFRED J. MARROW

contents

part one

Organizations and the Quality of Life

A Few Words in Advance

Not long ago a national magazine took note in a cover story of the increasing affliction of our municipal, business, governmental, educational, and health organizations by dry rot, rigidity, clumsiness, and ineffectiveness. The story reported that shiny packages often hide product defects, and that the low quality of many of the services offered in America fills customers with tension and frustration.

Many people, of course, have been aware of these unhappy developments for a long time. But now, more than in the past, the problems seem to be getting beyond the control of not only consumers but of even the participants in business organizations themselves. The pollution of our society by poor-quality products and services is lamented by the producers, denounced by the consumers, condemned by the politicians, carefully documented by the bureaucrats, and increasingly screamed at by the young. We seem well along on a course that could lead to the eventual collapse of many of our institutions.

What is causing so many of our society's organizations to malfunction so flagrantly? The behavioral scientists and practitioners who have contributed to this volume focus on several of the forces at work.

For one thing, we have designed organizations which have ignored individual potential for competence, responsibility, constructive intent, and productivity. We have created structures and jobs that at the lower levels alienate and frustrate the workers; lead them to reject responsible behavior, not only with impunity but with a sense of justice; and tempt them to fight the organization by lowering the quality of what they produce. Products and services thus become tangible expressions of the low quality of life within organizations.

Problems are equally severe at management levels, where incompetent organizational structures create executive environments lacking in trust, openness, and risk taking. The attitudes that flourish best in such environments are conformity and defensiveness, which often find expression in an organizational tendency to produce detailed information for unimportant problems and invalid information for important ones. This tendency ensures ineffective problem solving, poor decision making, and weak commitment to the decisions made.

None of this is new. And the effects are so pervasive that people throughout the world are beginning to believe that organizational entropy is natural and basic to organizational life. Herein lies the danger. It is sad enough to document organizational decay; it is tragic to see it accepted as natural and inevitable. Such acceptance makes organizational decay a self-perpetuating process which reinforces the alienation of employees, the frustration of consumers, the anger of bureaucrats, the outrage of youth. How can there not be a sense of helplessness all around?

Clearly, traditional managerial practice is a source of pessimism. It has produced a set of monumental problems that need to be tackled quickly at many levels, with the realization that every successful individual solution, no matter how small, helps.

Behavioral science research and practice provide the most hopeful alternative. The exciting conclusion that grows out of behavioral science research (whether carried out under laboratory conditions or based primarily on experience) is that *organizations can be made more humane and, at the same time, more effective.* It is possible to design organizational systems where individual participants can give of themselves—and not give themselves up.

This does not mean that there are no basic conflicts between the individual and the organization. There are, and probably will continue to be. But there can be new organizational structures, heightened competence in interpersonal relations among the managers, and increased group effectiveness. Instead of being stymied and frustrated by the basic organizational conflicts, the participants can gain a new sense of them as challenges which are to be overcome.

Examining the case studies in this book, I detect five major themes which, together and singly, hold out hope that the trend toward organizational decay can be reversed.

1. *There is increasing emphasis on designing and managing organizations more in congruence with the way serious research shows man to be.* The behavioral scientist's view of man is concerned not only with what he is, but with what he might be. Ways are being found to deal with such difficult subjective variables as satisfaction and happiness, commitment, responsibility, and effective relationships. These are variables that people participating in organizations rarely discuss with outsiders—except, sometimes, to report about how organizations try to snuff them out.

It now appears that assumptions about human beings and organizations, no matter what they are, become self-fulfilling prophecies in the minds and hands of managements.

2. *Research results increasingly question some basic managerial assumptions embodied in the pyramidal structure and in traditional administrative controls.* These include the unilateral use of power; the assumption that power is finite; the belief that subordinates can never be asked to select their superiors; the generalization, sacred to engineers and economists, that the simplest work is necessarily the most efficient. All are being actively and seriously reexamined.

To a surprising extent, organizations can benefit by freeing their participants to design their own world of work. By no means will all the choices inevitably be in the direction of satisfying immediate personal needs. Employees at all levels are able to recognize the necessity of organizational health. And they will aspire toward it. Employees see that some frustration of individual needs is inevitable; under certain conditions they will agree it is necessary and legitimate. Suppression of needs can win endorsement at all organizational levels when there is a gain in terms of other goals the institution and society have—*and* when individuals can influence the choice of what, and how much, will be frustrated.

3. *Behavioral scientists are becoming more assertive at the same time that they are becoming less authoritarian and manipulative.* It is hard to be a member of an organization and still honestly provide the service of continually questioning the organization's basic assumptions and values about the management of human resources. It is not uncommon for the management to view the professional behavioral scientist with some suspicion. Executives are apt to be concerned that he is striving to make the organization "soft" on people. It is also not uncommon for managers—even those who view themselves as being "strong"—to resist confronting this friction openly. A typical course is to withdraw emotional and financial support from programs that are telling them things they don't want to hear. In time, the professional may find himself exiled from the major arenas of organizational activity.

The behavioral scientists represented in this book seem to be escaping that fate. Many of them seem to have won the trust of top management without compromising their ability to challenge commonly accepted values and policies. Others, whose contacts appear to be less with top managers and more with middle- and lower-level people, are not only confronting accepted patterns—they seem to be producing some of the most rigorous knowledge about organizational behavior yet available.

4. *Behavioral scientists are worrying less about whether their activities invariably stay within the traditional confines of "rigorous" research.* Some of the professionals writing here have long-established reputations for conducting only studies whose designs would meet the expectations of their academic brethren. Lately, though, some researchers have come to realize that the only "rigor" worth pursuing is the capacity to obtain valid information that is relevant to basic problems of the organization.

The traditional path of scientific rigor has been to study those variables that can be easily measured and publicly verified. Research is so designed that, at any given period of time, it is as elegant and tight as possible. It is executed with as little tinkering as possible with the original premises.

The result, in my opinion, has been too much narrowing of the questions that could be explored and, consequently, too little relevance to real problems in the results. The lack of relevance does not arise because there was no attempt to be rigorous. On the contrary, it comes because rigor was carried to the point where the potential users found little help from the data obtained. Rigorous research procedures require control over the range of responses the subject produces. This control may assure the researcher that he is getting what he wants. It may also frustrate the subject, because he sees part of his response spectrum ignored. Even if he responds accurately within the terms of the study, he may well distrust the results.

I sense that behavioral scientists are now seeking to avoid the production of elegant but sterile studies by involving their human subjects more in the design, monitoring, and execution of the research. There are several chapters in which the professionals state that they are now more willing to sacrifice precise measurements in order to confront basic questions. What they lose, it seems to me, is more than made up. Instead of one elegant design—which, once put into play, is compulsively completed even if questions arise about the data being obtained—several less elegant designs are created. Each of these is more modest in its goals. The designs allow for early feedback of data. They continually request the subjects (and users) to examine the data and to voice any objections or feelings of disbelief they may have. This feedback is taken seriously, and new studies are designed.

It may be that these new procedures, in the long run, will produce information that is more useful to the clients. If so, we may wind up with clients who value behavioral science research highly. This, in turn, could create a deeper commitment toward such research. Such commitment on the part of the client, I believe, would do more to facilitate the collection of valid information than would the development of any new experimental design, questionnaire, or analytical scheme.

Basic research has tended to yield knowledge that merely explains. Applied research of the kind described in this book includes explanatory knowledge; but it goes beyond that in seeking knowledge for action.

5. *Clients now function as paraprofessionals—not only helping to design the research but actually executing it.* One example, among several, in this book is the use of line executives as professional evaluators in assessment programs. The managers find the experience a meaningful one, full of learning for themselves. And, they seem to collect data as valid as those collected by professionals.

Organizations require the cooperative efforts of many people. In order to gain cooperation, we design authority and control systems that make subordinates dependent upon superiors. We also work out competitive systems so that the superiors can play one subordinate against the other—or, even more insidiously, we teach men to compete with each other while their superiors talk of cooperation. All these designs, of course, work against the human being's orientation toward growth—personal and organizational—and point him, instead, toward closed-mindedness and stagnation. These are designs for dry rot.

The problems of integrating individual needs and capacities with organizational requirements is still a major problem in organizations. Organizations tend to be designed to minimize ambiguity wherever possible. This limits the potential for challenging new experiences. If the reward and penalty systems emphasize punishment of mistakes, then the people who prefer the new will suppress this quality and strive themselves to reduce ambiguity by staying within well-traveled pathways.

People have the capacity to go either way—toward growth or toward stagnation. The design of the system in which they work can significantly influence which way they go, and how far. The more they slide toward stagnation, the higher the probability of developing organizational illness. And, in general, the more they orient themselves toward growth, the better for organizational health. Beyond a certain point, however, frustration may set in, because there must be limits to how much growth orientation a system can permit and encourage.

We are beginning to learn from employees at all levels something that should have been obvious from examining our own lives: Human beings understand that it is legitimate to have their growth toward personal goals blunted in order to create and maintain organizations. They can be trusted to participate actively in the decision to determine at what point they cannot have new challenges. You may say that one characteristic of a person who knows he is free and autonomous is an ability to define and accept limitations of his growth and the growth of others.

For the near future, at least, the job of the behavioral scientist in organizations in the United States and elsewhere will be to develop and distill the themes that recur in these pages. This book lets you hear those themes as clearly as they are now being heard in certain advanced areas of American industry. You can be sure that they will soon reverberate almost everywhere that human beings form themselves into organizations.

The Failure of Success

The hero of Eugene O'Neill's play *Marco's Millions* cannot understand why there should be discontent and unrest in his land. After all, he cries, "I have passed a law that everyone should be happy."

> *There is the tragedy of the man who works hard all his life for something and then doesn't get it. There is the even more bitter tragedy of the man who gets what he wants and then finds it empty.*
> HENRY KISSINGER

This book is about good things and bad things happening in a country that was the first in the world to incorporate the word "happiness" in its basic founding documents. It is about discontent and unrest there. It tells something about a country which has succeeded beyond its wildest dreams—but whose success is seriously flawed. It is about American industry—personal industriousness as well as corporate ventures. It is about how American industry, in both senses, has reached a turning point. It is about what we may expect to encounter in the future if we are executives, workers, investors, and members of working families.

This is *not* one of those pessimistic, dispirited books about the gloomy state of American business organizations. This is a hopeful book, even an optimistic book, because it contains a wealth of ideas for finding solutions to some of our most urgent problems, and it provides many enlightening glimpses into the future.

Our focus is on people. Perhaps predictably, because I am a professional psychologist, I do not really see simply a political solution for the troubles that confront us. Nor an economic one. Nor a legal one. What I see, of course, is a psychological one that embraces, in a disciplined way, all the others. There may be political, economic, or legal solutions to the clashes between individuals or groups in organization systems, but if there are, those professions have yet to come up with them. I submit that the time has arrived to give profound consideration to what behavioral scientists are finding out about how individuals and groups perform best.

The chapters of this book are selected to illustrate a point: Management methods based on sound psychological principles have provided workable answers for American industry in the still-too-rare instances where they have been used with commitment and seriousness. These methods have repaired organizations that were in the process of collapse; they have effectively strengthened organizations in which farsighted men decided to commit themselves to new methods as a matter of prudence and planning. The behavioral science applications which will concern us in this book have actually been used to modify or completely change traditional management practices of business organizations into ones that operated much better. The methods are not short-term, first-aid gimmicks. They are not matters of merely changing a few tactics in sputtering organizations. They are long-term, deep-reaching, strategic changes in the way organizations deal with the critical matter of work and the people who do it. These methods are based on hard-gotten hard-tested behavioral science facts collected by trained psychologists and concerned businessmen who had a great deal at stake. Therefore, dismiss the notion that what we will get into here is speculative or softheaded or neglectful of the essentials of making businesses and organizations prosper. This is not weak medicine.

In each case we will examine the methods that were devised in order to improve a system that was failing because it was geared to outmoded practices. In most cases, the management system that was failing was based on authoritarian principles and was oriented almost exclusively to getting out production, production, production. Concern by management with the role of the worker in achieving that production was at best misguided. The time had already arrived when the workers were demonstrating the importance of their roles in ways that hurt production and profits.

Although many managers continue to regard psychologists with all the trust and confidence that Wells Fargo reserved for Jesse James, there are some who realize that firms operating under conventional management systems are barely clanking along. The realistic-minded companies that have seen the decline in performance have searched to find some better way.

One remedy for the malady that afflicts so much of industry today was found in the development of new, humanized management systems whose concern for people equaled the concern for production. The few enlightened companies who had the emotional commitment to change to this fundamentally different system found their success in higher production and improved profits. Their use of organizational development methods, job enrichment, team building, achievement motivation, sensitivity training, group incentives, and other techniques led to clear new potentials they had not even considered in the past.

These companies—the ones with a strong taste for survival and new success—are turning more and more toward psychological methods and the human approach to management. These include, among many others, A.T.&T., Detroit Edison, Fieldcrest, General Electric Co., General Motors Corp., J. C. Penney, Sonesta (the Hotel Corporation of America), Standard Oil of New Jersey, and others. Not all of these corporations are fully committed to new methods on all levels. Several are finding out, however, that significant progress can be made through psychological methods, and top management is growing increasingly receptive to extending the procedures to other parts of the organization.

The poor quality of the services and products we get from so many companies surely suggests that there is something wrong somewhere. It may be because only a handful of companies are truly making use of the behavioral science knowledge available. Or it may be because it is not easy to switch over to a new managerial system that seriously concerns itself with the psychological needs and human problems of people in organizations. Finally, it may be because many executives are unaware of the inconsistency between their expressed attitudes and their actual behavior. There are many executives who pay lip service to the concept behind the humanistic methods we are discussing, but among them there is an abiding fear of innovations that involve sharing decisions and responsibility with underlings. And that is essentially what we are talking about: employee participation in problem solving and decision making. Hence the wide discrepancy between creed and deed.

The reasons for such deep-rooted resistance appear sensible enough. Most organization decision makers rose to the top through a management system that put a premium on authoritarian practices. Along with harshness and guile, it was the hard-nosed I-am-boss quality that proved effective in the early days of the Industrial Revolution; with modifications, much the same qualities were expected of executives through the business boom of World War II and for perhaps a decade thereafter. But it grew increasingly clear, sometime around the middle 1950s, that there was a dinosaur's curse on the old-fashioned Tyrannosaurus rex of the executive suite. These men and their ways left deep impressions on corporate practices; their powerful influences are still to be coped with. These men and their proteges are naturally uncomfortable with the "humanistic" changes recommended by organizational psychologists, who have shown that a system based on a scientific understanding of how and why humans work at their level best is a system that will outperform for industry.

Behavioral science terminology is currently in fashion, and many bosses employ the new vocabulary to describe their management practices. The jargon shows up in the annual report or at staff meetings.

But in the way they run the organizations, these men act as autocratically as they always did. Only the words have changed. Except that there are now implied promises broken, expectations disappointed, and new grounds for anger and apathy in the ranks. The anger shows up in the poor quality, avoidable mistakes, and acts of sabotage that cut into the profit and productivity of so many companies, large and small. The apathy shows up on the balance sheets, too, and it is communicated to the customers and clients in ways that erode product loyalty. The heads of some of the largest and most influential corporations, some of whom are themselves guilty of playing games with the psychological vacabulary, say privately that the causes of restlessness, carelessness, vindictiveness, and hatred on the part of the employee toward his company must soon be eased if the prices of "made in U.S.A." products are to remain competitive in domestic and world markets. The popularity of the catchphrases "blue collar blues" and the "tight white collar" express the feeling of the present generation of workers toward their jobs.

Disruption of production by blue collar employees is a strategy more and more frequently being used to offset the feeling of powerlessness that the workers deeply resent. In the most highly automated plant in the auto industry, output was restricted by young workers (average age twenty-four) who refused to increase production unless they had a greater say in how jobs should be performed. They were determined to alter the dehumanizing aspects of their jobs. A worker spokesman said, "The robots are in revolt. The company has to do something to change the drudgery of assembly-line work or face further disruption. A guy can't do the same simple thing eight hours a day year after year. There must be an end to the dull monotonous jobs that destroy the satisfactions that work can yield. It's going to take something somewhere to change things to where a guy can take an interest in his job."

A significant step in that direction is already being taken at the Volvo and Saab auto plants in Sweden, where the traditional assembly line is being replaced with teams of four blue collar employees who will put together the entire engine. The company's aim is to reduce worker discontent caused by the back-breaking drudgery of the present system.

We must all know by now that productivity gains in the United States have been slowing for several years. From 1965 to 1970, the average annual increase in manufacturing output per man-hour in the major non-Communist nations was as follows: Japan, 14.2 percent; Netherlands, 8.5 percent; France, 6.6 percent; West Germany, 5.3 percent; Italy, 5.1 percent; United Kingdom, 3.6 percent. And where was the United States? At the very bottom of the list with an annual average increase of only 1.9 percent. In the auto industry, compensation jumped 43 percent over a five-year period and productivity accelerated only 13 percent. These figures tell much of the story of what is wrong with the American econ-

omy. They may also say something about the mood of the people working not only in business but in other organizations as well. It also says
something about the reasons why the chairman of General Motors stated,
"Every problem we have gets back to a people problem."

Our nation is in a period of transition. At such times there is always
discontent and confusion. Bewildered leaders feel they are subjects of
change rather than its master. Clearly there are monumental changes
taking place, and since it seems true enough that the business of our
nation is business, some of the most profound changes are taking place
in American organizations. This is why:

There are currently more than 80 million people at work in this country and the number is expected to reach 100 million within a decade.
Most of these people were taught to feel that there is great value and
goodness in work—aside from the fact that it pays the money that pays
the bills. Most of these people spend almost half their waking hours
at work. Think about that while you also consider the claim made by
so many people that satisfaction and performance on most jobs, both
public and private, have declined alarmingly.

Consider New York. It is a city paralyzed all too regularly by near-dis-
asters. Strikes of sanitation workers stop garbage and trash collection
and the city almost chokes in its own waste. Subways, buses, and taxis
halt because of labor trouble. Teachers walk out of their classrooms;
postmen stop delivering mail; hospital staffs abandon the sick; cemetery
workers refuse to bury the dead. They say New York is simply ungovern-
able because of the outmoded way it is managed. They are probably
right. Certainly not New York nor organizations of almost any size or
kind in the United States today can be run successfully under the systems
of yesterday. We all understand this in a visceral way and it makes
us ill at ease.

In 1962, a man named Frank Brugler, who was the controller of
Bethlehem Steel, made the following statement: "We're not in business
to make steel; we're not in business to build ships; we're not in business
to erect buildings. We're in business to make money."

Only eight years later, President Edward Cole of General Motors
said that industrial organizations must consider it among their "major
priorities" to achieve "improvements in the quality of life and more
effective management and motivation of people."

Not long after that, B. R. Dorsey, the outspoken president of Gulf
Oil Company, wrote: "The first responsibility of business is to operate
for the well-being of society."

The drastic change in rhetoric may, and I repeat *may*, reflect some
deep change in the executive point of view. But many executives who
speak about "business" and "responsibility to society" in the same breath
are merely offering their considered forecast of the years ahead. They
themselves are fearful of innovation and leery of tampering with the

traditional system that they know and have mastered so well, even though they can see clearly that employees resist many long-accepted practices, performance is inconstant, and complaints are increasingly strident.

Executives with unclouded vision can see how profoundly the social and technological changes of the 1960s have transformed our society. Indeed almost any open-minded business leader can see that, unless something is done, corporations large and small will be torn by the same sort of conflicts that have already erupted elsewhere. More and more stockholder meetings will be interrupted by angry investors who were rarely considered before. Boycotts of products based on social and political considerations will become commonplace. "Trusted" employees will leak out confidential information to the press or to government agencies to expose the company to charges of misrepresentation or fraud. False advertising will result in the setting up of picket lines that will be frighteningly effective in cutting sales. Plants polluting the water and air will be attacked in the courts. An army of Ralph Naders will march through the company's records bringing damaging shreds of information into the glare of well-organized consumer attention. To some executives this vision is a terrible nightmare. To others—the ones whose survival instinct is strong—it is a warning that the wheels of real management change must start grinding in a twentieth-century hurry.

"The Social Seventies," as they are called, may be remembered as the years when solving social problems became the paramount responsibility not of the impractical theorists and do-gooders, but of the tough-minded heads of business organizations. A few large companies already have taken strong positions in such fields as fair employment practices, the training of the hard-core unemployed, and pollution control. The practical executive recognizes that he now faces a new dilemma: Social responsibility may be good for society, but may not always be good for profits.

B. R. Dorsey of Gulf Oil found that out when he declared at a stockholders' meeting that the traditional business objective of "maximum financial gain" had moved into "second place whenever it conflicts with the well-being of society." A stockholder rose from the audience and cried, "Not with my money you don't!"

Of course business as we know it today cannot survive if it does not earn a profit. Where, then, is the line between responsibility to society and responsibility to stockholders? Nobody knows. But for businessmen even to recognize this problem marks a major departure from the kind of thinking that dominated industrial policy making in the past.

What most executives seem to miss about the whole issue of helping society versus paying dividends—and a point I hope will be made clear in this book—is that *business can best begin discharging its social re-*

sponsibility by humanizing its management practices. The company that acts on this insight and begins to operate on participatory forms of management is more likely to remain highly competitive. For it is only through a radical change to democratic governance that lower costs and higher performance can be achieved. It is this concern for its people that is the most direct social responsibility of business, yet it is the one most business leaders tend to overlook.

There is little need to list all the troubles that have recently flowed from the old-fashioned concept that a man's work can be separated from a man's life. Anguished stories appear, often on the front pages and the financial sections of the newspapers: On the automobile assembly line in Detroit (and elsewhere) as many as 20 percent of employees fail to show up on Fridays. Production is constantly disrupted. Turnover is high and quality is low. The cost in wasted time and lowered productivity is staggering. In addition, there is a tremendous and growing amount of sabotage of products by companies' own workers. Windshields are cracked, upholstery is slashed, coke bottles are dropped in the gas tank. This is matched only by the floods of negative, antibuying feelings so many company employees engender in the paying customers. It all builds upon itself. Feelings of carelessness, restlessness, anger, and hatred creep out of the factories and shops and office buildings and into the streets and the homes of America. They color the American mood. They transform the "can do" exuberance that characterized American industry and life in World War II, and for much of a generation beyond, into the "who cares?" cheerlessness about work and life that we now seem to encounter from coast to coast.

There is no doubt that the business climate directly and forcefully affects our social climate. How could it not, when we are a nation so absorbed with work that their jobs are largely the essence of people's lives? When the work is boring, monotonous, and constricting, and the boss dictatorial and insensitive, deplorable psychological effects are produced. The entire society is infected.

It is clear that there are systems with humanistic values that are superior to the conventional rigid managerial hierarchy operating in most organizations today. The malaise signaled by low output, poor quality, waste of materials, theft, and wildcat strikes cannot be cured by cracking down hard in the classic authoritarian ways. In the short run these may work. But in the long run this kind of response has proved a failure. Grudging employees have an uncanny ability to outwit every control device thus far invented. In many cases, the more sophisticated the devices for checking inventory or maintaining quality control, the more they seem to challenge employees to outwit them. These people do not wish the company well.

If it is obvious that the aggressive, frustrated, vengeful, and antisocial feelings an employee (on whatever corporate level) develops on the job are carried outside the plant gate or down the elevator from the skyscraper and into the street and home, it should also be obvious that the feelings of usefulness, participation, and worth developed in the work environment are carried outside. A company that is unconcerned with the human aspects of managing its workers is exhibiting equal unconcern about its responsibility to society, and is doing so in a way that will sooner than later cost it great sums of money to repair the damage, if the damage can be repaired. Organizations are in a position to improve and enrich directly the quality of life for people who work for them and for their families. This cannot but benefit society. This is the most direct social responsibility of business—yet it is the one business tends most to overlook.

There are good historic reasons why management remains shortsighted about new discoveries into the nature of work. Throughout the history of the Industrial Revolution, the crucial job of managing production (as opposed to inventing things or processes or putting up the capital and financing) was regarded as primarily technical. The men who knew best how to run and care for the machines were put in charge of the machines—and in charge of the workers who operated them. As technology grew more complex in the early and middle twentieth century, the skills required to manage the operation of an organization became increasingly specialized. Complex functions were divided among a variety of technical specialists: the systems analysts, the industrial engineers, the computer programmers. These men and women were fine at analysis, engineering, and programming—but were they skilled at managing people? Generally not.

The same man who could program a computer to pay everybody on time and simultaneously keep track of the entire inventory has had a terrible time managing his subordinates. The industrial engineer who could design a balanced production line and anticipate bottlenecks could be the cause of slowdowns and walkouts. For neither man had received any training in how to develop and carry through a program to lift morale, resolve conflict, introduce change, build trust, or improve organization performance. Consequently a huge number of people with no talent or no training in how to manage have succeeded in getting themselves ensconced in the position of "boss." Their only preparation was the traditional notion that a boss was supposed to boss, and the ones he bossed were supposed to do his bidding.

The manager-owners of enterprises in the period when labor was cheap and easy to get often ruled with unfeeling harshness. The Crash of 1929 and the disastrous Depression that followed were commonly held to have been caused by the rampant greed, dishonesty, and gross irresponsibility of business leaders. The assembly lines of the 1920s, whose inhumanities were so memorably satirized in Charlie Chaplin's

Modern Times, gave way to the breadlines of the 1930s. Businessmen found themselves operating in a world of distrust and hostility. Public disillusionment led to an avalanche of federal legislation that set up scores of regulatory agencies. This had a stunning impact on the way business could be done. The social and economic leadership long held by the "captains of industry" passed in large measure to the government agencies.

The "miracles of production" during World War II regained for the businessman some new respect and a degree of public confidence. But otherwise his image has remained much as it was after the Crash. You can still read on the front page of *The Wall Street Journal* (June 11, 1970) about the president of one of America's major airlines, who was described as a man who "unmercifully chews out underlings with one of the foulest vocabularies in any executive suite. . . . He absent-mindedly drops cigarette ashes on the floor while shouting obscenities at one subordinate or another . . . he rules with an iron hand, and his philosophy is simple: use the hell out of them."

Such men and women are not rare. They are found at every level of American organizational life from first-line foreman to president. They cannot distinguish between being in authority and being authoritarian. Even if there were an easy technique for making such bosses more sensitive to the devastation they create inside their companies, there would still be no easy way to heal the damage. When initiative is stifled often enough it hesitates to raise its head again. When staffs are kept dependent for many years, it is tremendously difficult to wean them. Intimidated people are shy of responsibility; it seems much too risky and threatening.

The problem for most authoritarian executives is that moves toward participation tend to redistribute some of their power to others throughout the organization. Since authoritarians like to hold tight to all the power they can, and because they have a great fear of innovation, they strongly resist change. It is only when the executive and his company are faced with overwhelming personal or organizational crises that the authoritarian takes a chance on the new way of doing things.

Autocratically managed organizations have survived and prospered until now primarily because high costs could be passed on to consumers in the form of higher prices, and automation made it possible to offset some of the excess costs resulting from low employee performance. But both employees and consumers, who are by and large the same, are growing increasingly resistant and antagonistic.

Though the opposition to major changes in management practices by most leaders of our technology-dominated society remains exceedingly strong, here and there initial steps are being taken. The tempo of change is certain to increase. The authoritarian system of management must be supplanted by the new logic of participative democracy. The retirement of the outdated authoritarian system is inevitable.

More and more the practical question is heard: "What do employees want?" For one thing, they want fewer restrictive rules. They also want less pressure, less bossing, more candor, and fewer mind-numbing jobs. They want considerably more responsibility and a real piece of the action. And they want the right to question authority. They regard being able to earn a living generally assured; what they seek is a fuller and more satisfying quality of life. The human-potential movement, encounter groups, and experiential seminars have taken hold in many business organizations. The mass media and the education system have taught employees the importance of self-realization at work as part of living.

Thus today's employees are more inner-directed and less satisfied with material things alone. With some of the same passion their forebears brought to the quest for good and steady wages, they seek self-esteem. The self-esteem they seek can be built only if their job asks for judgment and imagination. They are decidedly not like the immigrants who worked in the mines or the sweatshops in the early years of this century. They may be sons and grandsons of that earlier generation of blue collar workers, but they differ passionately with their elders about management's right to design jobs that bring in maximum profits irrespective of the cost to the workers' physical and emotional health. The present generation is not willing to pay the crushing price of filth, noise, mind-killing monotony, dehumanization, and stress diseases in return for wages. They know from research studies reported in *Fortune* and *Reader's Digest* that emotional factors are primarily responsible for the appalling toll from coronary heart disease and that "to a great extent the problem is the job." They answer charges that they goof-off and are indifferent to quality by pointing out that the way jobs are structured kills alertness and pride of craftsmanship.

Research studies indicate that psychic satiation results from the unending repetition of small tasks. Typical of the fuming dislike toward the excessively programmed job is this quote from a worker in a radio assembly plant: "I hate my job. All I can do to keep from going crazy is to daydream, to forget how I'm wasting my years. The manager gave me an official manual. It told me what to do with my right hand and my left hand, what time to take breaks, when to start, when to stop. It was demoralizing."

This feeling of being turned into a robot, of standing powerless before the screaming automatic system, leads at first to inner resentment and then to outer rebellion. A person with no power to change the drudgery and the dehumanized monotony of his job finds psychic withdrawal the only temporary escape against his growing fury. He does as little as he can get away with, and then joins his friends to find relief in excessive use of alcohol and drugs.

This kind of employee is not only expensive in terms of lowered productivity and profits—he is a potential saboteur whose silent acceptance of monotony hides volcanic feelings of bitterness at his helplessness. In the years ahead, if American industry does not recognize and deal clearheadedly with the problem, such men and women may act in concert against employers in a way students did against the unresponsive administrations of so many colleges and universities. The reasons people will give for their destructive behavior will sound wildly inappropriate to the tremendous damage they will cause. We have grown able now to understand demands for higher wages and shorter hours. Will we be able to understand demands that rise out of revolt against depersonalization, from the promptings of personal conscience, shattered ambition, and deadly monotony?

The sharing of power is what is at stake now. The tradition that power is finite and belongs on top is under attack not only in business, but in all spheres of contemporary life: the community, the church, the armed forces, the schools. These organizations have one thing in common: they have all been managed in the past by authoritarian leaders. Almost all such organizations are now coming to the end of their traditional governance procedures.

The millions of students of today—with larger than ever numbers being college educated—will be the employees of tomorrow. Sensible business executives realize that these young people are a different breed. They will not ask to be—they will *insist* on being—party to the decision-making process. They will press for genuine authority and autonomy. They will want challenges that seem beyond their capability in order to show what they can do. They will pick up and leave an employer who denies them opportunities for self-management or for building feelings of self-worth. Already more than 50 percent of all college graduates recruited at considerable cost on the campuses and trained at a higher cost still, leave their first employers within five years. On low-skill jobs in many industries it often takes as many as ten trainees to gain one steady employee. Many complain that the companies that recruited them with bright promises have built-in controls that stifle both self-reliance and initiative.

A good part of the answer, as I and my colleagues and friends who have prepared this book see it, is offered by management practices concerned with reducing the discontent rooted in boredom and loss of pride in workmanship. Such systems, when implemented thoughtfully and scientifically, blend corporate objectives and individual goals. They provide able people with a sense of involvement by showing them that their intelligence and responsibility are truly valued. An atmosphere of trust and mutual respect gives them the freedom to openly discuss problems that trouble both them and their company.

There are managers who mistake participation for permissiveness in the most pejorative and costly sense of that word. Time after time we will demonstrate that the two things are *not* the same. On the contrary, where there is true participation the abuses of permissiveness tend to disappear in the resulting mood of goodwill that suffuses a company from the top executive staff down to the machine operators on the shop floor. It is this spirit of team effort that must be instilled in industry. Then perhaps the constructive mood of cooperation will be carried by workers into the rest of our uneasy society. To accomplish this is the greatest challenge there is to the resourcefulness and foresight of management today.

Obviously, the redistribution of power has its costs, and these must be paid in coins of time, authority, and prerogative. But for American industry the rewards will be renewed pride, productivity, and strength.

Imaginative New Ways to Create Satisfying Jobs

America's factory workers have a message for any manufacturer who will listen: they can do more, and do it better, and contribute a flood of valuable ideas, if management will take steps to create the proper, stimulating kind of work setting. The workers know more about their jobs than anyone else—they spend forty hours a week doing nothing else—and most of their suggestions for improving methods are practical. The first requirement for unlocking this stock of energy, this rich source of ideas, is to make contact. First comes listening. Not talking, but listening. Listening to the workers tell what is wrong about their jobs, and listening to their ideas on how they can be made right.

Increasingly executives are turning serious attention to the problem of making jobs better, and they are investing growing quantities of time and money in job improvements. This reflects a gradual awakening of American businessmen to some central truths about this half century. Authoritarianism is on the decline. At the same time, a participative order is rising. The first response has taken place at the universities, the focus of youth in both its discontents and its aspirations. But a limited number of prescient industrial executives had already anticipated the change, some out of social concern, some out of sheer business sense.

These executives have now firmly established programs aimed at realizing the full potential of their production workers. They have carried out the ultimate executive function: to foresee, and then to move to resolve the consequences of what is foreseen. In so doing, they have boldly explored unfamiliar territory that many other executives will soon be forced to map out themselves.

Their explorations have not been without hazards. Some paths that seemed valid proved to lead nowhere, or even into trouble; fresh routes were hacked through administrative undergrowth, many of them only to be abandoned, at high cost in energy and money.

20

But some of the investigations have been rewarding in the extreme. These have led to startlingly higher production, better quality, greater profits, and lower turnover and absenteeism. They have also revealed that although significant improvements can be made in almost any kind of industrial job, the new concepts are more readily accepted by younger, smaller companies. This is because such firms are usually less encrusted by tradition and thus less hostile to new ways of doing things. Often the sheer scale of the productive process in big corporations limits their maneuverability.

Another reward to concerned managements that have acted to alter the workers' outlook has been the change in climate. No one pretends that in even the most enlightened factory the situation has become idyllic, that work has become play. But in some plants there is now a discernible mutuality of interest between management and the working force that results in a warmer atmosphere, an air of trust, so that workers who in the past might have spoken sullenly about what "they" want, now talk enthusiastically about what "we" are doing.

The industrial and social problems that led some farsighted executives to make changes are easy enough to see now—using hindsight. There was the obvious difficulty of getting and keeping good people in a competitive labor market. There was the equally obvious need to maintain production and markets against intensifying domestic and foreign competition. And, of course, profits had to be maintained despite the cost-price squeeze.

On the social side, the self-esteem of blue collar workers was diminishing rapidly, as a Department of Labor report to President Nixon recognized in devastating detail. More and more workers felt they were in dead-end positions, and many of them figuratively died at their work. Interest in doing the job well for its own sake, the old craft attitude, was vanishing, and consumer discontent over shoddy workmanship intensified. Both attendance and attention were becoming erratic; absenteeism reached new heights. Unions kept up the pressure to organize companies that had no contracts, stressing the advantages they could offer, and thus heightening awareness of discontent.

Beyond those specifics, and gradually coming to overshadow them in some areas of industry, was the increasing hostility of youth to the old authoritarian ways of running things. The challenge was acknowledged by some at least a decade ago, but increasingly that challenge became a strident demand. What's more, the challenge was posed by young persons entering the workforce in greater numbers, with more education, higher aspirations, and less willingness to accept old strictures. Youth has served as catalyst to climatic changes that would otherwise come more gradually.

While these realities keep many executives awake at night, those who had anticipated the growth of tensions and had moved to resolve them before they caused explosions were hearing comments like these from employees:

I'm doing a better job. I just like this place so much, I think it's wonderful. I've never worked in a place where we've had so much closeness with supervisors. RUTH MOULTON
ASSEMBLER, CORNING GLASS WORKS, MEDFIELD, MASSACHUSETTS

We work as teams, decide on our own goals—we're really involved in making the decisions. If everyone doesn't work, we can't make it, so we have a meeting and talk it over. JOHN MEYER
SHAPE CUTTER, DONNELLY MIRRORS, INC., HOLLAND, MICHIGAN

Now all the inspection is not left to the inspector. We all watch out for each other's defects. If one girl has machine trouble, other girls jump up and help her. It's wonderful to help each other.
MAE DARBY
MACHINE OPERATOR, R. G. BARRY CORP., COLUMBUS, OHIO

You don't have anyone hovering over you. We can make decisions. Now there's more responsibility on the individual. SHIRLEY MC CULLOUGH
WAX ASSEMBLER, PRECISION CASTPARTS CORP., PORTLAND, OREGON

It's a terrific place to work, you have freedom, you're on your own, you make it or not. Other places I've worked were controlled: "You don't leave that chair." Here, things are wide open for advancement.
RONALD WEINBERG
ASSEMBLER PROMOTED TO DRAFTSMAN, NON-LINEAR SYSTEMS, INC.,
DEL MAR, CALIFORNIA

It's a heck of a company—you're treated as a human being, you're made to feel a part of everything. Polaroid doesn't dog you. The responsibility they give you is just great. There are big opportunities to move up. MARTIN DEERAN
MACHINE OPERATOR PROMOTED TO PERSONNEL DEPARTMENT,
POLAROID CORP., CAMBRIDGE, MASSACHUSETTS

These words, from interviews by *Fortune* magazine reporters, provide an abundance of clues to solving the malaise affecting production workers across the country. There are several approaches to the problem, an apparently limitless number of charts and graphs, and countless words dealing with it. The solutions, however, have one common denominator: they treat workers as intelligent, distinguishable persons who can and will give everything they've got to a job if it is properly appreciated.

It seems genuinely applicable in the case of American workers that, if you assume they are slovenly sluggards who will work only when pressed by supervisors, that's what you'll get. If, however, you assume they can take pride in their work, get real satisfaction from it, and become personally involved in perfecting it, then this too may come to pass. Academicians and behavioral scientists would dispute this reductive view as oversimplified. But it is the common assumption that lies beneath the work of Rensis Likert, Frederick Herzberg, Chris Argyris, the late A. H. Maslow, Douglas McGregor, and other ranking prophets of work satisfaction.

The approaches differ from company to company, depending on the kind of product and on management's specific problems, as well as on which school of behaviorism is followed. The R. G. Barry Corp. in Columbus, Ohio, adopted the team concept when the firm's young president, Gordon Zacks, felt compelled to make changes in order to expand and to meet growing competition to his leisure-footwear business. Zacks relied on one of the country's longest established psychologists, Professor Rensis Likert of the University of Michigan, for guidance in restructuring his company. Corning Glass made rewarding changes at its Medfield, Massachusetts, plant at the urging of the firm's organizational psychologist, Michael Beer, who saw an opportunity to plant seeds of job enrichment that would take root elsewhere in the glass company. Edwin H. Land, president and board chairman of Polaroid, which has annual sales of $466 million, has been experimenting with different means of enhancing job satisfaction for years. His experiments have risen out of his eloquently expressed conviction that a central concern of a corporation should be to provide a worthwhile working life for each member of the company, allowing every employee to share in the responsibilities and the rewards.

Full-scale job enrichment for blue collar workers, with real commitment from management, is still comparatively rare in the United States. Experts who work full time on job enrichment and follow it closely can list only about forty companies doing important work, and their lists overlap. Most of the companies making noteworthy advances are small, or are small units of larger corporations. Almost all of them are nonunion. Apostles of job enrichment insist that dramatic improvements could be made anywhere, even in a steel mill or an automobile plant. The main difficulty, they say, is not the type of manufacturing but the inertia common to both management and labor in large organizations.

On the management side, the men who run plants for large corporations know that they will be moved fairly rapidly from one assignment to another, and they are reluctant to undertake long-term job-enrichment programs because such programs do not result in the immediate profit improvements they must show if they are to be promoted. The labor unions, for their part, tend to oppose job enrichment because they thrive on the present adversary system in dealing with management. Union spokesmen commonly denounce job enrichment as just another form of speedup inflicted on weary workers by harsh management. A few farsighted, usually younger, union leaders already favor job enrichment. However, as the contrast grows between the bitterness and indifference toward work on old-style production lines and the involved, concerned atmosphere in new-style plants, both reluctant managers and truculent union figures may have to revise their positions.

Job enrichment is a diffuse, open-ended kind of concept. It is more an attitude or a strategy than it is a definable entity. In fact there is no one term for it that is accepted by all the experts. But there are certain elements that characteristically appear wherever job enrichment is going on. Central, of course, is the basic idea of giving the worker more of a say about what he or she is doing, including more responsibility for establishing procedures, more responsibility for setting goals, and more responsibility for the excellence of the completed product. It can also mean, in appropriate kinds of plants, allowing the worker to carry assembly through several stages, sometimes even to completion and preliminary testing, rather than endlessly repeating just one small operation. Automobile assembly jobs offer dreary, repetitive, relentless work, and it is this dispiring monotony that managers seeking to enrich jobs strive to avoid.

Giving the worker more responsibility necessarily requires willingness on the part of management to delegate its authority and to accept decisions made by the workers. Diffusing authority does not mean managerial abdication; it simply means that decisions can be made by the persons most involved and thus best qualified. Supervisors are spared the need to relay routine matters up to management and decisions back down, a transmission procedure that often gets snarled, resulting in misunderstandings. A Precision Castparts worker says of this, "We can move around now and get information on a project without having to go through anyone or clear it with anyone. This saves time and means the information is firsthand. It saves mistakes to get it direct." One important benefit is that managers have more time to manage, instead of working on low-level problems.

Another concept fundamental to job enrichment is that of organizing the workers into teams, or groups. Individuals involved in small working units become concerned with helping their teammates and achieving common goals, just as members of a sports team do. It is hard for the most willing employee to feel directly concerned with production when he is just one cog in a 1,500-man workforce scattered throughout an automobile plant. But working jointly on a project with six other persons who count on you to be there, and will help you if you fall behind, can be highly rewarding, even stimulating. A bench worker at the Texas Instruments plant in Attleboro, Massachusetts, who does delicate welding, says of her job: "There is this team feeling—people seem to help each other. I feel as if, when I am out, they miss me."

One of the causes of blue collar discontent is the gap in status and perquisites between blue collar and white collar workers. Texas Instruments, with 58,974 employees and thirty-six plants in sixteen countries and with sales of $831,822,000 in 1969, continues to narrow the gap by consciously stamping out as many as possible of the visible distinctions between different categories of employees. The company has created a genuinely democratic atmosphere. No special dining rooms or parking spaces are designated for executives. Shirtsleeves and first names seem to be acceptable throughout the organization. Offices are purposely and uniformly Spartan at all levels of plant management. Other firms have taken other tacks; some ban the terms "blue collar" or "hourly," some have removed time clocks, and some have eliminated hourly pay by putting everyone on salary, with workers paid for time absent just as office employees are.

Although workers respond well to being members of a team and feeling they "belong," they also think it important to be able to move up, to improve their job status. One of the frustrations most often cited by Detroit auto workers is the oppressive feeling of being boxed in, of going nowhere. Therefore, most companies trying to increase worker satisfaction put careful emphasis on promoting from within. And they make sure the employees know it. Notices of available jobs are posted on bulletin boards at strategic locations, and the companies pledge not to fill the jobs with recruits from outside the company until after a period of one week or even longer so that employees have a good shot at them. At Polaroid, executives say that when a job opens up there are, on the average, three moves within the company before an outsider is brought in further down the ladder. This means a lot of paper work and expense, but it gives proof that promotion from within is definitely company policy. Last year, in a production workforce of 6,000, 163 persons moved up from operating to supervisory and administrative jobs. Texas Instruments goes so far as to distribute a big monthly "want ad" newspaper listing job openings at all its plants.

Huge firms like Texas Instruments, Corning Glass, IBM, American Telephone & Telegraph, and Procter & Gamble are all involved to varying extents in blue collar job enrichment. Donnelly Mirrors, Inc., with sales of $13,800,000, is a much smaller company that realized very early the remarkable promise of such changes. The company's 300 production workers are now organized into seventy work teams—groups that naturally take shape as a result of work assignments. All hourly paid employees were put on salary. All time clocks were removed.

Absenteeism and tardiness are both down, and "people are behaving in an increasingly responsible way," according to Henry Kort, the factory manager. Donnelly supervisors make an extraordinary effort to keep all hands fully informed on both prospects and problems. Charts of sales, production, inventory, and profits are prominently displayed in each division. Surveys and questionnaires are distributed frequently, and are discussed abundantly after they have been collated.

Management listens carefully to what the operators say—and it hears much more than complaints. Work teams work hard at, among other things, reducing the number of jobs, because they know that as production costs drop, bonuses go up (they have already increased twenty-one-fold since 1961). Quality-control personnel have been reduced from fourteen to four since 1967, while production has doubled. The percentage of returned goods has declined from 3 to 0.2 percent in two years. Scrap loss is down from 13 to 3 percent over eight years.

Implementing a job-enrichment strategy is an enormous challenge to management. It requires courage to overthrow long-established traditions, real discernment to make the right changes, and determination to stick with the new policies during the rough days when they seem to be hampering rather than helping. These requirements may explain why job enrichment is not more widespread. Perhaps most frightening for tradition-minded managements is the absence of any clearly delineated model to copy. Companies embarking on job enrichment programs have to be prepared to grope, to explore, to fail, before reaching the goals they seek. Edwin Land, with longer experience in the field than almost any other corporate executive, and with the added advantage of scientific genius, says quietly of Polaroid's effort, "Our greatest contribution has been to learn how to fail without guilt. The scientific notion is that you can fail, and fail, and fail, before you succeed. We are trying to apply this scientific attitude of tolerating failure to the social innovations here in the plant, making sure, however, that in all these efforts we do not fail the people."

Companies with some experience in job enrichment report that a certain amount of cynicism is commonly encountered, not only at the middle-management level, but also among foremen. Foremen resist handing authority down to the ranks because they don't think it will work, and if it does they fear their positions will be weakened or even eventually eliminated. The reluctance of some supervisors to accept the new concepts causes painful moments. Companies sometimes find themselves obliged to "resign" men who simply cannot adjust to the new ways.

The rush to conform has led some companies to embrace job enrichment overenthusiastically and often prematurely. The sudden interest has some of the unfortunate aspects of a fad, and has allowed the emergence of what motivation expert Frederick Herzberg, of Case Western Reserve University and a leading figure in the field, delicately calls "sellers of snake oil." Herzberg decries the "whole bunch of nondescript behavioral scientists who are selling love and sitting around in groups with their clothes on."

Danger signals that management should watch for when seeking outside advice are a penchant for cant, an air of mysticism, and a distaste for specifics, which the seer expects the customer to accept on blind faith. If they can't say it in intelligible English, it probably means it's not worth saying, or that they don't understand it themselves.

Plunging into job enrichment too precipitately, without careful preparation and advance planning, can cause severe disruption, as happened when Non-Linear Systems, Inc., of Del Mar, California (1969 sales: $5 million), set out to produce its complex digital voltmeters on a team basis rather than on production lines. The company founder and president, Andrew Kay, is an enthusiastic man who likes quick results, and he generated a whirlwind of change. One worker recalls the chaos: "They shuffled people around, built a wall here one day, tore it down the next, you work with this guy, then you don't. Furniture was moving by all the time."

Kay readily admits that he made some hasty moves. He was trying to get rid of very detailed tasks but, he says, "I went too far the other way." Later, after a number of older workers made plain their displeasure, he changed operations again so that most of the work was done in more specialized divisions. Both specialization and generalization can be good things, he points out, "but each one, carried to an extreme, can be the worst possible thing you can get." People doing production work, he says, "can get too damn much to do."

Even when job enrichment is carefully planned, workers often begin the program with grave misgivings. Basic among these is the common human resistance to change of any sort.

The most prevalent complaint heard in job-enriched plants is that there should be, but often is not, more pay for more responsibility and more production. A machine operator at the Texas Instruments plant in Attleboro, who was consulted by engineers throughout development of a new machine she was to run, was pleased to be included in this way. "I'm very satisfied, because I like the machine and I'm good at my work," she says. However, "the job grades aren't high enough for what I'm doing. I used to produce 8,000 parts a day, and now with the new machine I produce 15,000 a day, and they haven't changed the grade level." Another T.I. worker whose production has increased says, "I would like to see a financial upgrading of the job itself. I feel the additional responsibility warrants more money."

A woman who has been five years with Corning Glass in Medfield, and who in the last year has advanced from parts assembly to complete assembly of a complex $1,800 chemical metering device, says, "When we went for the total job concept, I thought we should get more. You have more responsibility, you are really doing the whole job." The company has higher pay for such job categories under consideration.

The benefits that flow from job enrichment far outweigh the drawbacks. With each employee doing more, and paying closer attention, there are often immediate dividends in the elimination of unnecessary jobs. Inspection and quality-control people are frequently among the first to be rendered superfluous. Since 1968, quality-control personnel have been reduced from ten to seven at the Corning plant in Medfield, although sales have almost doubled. Rejects in the instrument department dropped from 13 percent to 6.5 percent between 1968 and 1970. When inspection procedures were reexamined, it was found that certain of them could be completely eliminated: in one tedious time-consuming inspection procedure, initiated years earlier, not a single defect had been found over a two-year period. Delegating authority has allowed reduction of top-level production supervisors at the Corning plant from four to two. The savings this kind of cut brings are handsome indeed.

At Barry Corporation, where there were twenty inspection people, only five are needed now. All fifteen line inspectors have been eliminated, and yet the number of rejects has been cut in half. Still another advantage is the reduction in machine repairs. Since the introduction of teams, Barry has been able to cut the number of maintenance mechanics at its downtown Columbus plant from six to four, because the women are more careful with the sewing machines.

Perhaps the most important benefit of all is simply the change in atmosphere that characteristically occurs when job enrichment is attempted. The plant floor becomes a strikingly different place from the days when the work was a daily grind. A visitor to Precision Castparts, for example, senses an interest in the job being done, a purposefulness of activity, a feeling of initiative that is generally lacking along the automobile production lines in Detroit. When they are asked what they are doing and why, the men in the shell-coating room answer responsively, sometimes even enthusiastically, explaining why their operation is difficult and why its correct execution is crucial to making good castings. They look concerned, they are careful of their appearance and of their material. This is in sharp contrast to the indifference, sometimes even sullenness, often found among auto-assembly workers.

This atmosphere has a special appeal to younger workers. In the more open and more democratic kind of plant, young people get a fairer hearing. They feel they are not put down simply because of their youth. Says William Lane, a twenty-four-year-old technician at Corning: "I don't have any trouble talking with anyone here. A few years ago a person didn't get recognized unless he'd been with the company many years. Now you get recognized. It's in people's minds that you're doing something, that you're thinking." Looking at the potential of youth from the managerial side, Edwin Land said: "Our policy has always been to reflect faith in the maturity of youth as early as possible. A technique for putting an optical finish on Polaroid sunglasses was developed by a fourteen-year-old boy who worked summers at Polaroid. It's the putting off of faith in the maturity of young people that causes trouble."

In an era of increasing doubt about the validity of the usual corporate goals—doubt that has sharply reduced the desire of young people to enter business—making jobs better and more responsive to men's wants and ambitions becomes social service of a high order. Inventor-philosopher-executive Edwin Land expresses the aim well. "It is a wonderful phenomenon to see people serving a cause and working together to share a task. It is only through a unifying purpose that interpersonal aggressiveness and destructiveness can be subordinated."

Helping people to work together rather than in solitary competition, and to work together at more rewarding jobs—these are objectives that will attract idealistic young workers. Job enrichment can not only bring present profit, it can enhance the likelihood of constructive growth for the corporation and for the society in which it functions. Encouraging participation rather than rote learning, replacing ritual obedience with a sense of self-control—these are approaches that without question will benefit the company that dares to try them.

JOHN R. P. FRENCH, JR. / ROBERT D. CAPLAN

Organizational Stress
and Individual Strain

The large, bureaucratic organization, like other settings, exerts its own set of unique forces on the individual. Through the application of these forces, the organization is able to channel the individual's behavior toward certain goals and to direct his interactions toward certain people and away from others. This conformity to organizational norms is, of course, purchased at a price most often thought of in terms of salary or wages. But there are often other prices which the organization incurs for insisting that its members adhere in certain ways to certain goals—costs which are rarely, if ever, tallied in the quarterly reports of modern organizations; they are costs in the form of job-related pathologies of the people who make the organization run. These pathologies can manifest themselves in forms ranging anywhere from passive apathy, job dissatisfaction, and depression to violent acts directed against the organization. In some cases, the individual may even suffer a disabling ulcer or heart attack which forces him to withdraw from an active life in the organization before his full value as a human asset (Brummet, Pyle, and Flamholtz, 1968) has been realized. Thus, both mental and physical health may be affected by the continual pressures of the job over a period of years.

Although there are many clinical observations on the effects of job stress on mental and physical health, there has been very little systematic quantitative research. Accordingly, in 1957 the Institute for Social Research at the University of Michigan organized a program of research on the effects of the social environment, especially the effects of large organizations, on individual strain (including job dissatisfaction and tension, poor adjustment, physiological disturbances such as high blood pressure or elevated cholesterol, and diseases which are related to stress).

It is the purpose of this chapter to present some of the findings from this program of research, with particular emphasis on organizational stresses which produce psychological and physiological strains leading to coronary heart disease. We focus on this disease because it is so important in terms of death rates, disease rates, and costs. All forms of heart disease (including strokes) accounted for more than half of all deaths in the United States in 1963; about a quarter of the persons in the population between the ages of 18 and 79 had definite or suspected heart disease; and the costs (the sum of direct costs for medcial care

Figure 1. An outline of a theory about how organizational stresses affect individual strains contributing to coronary heart disease. The horizontal arrows show the effects of environmental stresses on individual strain which in turn affects heart disease. The vertical arrow shows the conditioning effects of personality variables.

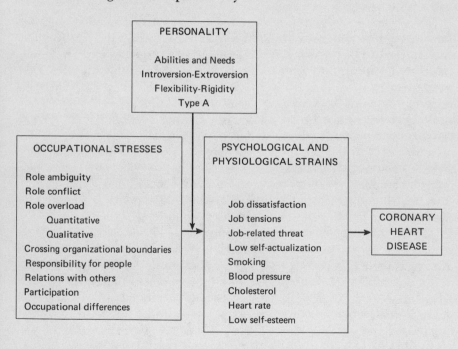

plus losses of output by members of the labor force due to heart disease) amounted to $22.4 billion, or 4 percent of the GNP in 1963 (The President's Commission on Heart Disease, Cancer and Stroke, 1964). By far the largest part of this burden of total heart disease is attributable to coronary heart disease, a disease which is more common in men than in women and has an especially high incidence in the age range of most business managers.

Our focus on coronary heart disease does not imply that there is a large body of dependable medical knowledge on the effects of organizational stress on this disease; on the contrary, we wish to warn the reader that many of our findings are new and have not yet been confirmed by other researchers. They deserve further research, but they also deserve attention from management.

Before describing our results, we will present an outline of the theory and research strategy which guided the studies and which can serve as a summary of the main findings. This outline, presented in Figure 1, can serve as a map to guide the reader through a complex set of findings. Then we will present our research grouped according to the following organizational stresses: role ambiguity, role conflict, role overload, organizational boundaries, responsibility for people, relations with others, participation, and occupational differences in stress, strain, and heart disease. Finally, we will speculate a bit about what management might do to reduce heart disease where organizational stress is a contributory cause.

Our theory, as presented in Figure 1, starts with occupations or roles as loci of stress in organizations. Public health statistics in England and in the United States show that there are large differences among occupations in rates of coronary heart disease. Studies by Russek (1960, 1962, 1965) reveal that different specialties within a profession have different rates of heart disease; for example, the general practitioner has higher rates than the dermatologist or radiologist. Similar differences are found for lawyers, dentists, and other occupations. However, these data do not tell us *why* one occupation has more disease than another. We have attempted to discover some of the specific variables which might account for such occupational differences. The occupational stresses listed in the first box of Figure 1 are the major ones which we have found to be related to individual strain.[1]

The first horizontal arrow represents our central set of hypotheses concerning the effects of each of the job stresses on one or more of the measures of psychological and physiological strain. These strains, in turn, are hypothesized to be risk factors (contributory causes) in heart disease as indicated by the second horizontal arrow. Some of these—for example, smoking, blood pressure, and cholesterol—are generally accepted as risk factors. Heart rate is strongly implicated by two recent studies (Hinkle et al., 1970; Stamler et al., 1969). Our own research suggests that job dissatisfaction may be a risk factor. Job tension and low self-esteem remain plausible hypotheses, but there is no direct evidence that they are risk factors in heart disease.

[1] Both the occupations and the specific job stresses associated with them are descriptions of the person's social environment. In our program of research, we have generally distinguished between the *objective* social environment and the *subjective* social environment, as it is perceived by the person. Where perception is veridical, the two environments coincide and the distinction may be disregarded. We have chosen to omit the distinction generally in this chapter in order to simplify a complex set of findings.

Finally we must qualify our central hypothesis about the effects of stress on strain. How a person reacts to job stress—that is, whether he shows strain or not—is a function of both the stress he encounters and the type of person he is. In other words, we assume in our model that part of the effects of organizational stress on the individual are determined by his personality. Thus, the top box in Figure 1 contains characteristics of the person which have this conditioning effect on the influence of stress on strain. For example, the influence of a heavy workload on job tension is very strong for persons low in the abilities necessary to do the work, but the same workload produces minimal tension in persons high in these abilities. It is the *goodness of fit* between the demands of the job and the abilities of the person which will determine the amount of strain. Similarly, the goodness of fit between the needs of the person and the degree to which these needs are satisfied in the job environment will also affect the strain. Other aspects of personality, such as the hard-driving Type A coronary-prone syndrome, are expected to have similar conditioning effects.

In order to test our theory about the effects of job stress on heart disease, we have chosen to deal with strains that are known risk factors in heart disease (for example, cholesterol and blood pressure). This strategy has been adopted for reasons of efficiency. One can demonstrate, using twenty men, that work overload influences cholesterol, but it would require 2,000 men to prove that work overload influences coronary heart disease because the disease is so rare.[2]

Now, with our model from Figure 1 in mind, let us turn to the evidence which links stress in modern organizations to coronary heart disease and other indicators of individual strain.

Studies of Role Ambiguity

In order for us to perform our jobs well in an organization, we have to have a certain amount of information regarding what we are expected to do and not do. We need to know our rights, obligations, and privileges—essentially our "areas of freedom" (Maier, 1965). Usually, we would also like to have some information regarding the potential consequences of anything we do in carrying out our jobs. Furthermore, we often want to know what the consequences will be for ourselves, other members of the organizaton, and the organization itself (Kahn et al., 1964). Typically, however, we have less than all the information we

[2] Although the theory outlined in Figure 1 does not show any causal relations among the various forms of individual strain, we do in fact assume that psychological strains affect heart disease by means of some intervening physiological strains. Also, one physiological strain such as heart rate may affect another physiological strain such as blood pressure. These mechanisms of the disease will not be discussed further because an understanding of them is not necessary to our major concern with the effect of environmental stress.

need, and so we may experience some degree of *role ambiguity*. In asking people to indicate the amount of ambiguity they have experienced, we have asked men to rate items such as the following:

1. The extent to which their work objectives are defined.
2. The extent to which they can predict what others will expect of them tomorrow.
3. The extent to which they are clear on what others expect of them now.
4. How clear the scope and responsibilities of their job are.

In other words, role ambiguity is a state in which the person has inadequate information to perform his role. Our particular interest in role ambiguity stems from its negative effects on the well-being of individuals in organizations, its potentially harmful consequences for the organization, and its prevalence in today's work settings.

Our findings on role ambiguity are based on data drawn from a wide variety of occupations. We started our research with an intensive study of the effects of role ambiguity on job satisfaction and job-related psychological tensions in six large business organizations in the United States (Kahn et al., 1964). Fifty-three persons were interviewed at length about various aspects of stress and strain in their jobs. The major findings of this study showed that men who suffered from role ambiguity experienced lower job satisfaction and higher job-related tension.

We found further support for these findings in a later study carried out at Goddard Space Flight Center, one of NASA's bases. In the Goddard study, 205 male, volunteer administrators, engineers, and scientists filled out a lengthy questionnaire describing various aspects of stress and strain in their jobs. As part of this study, we obtained blood samples from the men and took measures of blood pressure and pulse rate for later analysis as indicators of physiological strain. We will be reporting on the findings regarding physiological strain in a later section of this chapter. Our major findings with regard to role ambiguity showed that it was again significantly related to low job satisfaction ($r = -.42$)[3] and to feelings of job-related threat to one's mental and physical well-being ($r = .40$). In addition, we found that the more ambiguity the person reported, the lower was his utilization of his intellectual skills and knowledge ($r = -.48$), and the lower was his utilization of his

---

[3] r is an index of correlation between two variables; that is, it measures the extent to which two such variables are related to each other. Such correlations can mathematically vary only from $+1.00$ to -1.00. A correlation of $+1.00$ would indicate that two variables are perfectly and positively related to each other. A correlation of -1.00 would indicate a perfect *inverse* relation. A .00 correlation ($r = .00$) would mean that the two variables are completely unrelated to each other. A perfect correlation is rare in research in the social sciences; in this chapter

administrative and leadership skills. This lack of utilization also adversely affected satisfaction and increased job-related threat.

The latter two findings regarding low utilization of personal abilities suggest that people are unable to make their best contribution to an organization partly because the channels for utilization are unclear or ambiguous. Thus, an organization which is fraught with role ambiguity may suffer because it gets less than full use of its human resources. The individuals tend to see little opportunity for their own advancement in the organization ($r = -.44$), again because there is ambiguity about how to get ahead. This means that a person who wants to advance or improve himself in his job may feel that his efforts are quite futile. While we have no data on turnover from the Goddard study, it seems reasonable to assume that turnover is likely to be high in settings where people who want to advance feel unsure of what they should be doing, see themselves as being underutilized, and see no clear channels for advancement.

The upshot of all this is that role ambiguity may have far-reaching consequences beyond the strain which the individual experiences—consequences such as turnover of personnel and poor coordination which directly affect the efficiency and operating costs of any modern organization.

While role ambiguity is generally stressful for people, there are individual differences in how much ambiguity a person can tolerate. Persons with a high need for structure and a low tolerance for ambiguity are more likely to experience job-related tension than persons low on these needs when they are faced with ambiguity in their work (Kahn et al., (1964).

How prevalent is role ambiguity in our organizational society? Data obtained from another study, a national survey of 725 male wage and salary workers (Kahn et al., 1964), show that 34.7 percent reported role ambiguity. In the Goddard study, 60 percent reported some form of role ambiguity. These figures and others on the prevalence of stresses (to be discussed later) are presented in Table 1.

---

the correlations range from .22 to .68. The following table may help to interpret these correlations:

$r = .20-.29$ is a very weak relation
$r = .30-.39$ is a weak relation
$r = .40-.49$ is a moderate relation
$r = .50-.59$ is a substantial relation
$r = .60-.69$ is a strong relation

All findings presented here are statistically significant at $p < .05$ or higher unless otherwise noted. That is, it is highly improbable that they represent chance findings due to "luck" since they could not occur by chance more than five times out of one hundred. Our general rule has been to present only those findings which have been confirmed in two or more studies.

Table 1. The prevalence of several major types of job stress.

	PERCENT REPORTING STRESS	
TYPE OF STRESS	GODDARD*	KAHN ET AL., 1964†
Role ambiguity	60.0	34.7
Role conflict	67.1	48.0
Subjective quantitative overload	72.6	44.0
Subjective qualitative overload	53.8	—

* These percentages represent people whose average scores are equivalent to at least the "some" category on the measuring scale used.

† From a national survey of male wage and salary workers ($n = 725$). There is substantial, but not perfect, overlap between the measures of stress used in the Kahn et al. study and the measures of stress used in the Goddard study.

Figure 2 graphically depicts the findings. In summary, role ambiguity, which appears to be widespread, (1) produces psychological strain and dissatisfaction, (2) leads to underutilization of human resources, and (3) leads to feelings of futility on how to cope with the organizational environment. It is worthy of attention because it tells a great deal about the behavior of people in organizations.

Figure 2. The effects of role ambiguity on stress and strain in organizations.

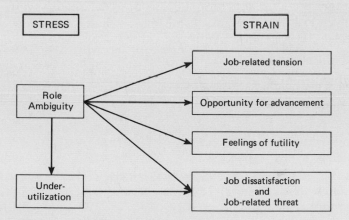

Role Conflict and Strain

If role ambiguity reflects a situation where there is a lack of information, role conflict reflects a situation where the information arouses conflict. The following items about the conflicts people experience are typical of those we have asked members of organizations to rate:

1. Being torn by conflicting demands.
2. The pressure of "having to get along" with people.

3. Differences of opinion between oneself and one's superiors.
4. Difficulties in handling subordinates, secretaries, and others.
5. Having to do things one really doesn't want to do, such as certain administrative duties.

The phrase "torn by conflicting demands" rings true to many employees, even in America's best-managed organizations. The very essence of an organization is the division of labor among jobs or roles and a clear agreement on who should do what. Nevertheless an interview survey of a national sample of male wage and salary employees revealed that 48 percent are sometimes caught in the middle between two sets of people who demand different kinds of behavior on the job. Fifteen percent of these employees report that such role conflict is a frequent and serious problem (Kahn et al., 1964).

Some organizations have more role conflict than others. Compared to the national average of 48 percent, we found that 67.1 percent of male employees at Goddard Space Flight Center reported some role conflict.

Similarly, some jobs in an organization have more role conflict than others. At Goddard, administrators suffer more role conflict than engineers and scientists. The administrator has more opportunity for conflict because he spends less time than the others working alone (34 percent of his time against 38 percent and 57 percent).

What are the effects of these variations in role conflict? Our first studies of role conflict examined the consequences for psychological strain and mental health, and it was only later that we included measures of physiological strain and physical health. We started with an intensive study of the effects of role conflict on job satisfaction and on job-related tensions in six large business organizations (Kahn et al., 1964). Fifty-three focal persons were interviewed, each of whom named an additional six or eight co-workers who were "role senders," that is, who defined the focal person's job, who made demands upon him, and who told him how he should perform his role. Next we interviewed all these role senders to find out what demands, instructions, expectations, and requests they sent to the focal person. From the interviews with co-workers we constructed a measure of role conflict which reflected the conflicting demands from these co-workers. The major finding showed that men who suffered more role conflict had lower job satisfaction and higher job-related tension.

This study also showed that how a focal person reacted to conflict depended on the type of position he held relative to his role senders. The greater the power of the role senders over him, the greater the job dissatisfaction and sense of futility produced by the role conflict. It is worse to receive conflicting messages from two superordinates than from two subordinates.

We say that any role senders who depend heavily on the focal person to complete some task in order for them to discharge their own responsibilities are *functionally dependent* on the focal person. To take an example, you may be unable to submit a report unless one of your subordinates does the job of gathering certain necessary information. In that case, you are functionally dependent on your subordinate.

Functional dependence, interestingly enough, creates some unique problems for the focal person as well as for the people who are dependent on him. When the focal person experiences role conflict, the fact that he has others who are dependent on him apparently makes it more difficult to resolve the conflict. Thus, in the interview study, we found that persons experiencing role conflict report high feelings of job dissatisfaction and futility in trying to deal with their organizational environment; but this is only true if these people have role senders who are functionally dependent on them for getting work done.

We also find that the personality of the individual is an important determinant of how he reacts to role conflict. Specifically, role conflict produces greater job-related tension in introverts than in extroverts. The findings show that introverts are less social, that is, they enjoy interaction with other persons less than extroverts, and they are more independent than extroverts. Thus, it may be that the introvert has more difficulty in coping with conflict because it occurs in social situations and threatens his independence.

Similar findings also appear for flexible people, who show greater job-related tension under conditions of conflict than do rigid individuals. Kahn et al. note that flexible people are characterized by their tendency to blame themselves when things go wrong, while rigid people tend to externalize blame and assume that the fault lies within the environment. Thus, it would seem that the flexible person, when confronted with conflict situations, would turn the blame for conflict inward and consequently experience more job-related tension than the rigid person.

An interview survey of a national sample of male wage and salary workers confirmed the finding that role conflict is associated with job dissatisfaction and tension.

Another study of over 800 salesmen examined the relationship between role conflict, measures of job satisfaction, and job-related tension. It was found that among managers, role conflict decreases satisfaction ($r = -.54$) and increases job-related tension ($r = .39$). In this study role conflict is weakly related to physical symptoms of anxiety as measured by eight questions about insomnia, nervousness, clammy hands, hard breathing, and so forth.

Although conflicting role pressures have their source in organizational variables, such as the conflicting goals of different departments, they have their expression in the demands which are made on a person. When these demands conflict, at least one of them must be rejected or ignored. It would not be surprising if such a rejection were resented and taken personally. In the study at Goddard we did indeed find that high role conflict goes with poor relationships with one's peer group ($r = .24$) and with dissatisfaction with one's subordinates ($r = .35$). Role conflict is also associated with job-related threat: the person under role conflict feels that this stress threatens his health, his feelings of pride, freedom from tension, and so on ($r = .29$). Given poor interpersonal relations and feelings of threat, persons under more role conflict experience a greater need for better relations with subordinates ($r = .35$).

Figure 3. The effects of role conflict on psychological and physiological strain.

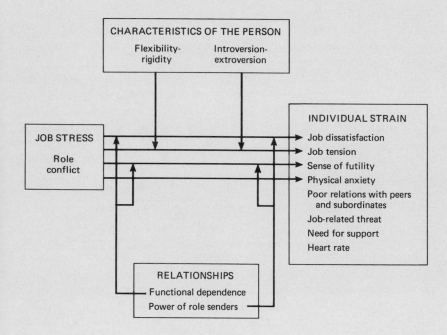

Finally, we have some preliminary evidence that role conflict is related to physiological strain. In a study of twenty-two men in NASA headquarters we telemetered and recorded the heart rate of each man for a two-hour period while he was at work on his regular office job. We found that mean heart rate was strongly related to the man's report of role conflict on a questionnaire ($r = .61$). However, in another study this same seven-item measure of role conflict was not related to pulse rate when a single, thirty-second, casual reading of pulse was taken instead of a two-hour-long measure as the person worked in his office.

Some major findings from these five studies of role conflict are summarized in Figure 3. The figure shows that this form of job stress produces a variety of psychological strains, but these effects of stress on strain vary depending on the personality of the individual and his relationships with others in the organization.

Role Overload

We have talked about role conflict as a situation in which a person finds, in essence, diametrically opposed demands being made on him. But very often a person is asked to work on one assignment when he already has some other assignments which also must be completed. If he is to work on the new assignment, he may have to stop what he is doing at the time. This is also a form of conflict, and it leads to a situation known as *overload*. When the issue concerns merely the sum total of work that must be done, irrespective of its difficulty, we talk about *quantitative* overload—the person has more work than can be done in a given period of time. When the work is overloading because it requires skills, abilities, and knowledge beyond what the person has, then we talk about *qualitative* overload.

Quantitative overload lies on a continuum running from "too little to do" to "too much to do." The continuum for qualitative overload runs from "too easy work" to "too difficult work." Either extreme on these continuums represents a bad fit between the demands of the environment and the ability of the organization member. A good fit would reside at that point on both scales of workload where the demands of the job just match the abilities of the person.

In our research, quantitative overload has been measured in a variety of ways. Our questionnaires contain items on "overwhelming workload," "not enough time," "the quantity of work you are expected to do," and others. The number of hours that a man works per week (as reported by the man and by his wife) is another measure. The frequency and severity of deadlines is still another measure. In order to avoid the biases in self-reports, we have actually observed the number of meetings, office visits, and phone calls; these form an index of workload since, at best, each event takes up time which could have been used in other work and, at worst, each event may mean the person receives additional work assignments. All these measures make sense as indicators of quantitative overload, all of them tend to hang together, and in general, they show similar effects of overload on strain.

The measures of qualitative overload are primarily questionnaire items referring to "the quality of work you are expected to do," "the demands of the job for training or knowledge," and "the difficulty of assignments."

The conceptual overlap between role conflict and overload is, of course, not surprising. Indeed, we have found in a reanalysis (Sales, 1969) of some of the findings from the study of role conflict that a good deal of the relationship between role conflict and job-related tension could be explained by a subset of three items in our measure of conflict which dealt specifically with quantitative overload. These items correlated .60 with job tension.

Overload is one of the concepts which receives a good deal of attention from general systems theorists. Miller (1960), for example, has shown that excessive overload leads to general breakdown in a system no matter what the level of the system is. That is, the finding holds true for systems ranging from single biological cells to individuals to organizations to states. Recent research has also indicated that overload resulting from excessive rates of change in the complexity of the environment (Terreberry, 1968) also leads to system breakdown. This process of "complexification" appears to be associated with systems dysfunctions at various levels ranging from individual suicide to bankruptcy of a business organization.

Quantitative overload is prevalent in our achievement-oriented society (McClelland, 1961). Even though their jobs do not demand it, university professors in one of our studies work fifty-seven hours per week. In the national sample survey, 44 percent of male white collar employees reported some degree of overload on our questionnaire measure. On the same measure, 45 percent of our small sample at NASA headquarters and 72.6 percent at Goddard Space Flight Center reported some degree of overload. On the average the men at Goddard spend about half their time working under moderate to extreme deadline pressure. At both NASA installations, persons who are high on the questionnaire measure of quantitative overload also spend more time in meetings, on office visits, and on the phone and correspondingly less time working alone.

The prevalence of qualitative overload is also high; 54 percent of the men at Goddard report at least some. This appears to be lower than the prevalence of quantitative overload in the same sample. In our sample of college professors, we also found more quantitative overload (a mean of 2.39) than qualitative overload (a mean of 2.13).

One of our initial studies of overload looked at the nature of quantitative as well as qualitative overload in a large university (French, Tupper, and Mueller, 1965). Questionnaires, interviews, and medical examinations to obtain data on risk factors in coronary heart disease were administered to 122 professors and university administrators. In order to see whether quantitative and qualitative overload were two different factors, as we had conceptually predicted they would be, we factor-analyzed the responses to the questionnaire items. This analysis confirmed our expectation that quantitative and qualitative overload are two distinct and separate variables.

Both quantitative overload and qualitative overload, as reported by the professors, were related to the same index of job tension which we used in the studies of role conflict ($r = .41$ and $.58$, respectively). These findings were supported when the overload was reported by the wife, although the correlations were not quite as high. These results together with the parallel findings in our studies of role conflict give us confidence that work overload is generally associated with job tension. One must be cautious in inferring causes from correlations. There are always three logical possibilities. In this case they are: (1) overload causes job tension; (2) job tension causes overload (perhaps because tension so interferes with performance that the man can't get his work done); (3) both overload and tension are caused by some third factor (for example, a harsh and demanding boss), and so there is a correlation between overload and tension even though neither causes the other. Our hypothesis states that overload causes tension, but we cannot rule out the other two possibilities on the grounds that they are implausible. So what we need is an experiment in which we systematically vary work overload while holding all other factors constant and observe the resulting variation of job tension. Such experiments are reported below.

Some professors did not understand the interview question that asked how difficult it is to "meet the demands of your job," because they did not experience their work as a response to demands from others but as self-induced activities (such as research, study, and serving on committees) which they were free to do or not do. When the meaning of "demands" was explained to him, one professor replied, "Oh, I could do that with one hand tied behind my back!"

Then what induces some professors and administrators to overload themselves, to work sixty or even seventy hours per week? In an effort to answer this question, we coded the intensive interviews for "achievement orientation," a syndrome which includes engaging in multiple activities, pushing oneself to achieve, reported achievement, taking leadership in accomplishing goals, and so on. As expected, this measure correlated .42 with the number of hours worked per week and .25 with our factor score on quantitative overload. More surprising, achievement orientation correlated very highly with serum uric acid ($r = .68$ in the first half of the sample, and $r = .66$ when cross-validated in the second half of the sample; Brooks and Mueller, 1966). This surprising finding was well replicated in a second study of professors, so the association between achievement orientation and serum uric acid may be taken as a fact. This substance in the blood is best known for its association with gout, and it has been observed long ago that gouty men often achieve eminence. Serum uric acid has also been considered a possible risk factor in coronary heart disease, but its causal connection is uncertain. It is known that serum uric acid tends to be high in occupational groups who are high in achievement, such as business executives; and we have found it to be low in a sample of unemployed men.

These facts suggested that serum uric acid might be the biochemical basis for achievement motivation. However, in a special study of this question we could find no relation between serum uric acid and two projective measures of achievement motivation. In another study of male high school students, a connection between serum uric acid and motivation to achieve was suggested: those who attempted college but dropped out had higher serum uric acid than either those who completed college or those who never tried to go to college. Within the group who attempted college (in spite of poor high school grades) those with higher serum uric acid persisted longer before dropping out (Kasl, Brooks, and Cobb, 1966).

The finding that overload is related to low self-esteem is confirmed in the total sample at Goddard. Qualitative overload is correlated with two measures of low self-esteem ($r = .27$ and $.30$); however, quantitative overload is not related to either. This effect is found primarily in the scientists, whose role is most like that of a professor. Among scientists as among professors, qualitative overload strongly lowers self-esteem ($r = .58$) while among administrators and engineers there is no significant effect.

Finally, we found at Goddard that both quantitative and qualitative overload correlate with job-related threat ($r = .22$ and $.29$, respectively). The number of cigarettes smoked, a much publicized risk factor in heart disease, also increases with increases in the actual number of phone calls, office visits, and meetings a person has (as tallied by each person's secretary). The correlation between cigarette smoking and this measure of quantitative overload is $.58$.

Having strong evidence that work overload is related to several forms of psychological strain, it was only natural to hypothesize that overload would produce physiological strains. Several studies have reported an association of work overload with cholesterol level, but in these studies only crude indicators of overload have been used: a tax deadline for accountants (Friedman, Rosenman, and Carroll, 1958) and an impending examination for medical students (Dreyfuss and Czaczkes, 1959; Grundy and Griffin, 1959; Horwitz and Bronte-Stewart, 1962; Thomas and Murphy, 1958; Wertlake et al., 1958). Accordingly, a preliminary field study at NASA headquarters tested the hypothesis that overload increases both cholesterol level and heart rate.

NASA was chosen as a research site because the Division of Occupational Medicine wanted to develop measures of job stress which would be useful in a computerized system for the early identification of those men who had a high risk of heart disease. NASA also seemed an appropriate site for the research, because the organization was reported to have strong deadline pressures and work overload.

Twenty-two white collar males were observed at work for a period of two to three hours on each of three days. A team of two observers recorded coordinated data on events occurring in the job environment and heart rate responses to these events. The heart rates were obtained by means of a pocket-sized telemetry device which did not interfere with the employee's freedom of activity and movement. On the same day of the observations, blood samples were drawn so that cholesterol determinations could be made. On the third day of observation each subject filled out a questionnaire which yielded a factor score on quantitative overload. This subjective measure could be compared with an objective measure constructed from the observer's report of incoming phone calls and office visitors. The two measures showed substantial agreement. Those men who reported that they were generally overloaded on their jobs were observed to suffer more interruptions from phone calls and visitors ($r = .64$).

As predicted, both objective and subjective overload were substantially related to heart rate ($r = .39$ and .65, respectively). Both were also related to cholesterol ($r = .43$ and .41, respectively). All the above findings are based on correlations across individuals; but analyses within individuals show that increases in observed workload were accompanied by increases in heart rate, a fact which supports our hypothesis that stress produces the observed physiological strain.

Although the association of overload with physiological strain has been strongly demonstrated in this study at NASA, it still does not prove that overload causes strain. In order to prove more conclusively that the stress of workload produces physiological strain, we conducted two controlled laboratory experiments. In the first experiment we found that men who were subjected to qualitative overload, as compared with those who received easy tasks, not only suffered psychological strain such as embarrassment and loss of self-esteem, but also showed more physiological strain as measured by the basal skin resistance level (Modigliani, 1966). In the second experiment those subjects who were given a substantial quantitative overload, as compared with those who were underloaded, showed lower self-esteem, made more errors, and had higher heart rates. During the one hour of working on the task, the level of cholesterol increased most for overloaded subjects. Together the two experiments prove that qualitative and quantitative work overload are the causes rather than the effects of physiological as well as psychological strains. When overload is reduced, the strain decreases.

In summary, our findings from several studies show that the various forms of workload produce at least nine different kinds of psychological and physiological strain in the individual (see Figure 4). Four of these (job dissatisfaction, elevated cholesterol, elevated heart rate, and smoking) are risk factors in heart disease. It is reasonable to predict that reducing work overload will reduce heart disease.

Organizational Territoriality

Robert Ardrey's armchair excursion into the world of *The Territorial Imperative* reveals the significance of territories for the behavior of animals and suggests the potential importance which personal space and territory may play in the everyday activities of man. To what extent is territory important to people in modern organizations? Do people develop feelings of ownership with respect to their offices or their own departments? Shouldn't the time a person spends in other territories prove to be a source of stress for the individual? What types of strains, such as insecurity, do people show when they cross the boundary between their own section of the organization and other sections—or move out from their own organization completely, as the salesman does routinely? Indeed, every time a person moves out of his territory, he invades the territory of someone else, potentially putting the other person as well as himself under stress.

What is the nature of territories and boundaries in organizations? These are essentially two. In addition to the external boundaries which

Figure 4. A summary of the effects of quantitative and qualitative overload on various forms of individual strain.

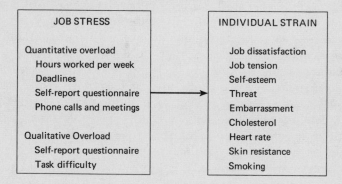

separate the organization from its environment, there is a set of internal boundaries correspondng to the functional division of labor among divisions, departments, and the like. NASA, for example, is broken down into various bases spread across the country, and a base, such as Goddard, is further divided hierarchically as follows: directorates, divisions, branches, and sections. In order to achieve the goals of the organization, it is necessary to coordinate the activities of all these "territories." Likert (1961) pictures the manager at each level as a "linking pin" who has primary responsibility for such coordination. The manager is the leader of his own unit and at the same time he is a subordinate in his boss's larger unit; he has a special responsibility for coordinating the work of the two units. Nonmanagerial employees may also have contacts across organizational boundaries. The salesman, for example, has contacts across the external boundaries of the organization, and he may find that his customers make demands on him which conflict with those from his superior.

There has been little research on organizational territories, and we are just beginning to explore the stresses and strains which may be involved. Here we will report on two variables which seem to belong to the domain of territorial behavior: having to make work contacts across organizational boundaries, and having your job located in a territory where the dominant occupation is different from your own (for example, the engineer who works in an administrative department where there are few other engineers).

Contacts across organizational boundaries are quite prevalent in organizational life. In our national sample survey 43 percent of the employees reported that they sometimes, rather often, or nearly all the time had contacts outside the organization; the corresponding figure for contact across departmental boundaries was 47 percent. Our sample at Goddard spent more than half their time "interfacing," as they call it, with other sections of the organization.

Contact across organizational boundaries, we discovered in our intensive study of role conflict in business organizations, is associated with role conflict. Those who are located on either the external or the internal boundaries of the organization have substantially more role conflict. Among internal contacts, those interactions with more distant departments are more stressful because the role senders have a less adequate understanding of the key person's job and hence they make more unreasonable demands. At Goddard, too, contacts with more distant organizational units are more difficult and they involve greater deadline pressures. The amount of deadline pressure decreases with the increase in amount of time spent in contacts within one's own branch ($r = -.31$). On the other hand, these deadline pressures increase with increasing amounts of time spent in contacts with other bases or centers ($r = .39$). The still more distant contacts involved in monitoring contracts with outside companies have other attendant stresses. The more time people spend in contract monitoring, the heavier is their actual workload in the form of meetings, office visits, and phone calls ($r = .61$).

Given all these stresses associated with interacting across organizational boundaries, it is not surprising to find that such interfacing also produces strain. Frequent boundary contacts are associated with high job-related tension in our national sample and with low self-actualization in our Goddard sample. In Goddard the amount of interfacing is associated with low self-actualization (that is, low utilization of one's best abilities and leadership skills), whereas the amount of time spent in contact with persons in one's own work unit is associated with high self-actualization.

We turn now to the effects of having one's job located in an alien environment. At Goddard our sample of administrators consisted of two subgroups: those in an administrative environment and those in an engineering environment. Similarly, there were subsamples of engineers in each of the same two environments. For each occupation, therefore, we could compare men in an alien environment with men in a better-fitting environment where most of the employees shared the same occupations.

As predicted, the men in an alien environment showed more stress and strain: (1) administrators in an engineering unit showed more quantitative overload, more qualitative overload, a larger percentage of time under great deadline pressure, higher systolic and diastolic blood pressure, and a faster pulse rate; (2) engineers in an administrative unit showed more incoming and outgoing phone calls, greater deadline pressure from their own branch, more contacts across organizational boundaries and less within their own unit, less opportunity to do the kind of work they preferred, less opportunity for advancement, and lower self-actualization.

It seems that crossing an organizational boundary and working in an alien territory entails stress and strain and poses a threat to one's health.

Responsibility for People

The responsibilities a person has constitute another frequent stress in organizations. In our research we have found it useful to categorize responsibilities into two types: responsibilities for persons and responsibilities for things. Responsibility for persons includes their work, their careers and professional development, and their job security. Responsibility for things includes budgets, projects, and equipment and other property.

In the Goddard study about 59 percent of the respondents reported at least some degree of responsibility for people, and about 59 percent of the respondents reported at least some degree of responsibility for things. We found that responsibilities for persons increase as one moves up the hierarchy of the organization (measured by government salary level in this study; $r = .44$). Responsibilities for things also increase as one moves up the status ladder, but the relationship between impersonal responsibilities and organizational status is not as great ($r = .26$). Thus, responsibilities for persons are fairly prevalent in Goddard and an increase in status is more likely to mean an increase in responsibilities for persons than in responsibilities for things.

People who have great responsibility for others at Goddard seem to pay the price in terms of large amounts of time spent interacting with people in meetings and on the phone, and in reduced amounts of time working alone ($r = -.47$). It is not surprising that such people also end up reporting they spend a good deal of time under great deadline pressure, often to the point where they can just barely keep up with their schedules ($r = .34$). Responsibility for things, on the other hand, has little or no effect on these other stresses.

We further found that the responsibility for people can hardly be considered conducive to good health and low risk of coronary heart disease. First, the more time the person spends carrying out responsibility for the work of others, the more he smokes ($r = .31$). Second, the more responsibility he has for the work of others, the higher his diastolic blood pressure ($r = .23$). On the other hand, the more responsibility he has for things, the lower his diastolic blood pressure ($r = -.32$).

Finally, when a person has either more responsibility for the work of others than he wants *or* less responsibility for the work of others than he wants, his serum cholesterol level tends to be higher than when he has exactly as much responsibility as he wants (the index of nonlinear association equals .23).[4]

If there is any truth to the adage that "man's greatest enemy is himself," it can be found in these data—it is the responsibility which organizational members have for other organizational members, rather than the responsibility for impersonal aspects of the organization, which constitutes the more significant organizational stress.

Poor Relations with Others

Psychologists and students of organizations have paid a good deal of attention over the last twenty years to the quality of working relations people have with one another. Many organization theorists have, in fact, suggested that good relations between organization members can be a key factor in improving organizational health (for example, see Likert, 1961, 1967; Argyris, 1964; and McGregor, 1960).

In the Goddard study we have examined the quality of the relations people have with their immediate superior, their colleagues or peers, and their subordinates as important sources of organizational stress. Poor relations have been defined as those which include low trust, low supportiveness, and low interest in listening to and trying to deal with the problems that confront the organization member.

Poor relations with one's superior, colleagues, and subordinates are likely to occur whenever the person experiences a good deal of ambiguity about what he should be doing as part of his role in the organization (the correlations range from .23 to .46). These findings are in keeping with those from another study, the intensive interview study of job stress by Kahn et al. (1964). In that study mistrust of the persons one worked with was positively associated with high role ambiguity ($r = .38$). Lack of information apparently leads to misconceptions about

[4] In this latter condition the goodness of fit between the person and his environment is perfect. That is, the person demands so much of his environment, and the environment provides just that amount. In the case of poor fit, the environment has either some deficiency or some excess of the desired supply. Additional research, not reported on here, also suggests that other conditions of poor fit between the person and his job environment produce strain in the individual.

people and how one should interact with them. As we might expect, poor relations with the people one works with are also likely to occur when conflicts arise over how jobs should be done and over what the priorities are for carrying out such jobs ($r = .24$). Often in an organization, the decisions on conflicts such as these are not easily resolvable by facts, and the decisions may rest on the weight of one person's subjective opinion against another's. It is quite conceivable that such conflicts often develop into sources of interpersonal friction with a consequent deterioration in relations between the persons involved.

Poor relations, perhaps generated by factors such as conflict or inadequate communication between people, go on to produce psychological strain in the form of low job satisfaction (r's range from .25 to .47) and feelings of job-related threat to one's well-being. Interestingly enough, poor relations with one's subordinates do not seem to affect feelings of threat ($r = $ only .12), whereas poor relations with one's colleagues and immediate superior do affect threat (r's $= .44$ and .41, respectively). Apparently an individual's feelings of threat are more likely to be reduced by improving his relations with his superior and colleagues than with his subordinates.

In summary, then, poor relations with other members of an organization may be precipitated by conditions of ambiguity—conditions where adequate information regarding roles and responsibilities and information necessary to carry them out are not provided. The misunderstandings and conflicts that may occur as a result of all this may in turn negatively affect the quality of trust, supportiveness, and willingness to listen to organization members' problems. Finally, these poor interpersonal relations generate dissatisfactions with the job and feelings of threat.

Participation

Participation refers to the extent to which a person has influence on decision processes of the organization. To the extent that people's knowledge, opinions, and wishes are excluded from such decision processes, we say that they have low participation. Of course, there is nothing inherently bad about being a nonparticipant. It all depends on the context. For example, you and I are often glad to be excluded from decision making because we do not have either the time to participate or the need to. We are concerned here, however, with decisions which the person might want to participate in, such as decisions about how he should do his job.

Early experimental research has shown that lack of opportunities to participate in such decisions can create strain in the person and even adversely affect productivity. One study of participation in a sewing plant (Coch and French, 1948) examined groups experiencing three different degrees of worker participation in making a major decision about a change in work procedures. The findings showed that the greater the degree of participation, the greater was the subsequent productivity, the higher the job satisfaction, the lower the turnover, and the better the relations between the workers and the managers. These findings were later replicated in a study in a Norwegian factory (French, Israel, and Ås, 1960). This line of research has also been extended to the study of the effects of employee participation in work-appraisal interviews (see "Feedback That Spurs Performance" in this volume). Such participation, when coupled with supportive supervisory practices, has produced improvements in relations between the employee and his boss and subsequent improvement in performance.

The findings on participation seem to hold across a very wide range of organizations. In Yugoslav factories, operated under a system of Workers' Councils, we also find that participation is associated with job satisfaction (Obradović, French, and Rodgers, 1970). Even more different from our large American organizations are the very small factories and poultry branches in the kibbutzim of Israel. Our study of forty-four such organizations revealed that high participation was associated with high satisfaction with the job and the organization, high self-esteem, low alienation, high commitment to work and to the organization, more innovation for better ways of doing the job, doing more extra work, reading more books and magazines related to work, a higher performance evaluation by one's manager, and lower absenteeism (Levitan, 1970).

Field experiments of the kind cited above have indicated that lack of participation can be a major source of stress. In the Goddard study high participation was accompanied by better relations with the person's immediate superior, colleagues, and subordinates (r's range from .24 to .52). We might expect that by participating in what is going on, a person reduces his ambiguity regarding relevant information for performing his work. This is in fact the case. High participators report low role ambiguity ($r = -.55$). As a result of lowered ambiguity, we would expect that people who participate a lot would utilize their skills and abilities more since they would have more information on how to best apply their talents. In fact, we found that high participation is positively related to high utilization of both administrative ($r = .50$) and nonadministrative ($r = .52$) skills and abilities.

Potential benefits to the organization may accrue from all of this. The attitude toward work by the high participators is quite positive. They tend to prefer more rather than less work than they already have ($r = .34$), which suggests that the involvement generated by participation makes people more willing to take on added tasks. High participators, compared with low participators in our sample of Goddard administrators, engineers, and scientists, also perceive greater opportunities for advancement in the organization ($r = .47$). This means that the organization is less likely to have turnover problems with these employees since they are less likely to be attracted to competing organizations.

We expect that with the right to participate in decisions goes the responsibility to enact and carry out those decisions. Our Goddard findings offer support for this expectation. The more a person participates, the more responsibility of all kinds he reports having, irrespective of his organizational status (measured here by government salary level; $r = .61$).

In the study at Goddard we found that people who report high opportunities to participate in decisions affecting the work they do tend to report both high satisafaction ($r = .50$) and low job-related feelings of threat ($r = -.51$). People who participate a lot also have high feelings of self-esteem or self-worth ($r = .32$). Thus, in terms of psychological well-being, our high participators are much better off than our low participators.

We have already mentioned a variety of other stresses, in addition to that of low participation, which are also accompanied by low job satisfaction and/or job-related threat. These stresses include poor relations with others, role conflict, role ambiguity, and quantitative and qualitative overload. Of all the stresses we have considered, low participation has the greatest harmful effect on job satisfaction and threat. This means that participation is a relatively important determinant of psychological well-being.

Since participation is also significantly correlated with low role ambiguity, good relations with others, and low overload, it is conceivable that its effects are widespread, and that all the relationships between these other stresses and psychological strain can be accounted for in terms of how much the person participates. This, in fact, appears to be the case. When we control or hold constant, through statistical analysis techniques, the amount of participation a person reports, then the correlations between all the above stresses and job satisfaction and job-related threat drop quite noticeably. This suggests that low participation generates these related stresses, and that increasing participation is an efficient way of reducing many other stresses which also lead to psychological strain.

We have discussed direct relationships between participation and its effects on organizational members. There is some additional evidence which suggests that the effects of participation on the person and his work may differ as a function of his personality or as a function of the nature of the decision he participates in making. Thus, if the person is given the opportunity to participate in trivial decisions or decisions unrelated to how work is done, satisfaction and productivity might remain unaffected. We have not gone into the specific findings here on the role of these context factors, because there have been only minor amounts of research in these areas.

Figure 5 summarizes our findings on participation. People who report high levels of participation are less likely to experience mental strain in the form of job dissatisfaction, job-related threat, or low self-esteem. The lack of role ambiguity which accompanies participation apparently enables the person to better utilize his skills and abilities in performing

Figure 5. Characteristics of persons who participate in decisions which affect their work.

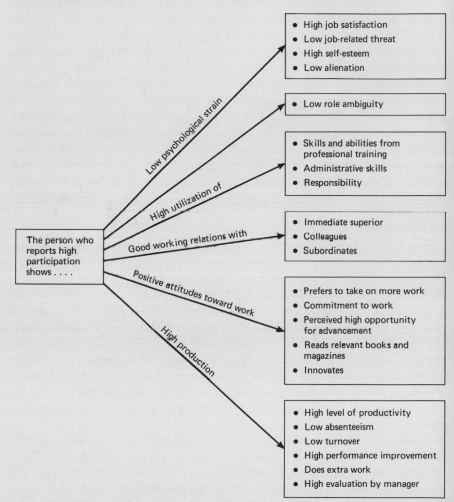

his work. High participation also is accompanied by high responsibility in our samples.

The high morale of the participators is seen in their positive attitudes toward their work. They prefer to take on more rather than less work, and they see the organization as a place where they have a good opportunity to advance. Some of our research indicates that under conditions of high participation one can expect to find low turnover, high productivity, and high performance improvement when employees participate in decisions on ways to improve their performance.

Occupational Differences in Stress and Strain

We have already noted that public health statistics, as well as specific studies by other investigators, have revealed large occupational differences in coronary heart disease. At Goddard we became interested in stress and strain differences between administrators, engineers, and scientists because NASA administrators have over three times as much heart disease as engineers and scientists. Our model of the effects of stress on strain, presented in Figure 1, suggests that there should indeed be such occupational differences in heart disease. First of all, different occupational groups are likely to experience different quantities of the same stress (for example, five deadlines per year versus five per month). Second, different occupational groups are also likely to experience different forms of stress (such as responsibility for the work of others versus responsibility for budgets). Third, occupational groups may differ in terms of the amount of strain they experience. Thus, recent research by Sales and House (1970) has shown that these occupational differences in heart disease are highly correlated with differences in the amounts of psychological strain (job dissatisfaction) that are encountered ($r = .49$). These findings hold especially for white collar occupational groups. Finally, different groups may react with different forms of strain (one group may develop coronary heart disease while the other group may experience low self-esteem).

An interesting example of these differences in stress and strain in occupations comes from a study of administrators and professors in a large Midwestern university (French, Tupper, and Mueller, 1965). Administrators experienced different stresses than did university professors, and each group's feelings of psychological strain were related to different types of stress. Administrators experienced more *quantitative* overload than professors. Professors experienced more *qualitative* overload than administrators. Quantitative overload produced feelings of low self-esteem in administrators ($r = -.65$) but not in professors. On the other hand, qualitative overload produced feelings of low self-esteem in professors but not in administrators. Thus what was psychological "poison" for one group was not so toxic for the other group and vice versa. Administrators would apparently rather do all their tasks sacrificing a bit on quality, while professors would rather sacrifice on quantity and do a high-quality job on a smaller number of tasks.

When we did the study of administrators, engineers, and scientists at Goddard we were curious to see if the scientists and engineers were like university professors in their concern with the quality of their work, and if the Goddard administrators were like the university administrators with regard to the quantity of work they had. This, in fact, turned out to be the case. The scientists reported the most qualitative overload while the administrators reported the least. On the other hand, the administrators reported the most quantitative overload while the scientists reported the least. In fact, the administrators scored the highest on a whole series of indicators of high quantitative workload including the number of phone calls, office visits, and meetings per week. They even took the longest, on the average, to return their questionnaires, suggesting that they indeed had many more items demanding immediate attention on their desk compared to the engineers and scientists.

We also found that administrators were highest on another important stress linked with coronary heart disease—namely, responsibilities for persons. The administrators reported spending the greatest amount of time, compared with the engineers and scientists, in responsibilities for the work of others and for others' futures. Our administrator group also reported the most role conflict.

Finally, we found that administrators, compared with engineers and scientists, spend the most time in contact with persons outside their own immediate part of the organization (that is, in other territory). They spend more time interfacing with persons in other branches, divisions, directorates, and bases. As a result of such contact across boundaries, they report greater stress from these other areas of the organization than do engineers and scientists.

We have already noted that quantitative overload and responsibility for persons are related to risk factors in coronary heart disease such as pulse rate, diastolic blood pressure, and number of cigarettes smoked. The next question, then, was whether we would find the administrators to be highest on these three risk factors. We did, although the differences in pulse rate and diastolic blood pressure were not statistically significant. The administrators also turned out to have the highest systolic blood pressures.[5]

Occupational differences in personality and their relevance to heart disease. In our theoretical model of organizational stress and its effects on individual strain, personality plays a very special role. If you look back at Figure 1, you will see that there is no arrow from personality to the risk factors. Instead the vertical arrow depicts personality as having a conditioning effect. If there is a particular stress such as quantitative overload, then we hypothesize that the Type A person will react by showing a good deal of strain (such as raised cholesterol, faster pulse, or more cigarettes smoked); on the other hand, the person who lacks the Type A traits will be relatively unaffected by the stress (that is, his cholesterol, pulse, or smoking behavior will remain unchanged).

---

[5] These physiological findings are age corrected.

The reader can probably think of everyday examples where personality plays this special role. Some people, for example, when faced with a good deal of job stress, become immobilized, make mistakes, or lose their tempers; others, under the same conditions, calmly go about the work before them. We usually think of these two types of people as differing in some relatively stable traits or personality dispositions. The stress is the same, but their reactions to the stress are a function of their respective personalities.

A good deal of research on the role of personality traits as a factor in coronary heart disease has already been carried out. Research by Friedman, Rosenman, and their colleagues (Rosenman et al., 1970; Rosenman et al., 1966) has shown that one can predict with some success the occurrence of coronary heart disease on the basis of the presence of a personality pattern known as Type A. These longitudinal studies have been carried out over a period of four and a half years using 3,182 males from a wide range of occupational groups. The Type A personality pattern includes traits such as high involvement in one's work (Involved Striving), a liking for deadlines and other job pressures (Positive Attitude Toward Pressure), a tendency to feel overburdened by one's work (Environmental Overburdening), and a tendency to take on roles of considerable responsibility—perhaps for the work of others (Leadership).

Having found that our Goddard administrators score highest on stresses commonly associated with coronary heart disease, we might wonder whether they would also be higher than engineers and scientists on the Type A personality traits. This is indeed the case. The findings are presented in Table 2. Administrators score highest on involved striving, positive attitude toward pressure, environmental overburdening, leadership, and on an overall measure of Type A called "What I am like." They also score highest on flexibility, a personality trait which, as we noted earlier, increases the effect of role conflict on job tension. All of these occupational differences in personality are statistically significant.

That the administrators score highest on the Type A personality traits means they are likely to react to certain stresses in ways which produce elevations in risk factors in coronary heart disease. On the other hand, since the engineers and scientists score lower on these measures of Type A, they are less likely to react to the same stresses in ways which will elevate their smoking, pulse rates, cholesterol, and blood pressure.

Our studies at Goddard provide some concrete examples of the difference personality makes in how a person reacts to stress.. We found, for example, that persons who are high on involved striving show increases in diastolic blood pressure and cholesterol as the percent of time they spend in responsibilities for others' futures increases. These people, who are so high on involved striving, apparently take their responsibilities for others' futures quite seriously. Persons who are low on involved striving don't appear to be affected by such responsibilities. As we have noted, administrators are the highest occupational group with regard to involved striving, responsibility for others' futures, and diastolic blood pressure.

There are similar findings of this type involving each of the other personality traits that characterize the administrators. In each case, the person who is high on the trait, compared with the person who is low, shows greater physiological strain in the face of some job stress.

Table 2. Occupational differences in personality.

| | OCCUPATION | | | |
| | ADMINIS- | | | |
MEASURE	TRATOR	ENGINEER	SCIENTIST	P
Rigid personality (flexibility-rigidity scale)	2.3*	2.4	2.5	.01
Involved striving	5.2†	4.8	5.0	.05
Positive attitude toward pressure	5.2	4.9	4.8	.05
Environmental overburdening	5.6	5.1	5.4	.05
Leadership	5.0	4.3	4.2	.05
What I Am Like (Type A)	3.5‡	3.3	3.2	.05

* These values are based on a four-point scale where 1 = flexible and 4 = rigid.

† The values for involved striving and the next three traits in the table are based on a seven-point scale where 1 = low on the personality trait and 7 = high on the personality trait.

‡ These values are based on a five-point scale where 5 = Type A and 1 = the opposite.

In summary, people with different jobs encounter different kinds and amounts of stress. Consequently, they experience different kinds of strain. Our own research shows that administrators, for example, are far more likely to develop coronary heart disease both because they experience different types of organizational stress linked to risk factors in the disease and because they experience more of those types of organizational stress than do engineers and scientists. It is important to consider the role personality plays in all of this. People with Type A personality traits are more likely to show strain reactions when they encounter organizational stress than are people who do not have these traits. Thus occupations (such as administration) which, for one reason or another, attract people with these personality traits will be higher risk groups for coronary heart disease then occupations which do not attract such persons.

Protecting Our Human Resources

The research we have reviewed clearly indicates that the stresses of today's organizations can pose serious threats to the physical and psychological well-being of organization members. When a man dies or becomes disabled by a heart attack, the organization may be partly to blame. But the assignment of guilt will not prevent people from dying or prevent the organization from incurring large losses in terms of the investments required to recruit and train replacements. What is needed, instead, is a program of organizational diagnosis and prevention aimed at curtailing the loss of human resources to an organizational enemy known as coronary heart disease.

As we begin to discuss prevention, some perspective is needed on what might be accomplished if we were to institute the ideal prevention program, given what we now know about coronary heart disease. First of all, if one reviews the medical literature, one finds that the known risk factors in coronary heart disease account for about 25 percent of the variation in the disease. This means that if you could perfectly control cholesterol, blood pressure, smoking, glucose level, serum uric acid, and so on, you would have controlled only about one-fourth of coronary heart disease.

Furthermore our data suggest that a perfect control of job stresses would control only a small part of the variation in these physiological risk factors. However, it may be that job stress also affects heart disease by means of other mechanisms which we have not studied. Thus there is positive evidence that the control of job stress should have a small effect on heart disease, but there is a possibility that it could have a substantial effect. This latter possibility is still a big unknown. We know just enough to justify thinking about programs of prevention and planning research to explore their feasibility.

We should point out that although our notions about prevention are concerned primarily with coronary heart disease, there is some evidence to suggest that reduction in job stresses may also lower the incidence of other work-related illnesses, such as ulcers (Dunn and Cobb, 1962). The fact that dispensary visits tend to increase under increased responsibility (Kasl and French, 1962) gives support to the notion that a wide variety of illnesses, such as respiratory ailments, headaches, anxiety attacks, and nausea, might be prevented by reducing job stress.

What should be done to prevent coronary disease and psychological strain in organizations? To answer that question, we must change hats and switch from the role of social scientist to that of consultant and adviser. This is a difficult switch for us to make, and we want the reader to understand the difficulties so that he can properly evaluate the nature of our recommendations.

For one thing, very little research has been done on experimental programs of prevention. It is one thing to know, on the basis of careful research, some of the organizational stresses which influence heart disease and its risk factors; it is quite another thing to know how to control these stresses. Although we will utilize the available research, our advice must often rely on interpretations which go beyond the established facts. We will not hesitate to use our experience in organizations and our creative imagination in trying to invent programs of prevention. In this section, therefore, we can no longer adhere to our standards of scientific reporting, namely, that we report only those findings where we can assess their probable truth and where the chances are at least 95 in 100 that the findings are true. Instead, we will try to generate a variety of suggestions for prevention which are implied by our research but whose feasibility must be judged by the reader. The ultimate effectiveness of these suggestions must, of course, be determined by trying them out along with a careful research evaluation.

A second difficulty which faces us as consultant but not as social scientist is that we must now pay attention to a whole series of constraints. Any prevention program designed to improve health must not cost too much, must not conflict with other organizational goals, must not violate existing policies, must be feasible to carry out with the available (or obtainable) personnel, and so forth. Our suggestions will try to take account of these constraints even though we do not have space to discuss each of them.

However, one constraint is too important to bypass: Will the prevention program interfere with productivity and profits? Our general answer to this question is no. The research underlying systems of management such as the one proposed by Likert (1961, 1967) shows that high productivity often (although not always) goes together with high morale and job satisfaction. Some aspects of this system of management seem well adapted to reduce organizational stress and individual strain. It seems possible to design programs that will reduce heart disease and in the long run improve organizational performance. Nevertheless, there can be cases, especially in the short run, where organizational goals and individual well-being are in conflict. An ambitious Type A man, for example, may voluntarily take on an extremely heavy workload and contribute greatly to the performance of the organization, but eventually he may die of a heart attack.

A third problem facing us in the consultant role is the fact that every organization has its own special environment, its own unique structure and procedures, and its own pattern of stresses. Just as stress and disease differ greatly from one occupation to another, so too they differ from one organization to another. As consultants we are in a position similar to the doctor who is asked to make a diagnosis and prescribe a cure without seeing the patient. The first step in devising a program of prevention must be to make an accurate diagnosis of the stresses and strains in the particular organization. Such a diagnosis would include answers to the following questions: (1) How is heart disease distributed among the different divisions, departments, and other organizational units and among occupations? (2) How are psychological and physiological strains distributed among organizational units, among occupations, and among individuals? (3) What are the patterns of stress in the various organizational units and occupations and on individuals?

Given the answers to these questions, we can concentrate preventive programs on those organizational units, occupations, and individuals where the risks to health are greatest. For example, we know that at NASA we should focus on administrators rather than on engineers and scientists. At a more sophisticated level of analysis, we might aim our program at those places in the organization where there is high overload and heavy deadline pressures, high role conflict and role ambiguity, many contacts across organizational boundaries, and a heavy load of responsibility for other people. Finally, this information would enable us to devise programs designed to alleviate particular kinds or patterns of stress.

We believe that the research methods we have employed can be adapted as useful instruments for the kind of diagnosis that will permit each organization to devise its own tailor-made program of prevention. In the absence of such information, the reader should recognize that our suggestions here must be rather general and, of course, cannot be specific to the special conditions in his own organization.

One can distinguish three methods of preventing the bad effects of disease: (1) primary prevention—that is, preventing the stresses from reaching the person; (2) once the noxious elements of the environment have reached the person, preventing the disease by, for example, early elimination of strain; (3) once the disease has broken out, preventing a later disability by proper treatment. Our emphasis will be on the first two of these, for they seem more desirable and more appropriate for action by management. The third method, the treatment and management of the cardiac patient, will not be discussed here because it is the special province of the physician.

In this discussion we shall be dealing with two broad classes of preventive actions which stem from our two main findings. The first main finding is that various organizational stresses produce strains in the individual which may eventually result in heart disease. This finding suggests a kind of primary prevention—the elimination or reduction of these stresses in the environment so that they do not impinge upon the person. The second main finding is that the effects of stress on strain will vary with individual differences in personality and with the goodness of fit between the demands and stresses of the job and the characteristics of the person. This second finding suggests a set of personnel procedures for improving the goodness of fit—namely, selection, placement, training, and job rotation. First, we will briefly discuss these personnel procedures because they are simpler and more familiar procedures. Then we will go on to consider the more desirable but more difficult possibilities of primary prevention, ending with an example of an experimental program of prevention designed to reduce several stresses in a specific organization.

Personnel Procedures for Reducing Stress

Selection and placement. Our research suggests that certain types of persons are more susceptible to stress than others. Current selection procedures are typically devoted to preventing qualitative overload by assuming that the applicant has the required ability, training, knowledge, skill, and experience. One could extend these selection criteria by also choosing people on the basis of their tolerance for ambiguity, their ability to handle role conflict, or their resistance to the stress of responsibility. There are problems with this approach, however, since we lack adequate selection tests for measuring such traits and dispositions. Our tests have been used solely for scientific research and have not been adequately validated in studies where we predict in advance who will and who will not show strain under certain organizational stresses. This means that one might make errors in selection by relying on tests of this sort.

At any rate, special selection to prevent coronary heart disease is not necessary because the effects of stress and strain on this disease are probably very gradual. The new employee probably won't die on the job the first month even if his selection was a mistake. Thus, the organization has time to observe the employee's response to his current job, and to work on placement and promotion decisions on that basis. It is probably easier to diagnose a man's susceptibility to stress by watching him perform under stress than by giving him a battery of pre-employment tests.

Training. Another procedure for improving the fit of the person to the job involves training. He would be taught skill in performing his job more effectively and consequently with less effort and strain. He might be shown how to reduce overload by taking shortcuts in performing his tasks, or he could be provided with certain skills. His relations with others might be improved and his conflicts reduced by training him in techniques for getting along with people and handling conflict. Some training techniques such as role playing and sensitivity training are well known to management, but their effectiveness remains to be demonstrated (Campbell and Dunnette, 1968), especially for the purpose of reducing strain.

Job rotation. This is yet another procedure to be considered in cases of high-stress jobs which cannot be easily restructured and where no one can handle the job without strain. In such cases, the exposure of any one person to these stresses is reduced by job rotation. Since jobs on organizational boundaries involve high stress, one might rotate people on and off these jobs to allow them to recuperate. One disadvantage of this procedure is that on the first rotation the new man will suffer the usual temporary stresses of a transfer: an increase in qualitative and quantitative workload and in role ambiguity. After he has had time to learn the new job, however, these stresses should disappear. There are, of course, limits to job rotation. Some people are "indispensable" and cannot be rotated (all the more reason to be concerned about their health). It is noteworthy that one of our most important and most stressful jobs, President of the United States, is subject to regular rotation.

Reducing Organizational Stress

Here we need to consider the possibilities for reducing each of the stresses we have identified: role ambiguity, role conflict, quantitative overload, qualitative overload, interaction across boundaries and in foreign territories, responsibility for people, poor relations with others, and low participation. For each of these we must look for possible preventive actions directed at both the job itself and the wider organizational environment.

Changing the stresses in the job. Some job stresses—such as role ambiguity, role conflict, and poor relations with others—seem to be bad for both the health of the individual and the health of the organization. Managers have a special responsibility for establishing an unambiguous division of labor within the organization which is understood and accepted by all. At the same time, the organizational structure should be maximally flexible and responsive to local needs. Perhaps this can best be achieved by avoiding formal job descriptions imposed by the superior and instituting a program, already used successfully in one company, of discussions between each man and his supervisor for the purpose of jointly redefining the man's job. If such discussions are held frequently and successfully, less ambiguity and conflict, better interpersonal relations, and improved organizational coordination should result.

The stress of overload is bad for the individual, but high workloads may be good for the organization; so there is often conflict between employees and employers over workloads, work standards, and piece rates. However, where individual jobs are definitely overloaded, it is probably to the long-range advantage of all concerned to correct the inequity by reducing the overload and redistributing the work.

One might also change the job by institutionalizing certain procedures for reducing stress when it occurs. For example, Kahn et al. (1964) suggest that persons who experience a great deal of role conflict or overload should be given the right to convene those people who make excessive demands on them, confront them with the conflicting demands they are making, and work out some acceptable solution. Similarly, a person could be given the right to delegate work to other people or to ask for more work or responsibility if he is underloaded.

It should be recognized that giving people such rights is not always a simple matter, for there are strongly held norms and values specifying who should do what and how policies, procedures, and jobs should be changed. There may be resistance to changing norms about subordinates delegating work, redefining their jobs, or taking initiative to get more responsibility.

Changing the wider environment of the job. A variety of such changes could be made. First, one could increase the resources available to the person to reduce overload and deadline pressures. More auxiliary help could be added. Immediate superiors could be trained in better management techniques to improve relations between the person and his superior and reduce role conflict. Better information transmission systems could be adopted to reduce role ambiguity.

Although many such environmental changes may be necessary to reduce stress, they may not be sufficient in and of themselves. If people are not *trained* to use their new rights or organizational resources, the structural changes may have little effect on them. Thus, many changes in the job or its environment will also require some changes in the person. Similarly, some changes in the person may have little effect if there are no structural changes in the job which allow the person to utilize his new skills, knowledge, or rights.

Large-scale changes in environment might also be adopted. If boundary stress is a problem, the number of boundaries within the organization, such as between different divisions, could be reduced by reorganization. Role ambiguity could similarly be reduced by reducing the number of hierarchical levels in the organization, thereby reducing the distances between organizational members who need to communicate with one another. New policies for the allocation of various forms of workload could also be introduced (such as workload on the basis of ability rather than role, with new roles added and subtracted to take up and let out slack).

Some of these larger system changes might follow models of "ideal" organizations suggested by Likert (1961, 1967), McGregor (1960), Argyris (1962, 1964), Katz and Kahn (1966), and others which are based on research in organizations. The implications of temporary work groups where roles constantly change to adapt to new organizational demands have been discussed by Burns and Stalker (1961) in *The Management of Innovation* and by Bennis and Slater (1968) in *The Temporary Society.* Both books lead the reader to conclude that organizations, particularly those in today's changing and unstable environments, have the best chance of adapting to new challenges from their environments if they utilize a flexible ("organic" rather than "mechanistic") structure of organization. This structure does not lock or freeze people into specific roles or jobs beyond the point where this is nonadaptive for the organization.

Using participation to reduce stress and strain. We have observed that low participation is related to psychological strains such as job dissatisfaction and job-related threat. We now wish to offer some advice on the use of participation, because there are ways of using participation which may have either no effect or may create even more strain and problems for management than if it is not used. This advice is based on some findings from research (French, Israel, and Ås, 1960; French, Kay, and Meyer, 1966) which, although inconclusive, nevertheless seem to be potentially too important to overlook.

We have already noted that one experimental program of participation worked best when the employee felt supported rather than threatened by his boss (French et al., 1966). Generalizing these findings a bit, we suggest that attempts to decrease stress by increasing participation should also provide a supportive supervisor and a cohesive and supportive group of co-workers. Such supportiveness will directly reduce psychological strain, and it will also increase the effectiveness of the participation.

Second, participation which is only *illusory,* as when management asks employees for their advice and then ignores it, may be perceived by the employees as an attempt at psychological manipulation. The end result of such an attempt by management to "win the hearts" of employees may be employee distrust of superiors, organizational sabotage, apathy, and turnover.

Third, participation in *trivial* decisions (should the company newsletter be on white paper or light-green paper?) are liable to have little, if any, effect on the employees. A fourth and related potential principle concerns *relevance.* If the aim is to reduce the stress of quantitative workload, then participation in decisions irrelevant to the workload are not likely to have ameliorative effects on strain created by quantitative overload. Participation, for example, in decisions about what hours the company cafeteria should operate to best meet the needs of employees would probably have little positive effect on strains caused by deadlines and other work overload.

Finally, the decisions which people participate in should be perceived as being *legitimately* theirs to make. If a group does not feel it is debating something within its area of freedom, the participants may feel anxious, threatened, even dissatisfied. Since strong norms or widely shared rules develop in organizations about who should decide what, it would not be uncommon to find people feeling that they were overstepping their bounds in making new kinds of decisions. Thus, increased participation may need to occur at a rate great enough for employees to perceive, yet not at a rate so great that they cringe in fear over new expectations they feel they have been saddled with.

In conclusion, the body of evidence we have reviewed here lends strong support to the notion that modern organizations have an impact on both the psychological and physiological health of their members. Many of the stresses that are fairly prevalent in national samples and in specific organizational settings appear to be linked in one way or another with strains which produce coronary heart disease. But the fact that coronary heart disease seems to be as much a part of organizational life as are other traits of organizations (such as size and structure) does not mean that steps cannot be taken to reduce the risk of disease. There are innovative measures available to management. Programs which involve the coordinated effort of management, medical personnel, and organizational psychologists can be developed. Careful evaluation of these programs can be carried out; and through such experimental programs, modern organizations can make potentially important contributions to both management and medical science, with benefits for both the individual's and the organization's well-being and strength.

REFERENCES

ARDREY, R. *The Territorial Imperative.* New York: Dell, 1968.

ARGYRIS, C. *Integrating the Individual and the Organization.* New York: John Wiley & Sons, 1964.

ARGYRIS, C. *Interpersonal Confidence and Organizational Effectiveness.* Homewood, Ill.: Richard D. Irwin, Dorsey Press, 1962.

BENNIS, W. G., AND P. E. SLATER. *The Temporary Society.* New York: Harper & Row, 1968.

BROOKS, G. W., AND E. F. MUELLER. Serum urate concentrations among university professors. *Journal of the American Medical Association,* 1966, *195*, 415–418.

BRUMMET, R. L., W. C. PYLE, AND E. G. FLAMHOLTZ. Accounting for human resources. *Michigan Business Review,* 1968, *20*, 20–25.

BURNS, T., AND G. M. STALKER. *The Management of Innovation.* London: Tavistock, 1961.

CAMPBELL, J. P., AND M. D. DUNNETTE. Effectiveness of t-group experiences in managerial training and development. *Psychological Bulletin,* 1968, *70*, 73–104.

COCH, L., AND J. R. P. FRENCH, JR. Overcoming resistance to change. *Human Relations,* 1948, *1*, 512–532.

DREYFUSS, F., AND J. W. CZACZKES. Blood cholesterol and uric acid of healthy medical students under stress of examination. *Archives of International Medicine,* 1959, *103*, 708.

DUNN, J., AND S. COBB. Frequency of peptic ulcer among executives, craftsmen, and foremen. *Journal of Occupational Medicine,* 1962, *4*, 343–348.

FRENCH, J. R. P., JR., J. ISRAEL, AND D. Ås. An experiment on participation in a Norwegian factory. *Human Relations,* 1960, *13*, 3–20.

FRENCH, J. R. P., JR., E. KAY, AND H. MEYER. Participation and the appraisal system. *Human Relations,* 1966, *19*, 3–20.

FRENCH, J. R. P., JR., C. J. TUPPER, AND E. F. MUELLER. *Work Load of University Professors.* Cooperative Research Project No. 2171, University of Michigan, 1965.

FRIEDMAN, M., R. H. ROSENMAN, AND V. CARROLL. Changes in serum cholesterol and blood clotting time in men subjected to cyclic variation of occupational stress. *Circulation,* 1958, *17,* 852–861.

GRUNDY, S. M., AND A. C. GRIFFIN. Effects of periodic mental stress on serum cholesterol levels. *Circulation,* 1959, *19,* 496.

HINKLE, L. E., JR., S. T. CARVER, M. STEVENS, AND S. SCHEIDT. Disorders of rate and rhythm as precursors of coronary death. Paper presented at the Conference on Cardiovascular Disease Epidemiology, March 1970.

HORWITZ, C., AND B. BRONTE-STEWART. Mental stress and serum lipid variation in ischemic heart disease. *American Journal of Medical Science,* 1962, *244,* 272–281.

KAHN, R. L., D. M. WOLFE, R. P. QUINN, J. D. SNOEK, AND R. A. ROSENTHAL. *Organizational Stress: Studies in Role Conflict and Ambiguity.* New York: John Wiley & Sons, 1964.

KASL, S. V., G. W. BROOKS, AND S. COBB. Serum urate concentrations in male high-school students: A predictor of college attendance. *Journal of the American Medical Association,* 1966, *198,* 713–716.

KASL, S., AND J. R. P. FRENCH, JR. The effects of occupational status on physical and mental health. *Journal of Social Issues,* 1962, *18,* 67–89.

KATZ, D., AND R. L. KAHN. *The Social Psychology of Organizations.* New York: John Wiley & Sons, 1966.

LEVITAN, U. Status in human organization as a determinant of mental health and performance. Ph.D. dissertation, University of Michigan, 1970.

LIKERT, R. *The Human Organization.* New York: McGraw-Hill, 1967.

LIKERT, R. *New Patterns of Management.* New York: McGraw-Hill, 1961.

MAIER, N. R. F. *Psychology in Industry.* 3rd ed. Boston: Houghton Mifflin, 1965.

MC CLELLAND, D. C. *The Achieving Society.* Princeton, N.J.: Van Nostrand, 1961.

MC GREGOR, D. *The Human Side of Enterprise.* New York: McGraw-Hill, 1960.

MILLER, J. G. Information input overload and psychopathology. *American Journal of Psychiatry,* 1960, *116,* 695–704.

MODIGLIANI, A. *Embarrassment and Social Influence.* Ph.D. dissertation, University of Michigan, 1966. Ann Arbor, Mich.: University Microfilms, No. 67–8312.

OBRADOVIĆ, J., J. R. P. FRENCH, JR., AND W. RODGERS. Workers' councils in Yugoslavia. *Human Relations,* 1970, *23,* 459–471.

The President's Commission on Heart Disease, Cancer and Stroke. *Report to the President: A National Program to Conquer Heart Disease, Cancer and Stroke.* Vol. 1. Washington, D.C.: U.S. Government Printing Office, 1964.

ROSENMAN, R. H., M. FRIEDMAN, R. STRAUSS, C. D. JENKINS, S. J. ZYZANSKI, AND M. WURM. Coronary heart disease in the Western Collaborative Group Study: A follow-up experience of 4½ years. *Journal of Chronic Diseases,* 1970, *23,* 173–190.

ROSENMAN, R. H., M. FRIEDMAN, R. STRAUSS, M. WURM, C. D. JENKINS, H. B.

MESSINGER, R. KOSITCHEK, W. HAHN, AND N. T. WERTHESSEN. Coronary heart disease in the Western Collaborative Group Study. *Journal of the American Medical Association*, 1966, *195*, 86–92.

RUSSEK, H. I. Emotional stress and CHD in American physicians, dentists, and lawyers. *American Journal of Medical Science*, 1962, *243*, 716–725.

RUSSEK, H. I. Emotional stress and coronary heart disease in American physicians. *American Journal of Medical Science*, 1960, *240*, 711–721.

RUSSEK, H. I. Stress, tobacco, and coronary heart disease in North American professional groups. *Journal of the American Medical Association*, 1965, *192*, 189–194.

SALES, S. M. *Differences among Individuals in Affective, Behavioral, Biochemical, and Physiological Responses to Variations in Work Load*. Ph.D. dissertation, University of Michigan, 1969. Ann Arbor, Mich.: University Microfilms, No. 69–18098.

SALES, S. M., AND J. HOUSE. Job dissatisfaction as a possible risk factor in coronary heart disease. To be published in *Journal of Chronic Diseases*.

STAMLER, J., D. M. BERKSON, H. A. LINDBERG, W. A. MILLER, E. L. STEVENS, R. SOYUGENC, T. J. TOKICH, AND R. STAMLER. Heart rate: An important risk factor for coronary mortality, including sudden death—ten-year experience of the Peoples Gas Company Epidemiologic Study (1958–68). Paper presented at the Second International Symposium on Atherosclerosis, Chicago, November 1969.

TERREBERRY, S. *The Organization of Environments*. Ph.D. dissertation, University of Michigan, 1968. Ann Arbor, Mich.: University Microfilms, No. 69–12254.

THOMAS, C. B., AND E. A. MURPHY. Further studies on cholesterol levels in the Johns Hopkins medical students: The effect of stress at examinations. *Journal of Chronic Diseases*, 1958, *8*, 661–668.

WERTLAKE, P. T., A. A. WILCOX, M. T. HALEY, AND J. E. PETERSON. Relationship of mental and emotional stress to serum cholesterol levels. *Proceedings of the Society for Experimental Biology and Medicine*, 1958, *97*, 163–165.

HARRY LEVINSON

Problems
That Worry Executives

Executives are mostly men of ambition who are powerfully motivated by distant goals of success. To get where they want to go, they have learned to be intensely self-critical.

As psychologist Lyle Spencer once wrote, "From the day they take over the reins of business control, most chief executives are secretly as dissatisfied with their own work as with that of their most bumbling employee, and their desire to improve the quality of their decisions and activities is as intense as their drive to increase company profits."

This intense internal dissatisfaction makes the executive both powerful and vulnerable at the same time. Although he may succeed in the eyes of others, his dissatisfaction with himself will frequently make him feel that he is a failure. He is only too keenly aware of how much more he might have done. Thus an executive may be buffeted constantly by profound and opposite feelings of failure and success.

Executives generally press themselves toward definable goals and naturally seek to create conditions under which they are most likely to attain them. On the whole, they prefer to guide and direct; they are reluctant to rest their fate on people whose actions they cannot predict.

The more ambiguous the environment in which they must operate, the more executives will feel threatened, for the steps to goal attainment will be less clear and the sources of potential trouble less discernible. Many executives, therefore, tend to concern themselves with procedures and to prefer well-defined organizational structure.

But the contemporary business environment makes organizations less subject to executive control and requires executives to interact with, and depend upon, others whose behavior is increasingly unpredictable. At the same time, business conditions in general are becoming increasingly ambiguous. Executive stress is consequently becoming more severe.

The Problems of Social Leadership

The most serious stress, and one which will become more pressing for many executives, arises from the executive's changing relationship to his community.

This shift in the role of a business executive, and the stress which goes with it, has been extremely rapid. When one prominent executive recently became president of his company, he was told by his predecessor (who remained as a consultant) that the new presidential job was so different from his own that he found it difficult to advise his successor. One of the new president's first major tasks: to serve as chairman of a state-government commission investigating race riots.

The readiness of the governor of a state to turn to a business executive to chair a social investigation is itself a significant sign of the times. The situation epitomizes a wide range of new executive stresses. These days the American business leader overtly wields social, as well as economic, power.

Henry Steele Commager has argued that the business executive has assumed and acquired extraordinary social power in American society because he developed his role in an otherwise empty social context. There were no already privileged groups like royalty, the church, or the military. As a generator of jobs and capital and a prime shaper of communities and social institutions, the business executive acquired power in this country earlier and to a far greater extent than his counterpart in Europe. One effect has been to thrust upon the American executive responsibilities and expectations that business leaders in other countries don't have to bear.

Today's American business leader may well have come to maturity accepting the widespread concept that his job was basically to make money and, only incidentally, to render a service or to produce goods. He is therefore astonished at being called upon to be a social engineer— to retrain the obsolescent, rehabilitate the impoverished and handicapped, abate pollution, give leadership to the political reorganization of communities and regions. He, who once had no reason to doubt that efficiency and effectiveness could be measured by a financial yardstick, is suddenly discovering that there are many other kinds of yardsticks which he has never learned to apply.

Many executives and their companies have long prided themselves on their good citizenship. In advertisements and annual reports they speak with self-satisfaction about their contributions to United Funds, community campaigns, colleges, and the like. They are dismayed when they are still accused of not doing enough. People today are ever more aware of the powerful crises of community living. They demand not merely financial contributions but the application of corporate power to solve community problems. In effect they are saying that with executive privilege must come executive responsibility. They may realize that a power center, such as a corporation, is likely to be hostile to change in its community unless it engages itself in bringing change about.

But most executives simply don't know where to begin with such problems. Furthermore, to undertake true community leadership inevitably will bring them into conflict with powerful vested interests, personified by their friends and colleagues in other businesses. This only increases their conflicts and guilt.

My impression is that most executives are caught in this kind of dilemma. Few are skilled agents of social change; nevertheless, all in senior leadership posts are being asked to assume that role. It is one laden with responsibility, with potential threat, and with the possibility of dismal failure. But the business executive has no escape. As long as he wields economic and social power there will be pressures on him to be a social engineer.

The social leadership roles the businessman is being asked to assume are often based on values and ideals far different from his own. Most business leaders in established organizations come from self-controlled, socially mobile families with strong prohibitions against overt expression of personal aggression. They are imbued with concepts of good manners, gentlemanliness, gradualness, and the suppression of conflict.

In dealing with those who demand more active leadership—and simultaneously criticize the leadership they are getting—the business leader must interact with and accept hostility, must cope with conflict, and must move more quickly than he does ordinarily to alleviate urgent social pains. The issues he faces, and the people who attack him, increase his discomfort. As much as he sometimes would like to fight back aggressively, he cannot allow himself to do so. Nor can he remain patient with business colleagues whose passive resistance to change complicates his task.

A second value conflict stems from the fact that he and his company may be criticized for the outcomes of activities which only a few years ago were almost universally applauded. For example, communities used to compete with each other to obtain new manufacturing plants, with little concern for their effect on the environment. The executive who brought a new plant to a community became a local hero. Now he must justify himself to a prospective host community if he wants to establish a new plant; he is perceived as a possible threat until he can demonstrate otherwise.

The business leader's new, unasked-for role in the glare of the spotlight is likely to be permanent. Henceforth all organizations that have power, and all people who exercise power, will be under continuous scrutiny.

Problems with Young People
A complicating factor for the executive, in both his business and community leadership roles, is the problem he has in dealing with young

people. Every new generation throws off some of the controls and values of the old. Each questions its predecessor and each accumulates experiences, directions, styles of behavior, and goals foreign to those who have gone before. Such behavior flies in the faces of men who seek stability, predictability, and control to realize their own goals. Many executives are therefore uneasy about working with young people and even more uneasy about sharing power with them. They react to young people with a confused amalgam of anger, disdain, admiration, envy, and rejection. Yet executives must work with the young, no matter how distant from youthful culture and values they may feel.

The conflict is most vividly observed at recruitment time in business schools. On the one hand, executives want young graduates who will do a job and fit into the organization while awaiting their turn for advancement. On the other hand, they want their graduates to be innovative and intensely ambitious. They are chagrined to discover that they can't enjoy the benefits of creative and profitable change without changing the way they have been managing. This often means relaxing some of the controls they have maintained.

The conflict is exacerbated when the young question executive perquisites heretofore taken for granted. For example, when a panel of college students was invited to speak at a convention of executives from a utilities company, the students chided the executives for not acting on a wide range of community problems—including using some of their profits for rehabilitating the economically disadvantaged. The executives said they could not afford to do so. The students pointed out the paradox of crying poor while waiting to get out on the golf course of the luxury hotel in which the meeting was taking place at company expense.

Executives are increasingly threatened by their *own* children too. They worry about being rejected, as do all parents. But they have more difficulty than some because they are so heavily geared to "making it" in the already established social patterns. When their children get into difficulty, the executives are disappointed in themselves as well as in their children. Among executives who travel frequently, guilt feelings are honed by the fear that they are ignoring or neglecting their families.

The Problems of Scientific Management

Another and quite different source of stress grows out of traditional conceptions of management practice. For many years executives have operated under the constraints of a conceptual straitjacket called "scientific management." Scientific management refers neither to science nor to management. Rather, it is industrial engineering upgraded and given a fancier name. It depends on "hard data" about matters which can be counted, measured, categorized, catalogued, and tabulated—in short, numbers. But the assumptions about motivation underlying those data are often questionable. At lower levels scientific management has resulted in alienation of employees, in a hostile manipulative relationship between management and employees, and in an increase in unionization. It is beginning to produce the same trends—unionization and alienation—among professional employees and middle management.

Measurement and control are what executives are taught as fundamentals of scientific management, and these are the techniques they try to apply. The application of such techniques forces executives into ever tighter profit squeezes and requires them to focus on short-term results at the cost of long-term organizational health.

They know that. But they feel they have practically no choice in how they manage if they are to be "scientific."

Thus businesses are often run under the constraining influences of accountants and financial experts, more for the approval of security analysts than for their own well-being. This is much like rearing a child for the approval of his teachers, with primary emphasis on his report card; the interests of the child can easily be sacrificed to the need for external approval. The true interests of many businesses are so sacrificed. Executives feel disloyal to stockholders, superiors, and themselves when they are compelled to focus on the short-term profit picture. At the same time, their tasks of providing social leadership, adapting to new values, and interacting with young people are made even more difficult.

Coupled with the limitations and fallacies of scientific management is the fact that most organizations operate with obsolete organizational structures. The historic bureaucratic model no longer functions well, even for bureaucratic organizations. Many government agencies, larger manufacturing firms, banks, public utilities, and similar organizations that have been thought to operate well bureaucratically have become so sluggish that it is impossible for them to maintain effective quality control.

There are many reasons why organizations resist change and why executives do not seek more actively to change them. But one important reason has been relatively obscure: many executives feel that to do so would be disloyal. On the way up executives must operate within the structure in order to achieve position and power. Once in a position of power, they feel they must allow those below them to establish their own track records. To change organizational structures implies changing criteria of performance, thus perhaps impeding the career prospects of loyal subordinates. Furthermore, executives are naturally frightened of making drastic changes in organization style and structure for the same reason that individuals may be frightened of seeking psychological help despite their misery and unhappiness—they fear it may change them. As a result of this executive fear, anachronistic organizations burden the economy. The executive knows they are ineffective. He simply doesn't know how to cope with his conflicts about it.

Like it or not, though, he is being pressed by a rising tide of employee resistance and angry consumerism to cope with the problems brought about by scientific management and bureaucratic structure. This consumerism even threatens his board room. He struggles with feelings of guilt because he is not doing as well as he should; because of all the criticism that is being heaped upon him; because he and his organization are less efficient and more obsolescent than either ought to be; because he has luxuries that others do not have; and because in times of recession, he must cut back arbitrarily to preserve a short-term profit picture no matter how much that cutback may ultimately cost him in terms of organizational commitment and loyalty.

The Problems of Obsolescence
Executives are also under more severe personal competition than ever before. As the average age at which men become company presidents declines, the competitive time span for achievement becomes narrowed. You have to make it more quickly, or you lose out entirely.

In addition, historically valuable skills are no longer so useful. I have seen a number of executives in consultation who have been told after many years of presumably effective performance that they are too authoritarian. Men who had previously been praised for taking charge of situations and operating them efficiently are now being taken to task because they are heavy-handed. They don't know how to be light-handed. They were taught to be men in control; they *are* men in control. Their major problem is that today people don't want to be controlled. As a result, these executives are now a drug on the market.

Yet their problem is much more complex than one of authoritarian personality. While they are being asked to be more diplomatic, their superiors nevertheless expect them to retain control by means of organizational devices like compensation systems, job descriptions, management by objectives, and other maneuvers largely intended to disguise control. Thus the basic underlying management values have not changed significantly. Only the mode of applying the assumptions which lie behind authoritarian control and bureaucratic structure is different.

This sometimes almost farcical divergence between appearance and reality creates more difficulty than ever for executives and for the people who report to them. It can be seen quite clearly that when executives change their behavior without changing the underlying control and the overriding structural forces, the result is likely to be even greater ineffectiveness when people discover the change to be only an illusion. That illusion may be more easily tolerated by younger, less experienced executives who have not yet learned to distinguish a slogan from an underlying pattern of manipulative behavior, and by those who have not yet reached that period in middle age when their conscience demands a price for manipulation.

There are other ways in which individual executives become obsolescent. As they grow older, they go back to school less frequently. They tend to exaggerate their own way of doing things as it becomes obsolete, for like most people, their first step in coping with stress is to become conspicuously more like they always were. This heightens obsolescence and intensifies the fear of being displaced.

That fear has increased, at least according to my impressions. Few people trust organizational loyalty these days. Even paternalistic companies that have valued their own loyalty to their employees find themselves under competitive pressures that require them to demand results and competence. When short-term spectacular results are at a premium and long service is correspondingly less valued, an executive's identification with an organization is undermined and loyalty becomes an anachronism.

The Problems of Dependency

Increasingly the executive must depend on other people who have skills and specialties he doesn't understand and cannot control. He is dependent on a technical infrastructure, so aptly described by John Kenneth Galbraith in *The New Industrial State*, which limits his alternatives and competes with him for power and authority. Often he discovers, sometimes painfully, how weak that infrastructure is. The discovery fans anxiety.

The chagrined managing director of an engineering firm, for example, tells this story: His subordinates, called upon to produce designs for buildings, decided to draw on already established analytic data for much of their work rather than redo the analyses themselves. They leaned heavily on the published analyses of an excellent specialist in their field. One day the director met the specialist and congratulated him on the usefulness of his work. The specialist was astonished to be congratulated. He was using as a basis for his analyses designs published by the director's own firm! The specialist and the director each thought the other had firm facts, and depended on those data.

This same executive and others report that increasingly all kinds of organizations—business, government, nonprofit—are sponsoring second and third studies of the same issues by different consultants. This seems to be happening with all kinds of problems in an effort to spell out in detail as many alternatives as possible. Apparently executives need to have such repetitive studies to feel secure and to be certain there is ample evidence to support their actions. The wish is commendable, but its manifestation in this form is pathological. Repetitive studies of the same problems cost money and thereby increase ultimate costs. Knowing that their clients want alternatives, consultants produce them. But the assumptions behind many of the alternatives are often so farfetched as to be useless. Action is delayed and certainly is diminished rather than enhanced.

Sometimes the difficulty is of the executive's own making, usually because he cannot accept his dependency on others. If, for example, he forces his subordinates to make projections in a vacuum, without discussion with him, and requests them immediately, he is likely to get wild guesses. All too often these wild guesses then become goals and targets. When these goals cannot be met, he feels let down. Indeed, he may be subject to considerable criticism from his board, clients, customers, and others as a result of not delivering what he had promised. This problem occurs frequently in government. Top-level executives ask their subordinates for hasty projections as a basis for political statements. When these prove to be unrealistic, government executives must go to great lengths to defend themselves from the criticism of congressional committees.

The Problems of Ambivalence

Most executives become executives because they want to wield power. But nowadays consultation, coordination, and cooperation are common practice. This means that executives increasingly must yield decision-making power to subordinates, or at least consult with them more frequently. At the same time, organizational decisions are more heavily influenced by outsiders.

The executive is torn between his wish to act autonomously and the need to share power. As a result, many business leaders act erratically. They tell their subordinates they want more ideas, but have no time to listen. They invite participation without adequately preparing their subordinates in the skills and understanding required for participation. They present unchangeable programs, invite criticism, and then wonder why it doesn't come. They permit other top executives to dominate their own subordinates in open meetings. These are only a few of the ways their mixed feelings show.

The same problem of authority and power enters into other forms of relationships with subordinates. Just as the cadaver is the model of the ideal patient for many physicians—something they can act upon as technicians without considering human feelings—so the automaton is the model subordinate for many executives. He is the man who does what he is supposed to without anxiety, concern, doubt, or question. I asked him what his own work was—what a boss was supposed to be a father confessor to my men." The boss had his own work to do, he said, and that didn't include answering questions on matters that his subordinates might just as well look up for themselves. But when I asked him what his own work was—what a boss was supposed to do, how much of his time was taken up repetitively dealing with the same problems because he hadn't listened in the first place—he was stumped. Like this man, many executives simply do not know what behavior is required of a boss if his subordinates are to function effectively.

The Problem of the Future

Business leaders have always had to predict future trends. A large part of their success hinges on such predictions. Today's business leaders have much more difficulty understanding, anticipating, and working toward future events than did their predecessors. Not that there aren't plenty of statistics and trends; every computer is a storehouse of them. Rather, it seems more difficult to assess the probable direction of the quality of life, for which the statistics are only an elementary skeleton. Specific needs for goods and services, and therefore business decisions and business leadership, will depend on the style and quality of life.

Executives are being asked to look further ahead, to probe deeper into problems, to look behind them to history, literature, and life experience—in short, to become deeper, broader, and more sensitive. But most executives are men who chose business, or were recruited into business careers, because they were men of practical action who eschewed "long-hair" theorizing.

Available figures can indicate and project many trends. But what about the problems that are not predictable? And what about those that are not quantifiable? To whom does the executive turn to find out about these?

Who, for instance, would have predicted the influence on life styles of hippie and mod trends, from miniskirts and vibrant colors to "doing your own thing"? Earlier figures could have projected the number of middle-class men in white collar ranks, the frequency with which they were likely to get haircuts, and the probable gross of a barber shop in a middle-class white collar residential area. But who could have guessed that hippie-originated long-hair styles would be adopted by middle-class men and send the whole barbering industry into a slump?

So the executive is up against the future, which becomes the unpredicted present more quickly than ever. The fate of many people depends on his capacity as a seer. More than anyone else, he knows how inadequate a seer he is.

The Problems of Motivation

All these problems have been added to his ordinary, everyday problems of choosing competent subordinates, creating highly motivated work groups, dealing with those who falter or fall by the wayside, and giving constructive leadership to those who are dependent upon him. He is only too keenly aware of his many mistakes in these areas and is usually burdened with guilt about them. He frequently carries a heavy emotional load, often feeling that when his subordinates fail, he has failed. More often than not, he is reluctant to discharge men who are not performing adequately. He burdens himself with the assumption that they might have done better if he had chosen or supervised more wisely. His problems of motivation and supervision have become more acute as social changes make increasing numbers of people reluctant to be ordered about or to operate mechanically on tasks that are not psychologically rewarding.

So here we have him, the American business executive: thrust into the forefront of social leadership, for which he is totally unprepared; required to cope with an increasingly competitive business environment with inefficient, sometimes self-destructive, organizational structures and management conceptions; afraid he himself is obsolete and expendable. This man is being asked to anticipate a vague and uncertain future with too little background in the past. He is forced to depend on inadequate authority for making decisions about unprecedented risks, while he struggles with ambivalence about the use of power.

In sum, there is a radical change in the quality and direction of society's problems. Not only do they increase in complexity; they become more urgent and more highly charged with emotion. Often the most pressing problems are those of attitude and feeling.

Dealing with these problems, both internal and external to business organizations, requires high skill and great sensitivity to people's feelings—one's own as well as others'. Already we have seen the displacement of the salesman-fundraiser college president by a new kind of college leader who can interact with his followers. We will soon be seeing similar displacements in business leadership, if we haven't already.

Nevertheless, of all the skills executives need, psychological competence is the least well taught and the least well understood. There are a number of reasons why this is so:

□ There are few places where executives can really learn how to apply the psychological aspects of management to the resolution of organizational and social problems. The available courses are mostly quite brief and take the form of seminars or laboratory training groups. Most confrontation or sensitivity training groups offer the executive little by way of a conceptual framework.

□ University courses emphasize normative and descriptive psychology and sociology. These describe behavior in general, report how one variable correlates with another, and usually offer gross generalizations. They are not intended to be diagnostic and prescriptive. They offer the executive little that he can work with, and are most often taught by people with no experience in management problems.

As a result, while today's executive faces the most complex tasks any leadership class has ever had to face, he has almost no preparation for dealing with them. In my judgment, given the problems and stresses with which he must now cope, every executive should have a reasonable understanding of his own conflicts about his leadership role, and he should also be as fully trained in psychological aspects of management as he is in accounting, finance, marketing, and similar dimensions of the executive role. But he is not.

To be well trained psychologically requires, in particular, an understanding of individual motivation. All conceptions of the motivation of organizations are built upon some assumption about what motivates the behavior of individual people, however obscure the assumption may be.

Despite differences in opinion, there is a systematic body of theory and knowledge about the origin and development of individual feelings and thought processes. This body of theory and knowledge is largely based on psychoanalytic concepts, supported by current findings in the psychology of thinking, child development, ethology, sleep and dream research, brain studies, and similar fields.

The executives does not need to know either the theory or its applications in minute detail any more than he needs to know the fine points of law or accounting as they apply to his work. But he does need to know enough to avoid doing his work blindly. Whenever an executive makes a decision or takes an action, he is making a prediction that certain outcomes will result. Inevitably his decisions and actions relate to other people. He wants to obtain certain behavioral results. But if he does not know basic scientific conceptions about the way people feel, think, and act, he may find himself shooting in the dark. He can only dimly assess the likely effect of his decisions or actions.

What is worse, he may get a behavioral result which meets his short-run expectations but which may mask harmful later consequences. It is not hard to get higher productivity at the cost of lower quality, as some manufacturing firms are now discovering. Industrial engineering efficiency, extremely logical in its own terms, is not without its price.

Failure to understand personal psychology may frequently lead to unanticipated consequences. Much of the contemporary emphasis on job enrichment and participation in decision making, about work processes for example, is derived from studies of groups over the short term. These practices may well produce subsequent problems, because the emphasis of both techniques is on the immediate work alone. An understanding of the individual would make it apparent that people are fundamentally concerned with being in charge of their own fate. Offered the opportunity to be more concerned about their jobs, quite naturally they then want to be concerned about their organizations. They want to have some effect on policy and practice, on decisions which may affect their lives. When they are denied that opportunity, they may become cynical. Unable to influence the work organization, they may well feel manipulated. When programs based on inadequate knowledge of the individual begin to falter, both executives and behavioral scientists will become discredited. Everyone involved will be left even more frustrated and angry.

If only to protect himself, the executive therefore must become more knowledgeable about human feelings. Before he can do so he must overcome his own resistance and denials. Despite the advances in public understanding of psychology in the years since World War II, many executives are still frightened of it. They assume that people's feelings about themselves, their work, and their organizations can be disregarded, suppressed by managerial control mechanisms, or assuaged by kind gestures. Furthermore, they take it for granted that every executive is an expert in those matters—or, if not, that he is weak or inadequate.

Once he overcomes his own resistance, the executive can follow a two-step process toward becoming more knowledgeable and competent. First, he can learn about the power and importance of people's feelings through group laboratory experiences. And he can learn more about his own feelings through individual professional consultation with psychologists and psychiatrists. No amount of intellectual discussion about feelings can be as enlightening as direct experience. Nor can an executive gauge the effect of his own feelings and behavior on others until he has had a good opportunity to observe himself in relationship to others. He must look introspectively at those problems and feelings which give him the most difficulty.

I am not saying that every executive is sick and therefore should seek treatment. I am saying that psychological insight is most easily derived from living experiences, and that many executives have received tremendous relief and benefit from being able to take a look, with a competent guide, at some of the issues that burden them most heavily. They often learn how to deal better with hostility—their own and that of others.

One caution, however.

The executive should be extremely careful to investigate the training and qualifications of the sponsors before he undertakes participation in a group, for many untrained and poorly trained persons are offering encounter groups and other forms of confrontation. The same is true of individual professional consultation. The executive should know what the professional's training and experience is. There are many sadists, faddists, and quacks in these fields. One way to check is to look at professional directories, another to inquire of established and respected professionals.

However good such experiences may turn out to be, neither group-dynamics laboratories nor personal counsel provides an adequate conceptual grounding in the whys of individual behavior and their translation into the practice of organizational leadership. For that, the executive needs a systematic, guided learning experience.

As with any other effort to learn and apply a body of theory and knowledge, such an experience should be provided by people who are expert in the application of the theory. Psychoanalytic or other treatment requires a specially trained clinical psychologist or psychiatrist. The experience takes some time, because it is a learning process, and nothing important can be learned well without supervised practice. Even in golf it is advantageous to have the help of a professional until one's skill is established. Executive participants must have ample opportunity to review both their business and family behavior.

It is extremely important that the executive make use of the consultation to take up his feelings of failure. Since he is so vulnerable to this experience, he can understand it better and relieve a lot of internal pressure.

It is particularly important for the executive to seek this kind of counseling as he grows older. There is a great tendency in later years to look back on what one has done and to belittle it, thus undermining one's own mental health. Successful aging requires coming to terms with one's own life experience, accepting it, seeing it to be worthwhile, and being content with one's contributions.

A good beginning can be made in a one-week seminar. Such an experience should establish a frame of reference in psychoanalytic theory for the understanding of individual motivation, and then translate that understanding into applications in supervision, leadership, motivation on the job, and organizational structure. It should avoid global recipes— glib generalizations for problem solving, like "democratic management." It should include an understanding of drives, defenses, and the pressures of conscience; of the meaning of authority to both the leader and his subordinates; of the psychological significance of the organization; and of the personal problems of executives.

It should help the executive examine the psychological assumptions he is making whenever he formulates a policy of practice, alters organization structure, or takes action in or on behalf of his organization.

Most executives tend to think of motivation as a form of manipulation, and of the application of psychological conceptions as something to be considered, if one has time, after dealing with more important matters, like finance. The emphasis of a course or seminar should be on helping the executive understand that everything he does has important psychological implications, and on showing him how to examine the psychological assumptions he is making. The discussion of psychoanalytic theory will also open up the opportunity to talk about the problems of rearing children and dealing with young people.

It is very important for an executive to understand the psychological role of a leader and the implications of people's expectations of him, as well as the influence of his behavior on that of his subordinates. With this understanding, he can shift from thinking about himself as administrator, manager, or executive to considering what it means to be a leader, and what a leader does in practice to build identification between himself and his organization. When the executive can see that other executives have problems similar to his, he is likely to feel less guilty and inadequate. In discussion with them he may evolve new ways of using himself and his newfound knowledge.

In group discussions, the executive develops a better understanding of his own power in relation to his followers and of the psychological significance of leadership itself. He gets a better sense of the meaning and strength of conscience as a major motivating force. He becomes aware of the human wish to be able to like oneself for working toward an ideal self-image. He comes to appreciate the power of guilt feelings. All this will provide him with a more acute awareness of psychological pain and the ways people cope with it. He also learns more about the creative and constructive uses of aggression, the difficulties inherent in encouraging and permitting hostility to surface, and some ways of deflecting aggression into problem solving.

Newly aware of the psychological assumptions behind all managerial techniques, he takes another look at the hazards and limitations of scientific management, as well as the constraints of traditional organization structure. In the process he also examines the fundamental purpose of the business and his role in its perpetuation. He examines sources of feelings of guilt, anger, fear, self-doubt, rivalry, dependency, achievement, and mastery and their implications. He learns to distinguish between motivation and manipulation, and he learns how he can creatively ally himself with his followers to further both their individual and organizational goals. He learns more about power—how to use it creatively rather than abandoning it or using it clandestinely to apply clichés about democratic or participative management.

Of course, a one-week session can do no more than touch on these varied, complex issues. No short course can do more than create a frame of reference or establish a perspective for experimentation, further reading, and keener observation. To supplement his initial learning, the executive should seek follow-up experiences, such as continuing case discussions on a monthly or bimonthly basis. Some do this in small groups with local psychiatrists and psychologists. Others take advanced or refresher seminars. Still others use consultants with whom they can discuss applications in specific situations.

As with all psychological training, and even with intensive psychotherapy, evaluation is difficult. The executive's best clue to the usefulness of the learning is his increased personal comfort and his greater satisfaction with the way his work is turning out.

part two

Harnessing the Skills of Behavioral Science

Participation:
How It Works

A not-so-big plant (about 750 employees in Marion, Virginia) belonging to Harwood Companies, Inc., a corporation that itself is rather small in today's business terms (3,000 employees), has made a number of significant contributions to the understanding of human behavior in organizations.

The Marion plant and its employees have been examined, tested, experimented with, and reported upon by behavioral scientists for more than thirty years. The research findings have provided insights into many causes of the stresses that develop in the interaction of those who manage and those who are managed. The practical application of the findings within the company has been a prime cause of a high and healthy level of employee productivity.

This apparel plant has by far the largest record of experience in harnessing the skills of behavioral science to improve employee performance and job satisfaction. The collaboration at the plant between psychology and management was begun in 1939 and has produced practical results in terms of employee loyalty, productivity, and trust. It has also created a considerable body of knowledge about the factors that influence quality of work life and the methods that are effective in developing interpersonal competence. It is a story I know intimately, because I directed the program for nearly thirty years and was fortunate to have as collaborators a number of distinguished psychologists, among them Kurt Lewin, Alex Bavelas, John R. P. French, Jr., Gilbert David, Ian Ross, Stanley Seashore, and David Bowers. The studies on which we collaborated are now well known both in the United States and abroad.

The story of how this research program began shows how chance sometimes influences the long-term direction of scientific inquiries.

During the mid-1930s, I was earning my way through graduate school by working in a small company that had been hard hit by the Depression. The firm was a successor to a company that had been founded by my grandfather and father.

For my doctoral thesis in psychology I had chosen to verify experimentally a series of concepts developed by Professor Kurt Lewin, a world-famous German psychologist. The rise of Hitler had convinced Lewin that he could not remain in the country of his birth. He resigned from the University of Berlin and accepted an invitation to join the faculty of Cornell University. A few weeks after his arrival in the United States I arranged to meet with him. It was the start of a relationship that grew closer as the years passed. By the time I received my doctorate in 1937 we were warm friends.

When I discussed with Lewin my plans for an academic career, he pleaded with me not to leave the industrial firm I had helped establish. He observed that industry offered a fertile laboratory for scientific inquiry and pointed out that I was in a unique position because I had learned the practical aspects of managing an enterprise and could also carry out significant research in the field of human relations. He offered to collaborate with me on long-term research projects if I would stay with the company where I had already been asked to serve as president.

I decided to follow Lewin's advice. I realized that with the power of chief executive, I could set up research programs that would provide insights into the management of people in organizations and thereby discover new ways to get people to attain their potential and work at their best. Since the survival of the company depended in large measure on the productivity of our employees, I was hopeful that the application of psychological knowledge to practical problems would improve profits and performance.

About six months later, in 1938, the first opportunity to plan a major research project with Lewin came. The firm had closed its New England factory and opened a new manufacturing plant in Marion, a rural community in the mountains of Virginia. Among the most critical of the problems that troubled the staff of the new plant in 1939 were two that plague great segments of American industry today: low productivity and high turnover. The plant manager had had more than twenty-five years of experience running similar factories in New England, where there was always a pool of trained employees with industrial experience. In the mountains of Virginia, however, he had 150 inexperienced apprentices—more than 50 percent of the total workforce. They were eager to work, but their pace was halting and their output discouragingly low. If the company were to remain competitive, a way had to be found to bring these workers up to the high standards of production that prevailed in New England.

For many months this seemed an impossible task. After the twelve to sixteen weeks of training customarily required for an apprentice to reach the skill level of an experienced worker, our trainees—despite their great enthusiasm at the start and the good wages they were getting—could produce only 50 to 75 percent as much as workers doing similar jobs in New England.

Even more serious was the high number who simply quit. Since the cost of labor then represented half the selling price of the product, the level of worker performance in the new plant could well be the key factor in the survival of the company. It was obviously urgent to find ways to increase individual productivity, reduce the high cost of training, and lower the quit rate.

The employees worked on an individual incentive basis: they were paid more for producing above a standard production rate. But what was happening was that most trainees could not even acquire the skills to approach the standard, much less respond to the incentive for producing above it.

In an attempt to find out why the turnover remained so high, the supervisors were interviewed. They gave the usual explanations: the jobs were too difficult for the rustic local people; families had moved out of town; transportation was unavailable; work was too tedious; and so on. Interviews were then held in the relaxed atmosphere of their homes with workers who had quit during the previous two months. They gave about the same explanations as the supervisors.

Yet none of the reasons seemed truly convincing. For one thing, unemployment at the time was high in the region. Applicants would assemble hopefully at the employment office at 5 A.M. for job interviews. If they were selected they were delighted. The pay scale was as high as in any competing plant. The kind of work was no more difficult than that being performed elsewhere. The plant was new and contained all the most modern facilities. The location was close to public transportation, and car pools were available.

Nonetheless, as many as half of those who had been so excited about going to work at first were quitting during their first twelve weeks. Why? Evidently none of the "good" reasons given by the supervisors or the people who had quit were the *true* reasons. The plant managers were deeply troubled. They wanted help in finding out the real reasons why employees were quitting, and what could be done to keep them. I arranged with Lewin to visit the plant and to begin our first joint research project. What happened will be discussed in the next chapter.

This study was the first of a series of practical experiments which were carried out by professors Lewin, Bavelas, and French during the succeeding five years. It is a good example of the kind of action research we advocated and which the managers used when feasible. The results provided convincing evidence that open communication, greater self-direction, and broadly based participative approaches were a considerably more practical and profitable way to use human talent than the traditional approach, in which management decides what employees should do and then orders them to do it.

During the next twenty years the company expanded its manufacturing facilities by six plants: two new units in Virginia, three in Puerto Rico, and an established plant (Weldon) in Pennsylvania. In each of these units the training program for the local supervisors and managers was directed by members of the Marion staff and was designed to increase managerial competence, improve interpersonal relations, and educate supervisors in the principles of participative management.

The performance in each of these units is remarkably like that of the Marion plant. Productivity is high, costs are competitive, the employees are gratifyingly satisfied. The acquired Pennsylvania plant, the Weldon Manufacturing Co., was successfully converted to participative practices in a classic experiment, published in full detail in a book entitled *Management by Participation*. A summary appears in this book in a chapter called "Managing Major Change."

In 1968 Harwood purchased two other companies, which manufactured related but not similar products. As part of the purchase, Harwood took over two of the plants of one of the acquired companies and one plant of the other.

It soon became clear that all three plants (about 200 employees in each) were typical of the small owner-managed shops that still survive in some segments of the apparel industry. Each unit was autocratically managed, conflict-ridden, beset by low productivity, plagued by high costs, controlled by petty tyrants, and given to finagling of records.

The Marion staff could not be spared from their regular duties to take on the time-consuming task of trying to develop an understanding of participative procedures in these moribund factories. It was obvious that such reeducation of the personnel and a change in their attitudes would take many years, even if a consultant team of practitioners, engineers, and behavioral scientists could be assembled. Nevertheless, a process of technological rebuilding was tried without the behavioral science support given to the Weldon acquisition. The effort failed. After severe losses for nearly three years, two of the plants were shut down. The third is kept in operation for special reasons, but it continues to be an unsatisfactory high-cost production unit.

We have found that a participative approach can succeed only if there is an ongoing program of continuing education. When managers or supervisors retire, or leave, their replacements are likely to bring with them the managerial practices of the traditional authoritarian organization. Changes in personnel, especially at the top of the organization, can have an adverse effect on morale. Trust that took years to build can be obliterated in weeks.

Since it is sometimes thought that deviations from traditional management procedures are resisted by trade unions, it is interesting to note that all the Harwood plants operate under collective bargaining agreements with two international unions. The relationship between the company and the unions has generally been constructive, characterized rather by mutual respect than by "win-lose" conflicts with each side fearing to concede that the other side might be right. The union position has been that they must protect any employee whose interests are endangered by the application of behavioral science methods. But complaints on this score have been rare. Unionization, we have found, is not an obstacle to the effective use of participative procedures. Companies affiliated with other unions may encounter different reactions. But we believe that if the union representatives are encouraged to participate in the planning, cooperation will be forthcoming.

Managers' doubts about the participative system may arise from misconceptions. They may assume, for example, that arbitrary boundaries exist between management systems, so that any two systems are mutually exclusive. The fact is, there are gradations of practice. It is primarily a matter of convenience, in discussion, to divide managerial approaches into two opposites: the authoritarian, based on centralized control and direction with strong individual leadership, and the "participative," based on shared responsibility and group collaboration.

Participative management is the practical expression of what McGregor calls Theory Y, what Likert calls System Four, and what Blake refers to as a '9–9' management style. The evidence from the experience of organizations here and abroad is that participation is accompanied by greater job satisfaction, increased self-esteem, and heightened motivation; moreover it improves and strengthens psychological well-being. Warren Bennis summarized the view of leading behavioral scientists when he wrote, "Democracy in industry is not an idealistic conception, but a hard necessity in those areas in which change is ever present and in which creative scientific enterprise must be nourished. For democracy is the only system of organization which is compatible with perpetual change."

Although the number of companies that are adopting participative methods is increasing, the methods are still very far from having wide acceptance. The reasons are many; they range from fear of change to anxiety about loss of power. Often the resistance stems from misunderstandings. Some executives still naively imagine participation is permissiveness or paternalism, or a sacrifice of efficiency to "keep the workers happy." Others believe that the method is a manipulation of the employees, an act or charade to fool them.

The method of participation is not any of these. The expression denotes an overall attitude of management, not a particular tool or technique. It is based on the belief that workers are most productive only when they feel fully committed to their goals on the job. The degree of commitment depends on how much they have shared in both setting the goals and defining the methods of achieving them. It is their payment in return for getting a piece—just a piece—of the action. They don't want to run the organization; they just don't want to be thought of as robots. The aim of a "participative" manager is to enable his subordinates to make the fullest possible use of their knowledge, skills, and talents in setting goals or solving problems. He prefers not to rely solely on his personal experience. When management encourages employees to share in planning, management convinces them that it respects their knowledge and interest.

In the present context, participation signifies a person's power to influence the decisions that affect him and his job. His participation is high or low to the degree that his knowledge, ideas, and experience affect decision making.

Of course not to be asked to participate is not necessarily harmful. It is good or bad in relation to goals to be reached or problems to be solved. Nonparticipation can be a good thing in matters that do not concern the employee, or when decision making calls for more time than he can afford.

Nor does participation mean that everyone decides on everything. The degree of anybody's participation varies with the situations that call for decisions. Sometimes people will be asked for their counsel and advice, but not their consent. At other times, they will be told the decision is up to them. "The more the merrier" is not true of participation, since its effectiveness is tied closely to how much the participants know and contribute.

From the manager's standpoint, participative programs tend to be more demanding than conventional practices. In addition, the underlying philosophy of participation conflicts with authoritarian bureaucracy. Many men in positions of power continue to believe that only a tough-minded dictatorial boss can spur production and earn profits, but thoughtful executives are beginning to see the fallacy of this belief. Rapidly accumulating evidence confirms that autocratic practices lead to unsatisfactory profits because of low performance, poor quality, and high turnover.

Low participation is also a major source of employee stress. It results in poor relationships among co-workers and contributes to misunderstandings and conflicts. Very significant recent findings show that the tense climate created in low-participation organizations actually impairs the emotional and physical health of the employees. It has been found, for example, that employees who feel they have many opportunities to influence the way work is done are absent one-third as often as workers who report they have no opportunity to influence their work. A similar finding holds true of lateness. Moreover, employees who express feelings of alienation and who report that their jobs offer little or no opportunity for social interaction have been found to have visited physicians for medical care three times as often as those whose job provides an opportunity to work as a member of a team.

In case after case, the organizations that have used participatory methods have found the results worth the cost. The greater the participation, the greater the subsequent productivity; the higher the job satisfaction, the lower the turnover and the better the relations between employees and managers. But multi-unit companies planning to convert from the traditional authoritarian system should be cautioned that making the change throughout the entire organization can require as much as five years. Some results will be apparent quickly, but the process of change must be gradual since people need time to adjust to new methods, particularly methods that may be totally unlike any they have known before. Attitudes are hard to change and trust develops slowly. Moreover, under the decentralized structure of most large organizations, it is unlikely that a participative managerial system can be introduced and accepted into all parts of the organization simultaneously.

Before introducing practices that involve employees in problem solving and decision making, many questions have to be resolved. If employees are asked to suggest changes, what will happen to their confidence in the system when a suggestion is rejected, as sometimes it must be? Will resentment follow? And what if, having invited a frank expression of opinion, top executives feel criticized and embarrassed when they hear things they might prefer not to hear? Will executives regret having asked the employees their opinions in the first place?

These are real questions, and there aren't any blanket answers. But the power of participation to foster candor is one of the method's virtues. In organizations that operate in an atmosphere of mutual trust, answers to these questions can be worked out.

Are participative techniques applicable in all kinds of companies, or only in those with certain characteristics? The crucial question, it has been found, is not the nature of the product, the service, the size, location, or any other objective consideration. Rather it is the attitude of the key executives toward a major change away from bureaucratic management practices. A participative system can succeed only if traditional attitudes and values are unfrozen. Openness to change must be stimulated, trust must be increased. These processes should start at the top of the organization, although it is occasionally possible to begin at other levels.

Participative procedures, research tells us, lead to more loyalty, more flexibility, fewer costly mistakes, more efficiency, and greater job satisfaction. It can flourish, however, only in an atmosphere of mutual confidence.

The Effect of Participation on Performance

The stage was initially set for our first research project when Lewin accompanied me on a three-day visit to the Marion plant. At the time I did not know that this beginning search for a more scientific understanding of the management of people in industry would continue for thirty years. Nor did either of us foresee that the practically continuous program of research and application would provide data for a scientifically grounded view rare in the behavioral sciences.

We were agreed that the emphasis was to be on action, but action as a function of research. Each step taken was to be studied. Continuous evaluation of all the steps would be made as they followed one another. The rule would be: No research without action, no action without research.

We knew that we faced many uncertainties in our effort to get better utilization of our human resources. Could we introduce a new pattern of management emphasizing participative leadership? Would participative practices be acceptable to people who had spent their lives at work in an opposite condition? Our only certainty was that improvement would not come from mere alterations in work methods and work technology.

On our arrival at the plant we began a series of discussions with the staff on the serious problems they had reported of high turnover and slow learning pace among trainees.

At one point Lewin suggested that the answer to why so many were quitting might be found if we could answer another question: Under what circumstances do the people who quit experience success or failure? We went back and looked at all the data again. The harder we looked, the clearer it became that in some unknowing way the management might be responsible for the high turnover rate. Perhaps the reasons offered in the interviews were merely a cover-up for the apprentices' embarrassment at not seeming capable of reaching the production standard.

We made an exhaustive study of the "fear of failure" hypothesis and found some fascinating answers. The first question we asked was: What happens in the training period that is likely to create a fear of failure? The simple, basic answer was: Trying to reach sixty units per hour—the number needed to reach standard production.

Typically, a girl just hired would enter the training program full of high expectations and gratitude for having a job. One of the first things she would find out was that the "standard" she would be expected to reach in a reasonable length of time was sixty units. A sixty-unit operator, she would come to learn, had status, self-esteem, and security. That was the least the company expected of her. Consequently, being a sixty-unit operator became her goal. The first few weeks' experience encouraged her. This is the period of most rapid improvement. But then, as is generally known, the motor-learning curve decelerates and further improvement comes much more slowly.

Here the trainee began to wonder if she was capable of reaching that goal of sixty. All around her were skilled operators producing at the rate of sixty units or better, seemingly without great difficulty. Yet despite her intense, sometimes almost panicky, efforts to do well, she would make only small progress. The goal of sixty began to seem unreal, beyond her capacity. Frustration welled up, fed by an inner fear of failure. This fear was not related to how much money she was making; the standard wage was guaranteed no matter how little she produced. But tension mounted day by day, and by the end of the twelfth week the chances were one in two that she had given up and quit. Interestingly, there was no correlation between the level of performance and the individual's feeling of success or failure. Earlier research had already shown that the same person can feel success on one occasion and failure on another, though the objective level of achievement remains the same. A golfer, for example, may break 100 for the first time and feel highly successful. A week later he may play around in 95 and feel more elated still. If, however, the next week he just breaks 100 he will feel failure even though two weeks earlier that score was regarded as a triumph. The same holds true for people trying to better their production levels.

Another meaningful finding was that the quit rate jumped dramatically for the trainees who *were closest to reaching the sixty-unit goal.* Among the workers who had reached thirty units, the annual quit rate was just 20 percent; among those who had reached forty-five units, the quit rate was 60 percent; among those who were at fifty-five units, the quit rate was at a startling 96 percent. For workers who attained the magical sixty-unit level, the turnover rate dropped dramatically down to just 11 percent.

It seemed that workers did not feel too anxious during the starting weeks when they worked at ten, twenty, or thirty units per hour. But when improvement became more difficult, as the forty and fifty levels were reached, the quit rate soared. On the last stretch toward that shiny goal of status and security, anxiety about the possibility of failure became intense. Those who couldn't cope with the pressure were suddenly "needed at home." Withdrawal from the job was an escape from excruciating tension and embarrassment.

The high turnover was due to increasing frustration as the workers approached their goal. This frustration was produced by the conflict of two factors:

☐ The strength of his desires to reach his goal increased as he approached it—a typical goal gradient behavior.

☐ On the other hand, the difficulty of increasing production grew greater as the distance to the goal decreased. Thus the higher the level of production, the greater the difficulty of increasing production.

What these workers plainly needed was a more understanding and supportive training environment. We found it was vital to reassure the trainee before too much frustration set in. The first step was to do away with the golden long-range goal of "60" and substitute instead more easily attained short-range goals. It was clear that the new worker needed to experience frequent successes to build self-confidence. If the reachable goal during an early training week was, perhaps, thirty units, the next week the target would be a not-too-difficult thirty-three or thirty-five units. The steps would be small ones, and the hard-working apprentice would recognize that just three or five more units was not an impossible effort. When the learner finally approached sixty, she would find she could reach it without undue strain.

The results were striking. In the year after the new program was launched, the quit rate among trainees dropped by more than half. There was no change in the rate of pay or in physical arrangements. The reduction was due entirely to providing for a series of step-by-step success experiences.

Shortly after Professor Lewin began to visit the plant, he recommended that a full-time psychologist be employed to carry out research on practical problems. He suggested Dr. Alex Bavelas, who came to us from the University of Iowa. When Bavelas had to return to the University, Dr. John R. P. French, Jr. succeeded him. Dr. French continued to serve the company in various capacities for several decades and directed most of the research reported in this chapter.

At the plant, French was seen as an informal member of the management team. He attended meetings and participated in whatever activities he was interested in.

Both he and Dr. Lewin had observed that in the Marion plant, as in most mass production plants, the job of foreman traditionally went to the person with the greatest technical competence. But the man who knows how to keep the machines running or how to maintain exact records does not necessarily know how to handle the people who run those machines. Being able to win cooperation, build trust, and improve morale is very different from technical know-how and, as we came to understand, is more important in raising production and improving quality.

Yet under the traditional system of factory management, which has changed little since the turn of the century, nothing significant has been done to provide leadership training for supervisors. Few companies have given even a passing thought to the notion that a foreman must be helped to acquire the knowledge and skill needed to win the willing cooperation of those who call him boss.

Learning how to evoke cooperation and improve morale, how to discipline, or how to conduct interviews takes more than a well-intentioned lecture from a predecessor. Sage advice on how to deal with troublesome subordinates can be interesting to listen to, but it rarely helps much when real-life problems arise. Being told how to discipline workers or how to be fair and firm will not change a foreman's underlying perception of how to do things without actual practice under expert guidance.

Dr. French initiated an experimental leadership training program at the Marion plant. The aim was to provide foremen with an opportunity to examine—in the presence of other members of the group—their customary way of dealing with such typical problems as interviewing a frequently absent worker. The atmosphere would be supportive, and there would be a minimum amount of time spent listening to lectures or reading "how to" books.

Dr. French explained at the initial meeting that with reactions from the group, each supervisor could develop a clearer view of the merits and demerits of his approach, and risk altering it. Without such feedback, Dr. French explained, a supervisor might live out his working days being thought of as sarcastic, threatening, inconsiderate, or unclear, and never know it. But if he could see himself as others saw him, facts he formerly rejected or insights he never had would begin to make sense to him.

Role playing was one of the techniques employed most frequently. No script was used. The action was unrehearsed, and participants were encouraged to act spontaneously. The episodes grew out of situations the supervisors might face on the job. This method enabled them to see the issues in concrete terms, yet allowed them to play out realistic situations without real-life penalties for mistakes.

The group members were critical of each other in both negative and positive ways. While some of the harsher criticism was difficult for the participants to swallow, they discovered how others whom they respected might have handled similar situations. A man might be told after a simulated confrontation with one of his workers: "You were too apologetic." "You were not concrete enough." "You didn't listen." The comments might sting a bit, but the men learned something. The program emphasized self-examination, feedback, openness, and trust—all quite unusual in industry.

The effect on productivity was direct; the groups working for the newly trained supervisors increased their output. The supervisors themselves reported that they found it far easier to deal with their superiors and their peers, and that their skill in handling and getting cooperation from their workers had improved.

The success of the experiment encouraged Dr. French to employ many of the same techniques at the first session of the National Training Laboratories in Bethel, Maine, in 1947. These pioneer leadership training methods for industry have since become an integral part of what we all know now as sensitivity training programs.

At a number of staff meetings in the early 1940s Dr. French heard worried discussions about an increasing shortage of applicants for jobs. The company was growing rapidly and the workforce was being expanded. Turnover, though much lower than in the early days at Marion, remained high for reasons common to all plants with many female employees—marriage and children. Thus, when the employment manager complained that he had reached the bottom of the barrel in digging up recruits, there was considerable concern.

Then, as now, the belief in most mass production industries which require semiskilled, repetitive types of assembly work was that older women (those over thirty-five years of age) cannot maintain the same work pace as younger people. Before the current legislation declaring it illegal to discriminate on the basis of age, this prejudice frequently determined hiring practices. Many organizations simply refused to hire anyone thirty-five or older.

At Marion there were a good many applicants thirty-five or older, but when Dr. French recommended a change in policy to allow hiring of older workers, he was resisted at all levels. Dr. French argued that psychological findings elsewhere cast doubt on the notion that older women learned more slowly, produced less, and were absent more. But he was answered with one of the stock phrases of conventional prejudice: "Everybody with practical experience knows that it isn't so." Dr. French responded by producing high production figures that applied to workers in our own plant who were over the age limit but still on the company payroll for one reason or another. The staff, almost unanimously, said that these were "exceptions."

Prejudice, Dr. French realized, cannot be changed by stating more facts. Therefore, he devised a program which he hoped would allow the staff to discover for itself the facts he was trying to present. He hoped that in this way the staff would develop the necessary insight to recognize the discrepancy between what was true and what they believed. He suggested a modest project that was difficult to refuse. If older workers were indeed inefficient, then it only made sense to determine how much those already working for the company were costing in additional payroll. Most of them had been employed for a long time, or—as with a widow, possibly, or a hardship case—had been taken on as a favor to the community despite the age limit. His suggestion of a study of this situation was accepted.

He then called on the staff to decide just what to measure in order to find out how much money the company was losing on these older women. They hit upon productivity, turnover, absenteeism, and speed of learning new jobs as the main cost factors. The project was put entirely in the hands of a group of staff members. Dr. French would simply serve as a guide if he were asked. The staff group set up its own methods for collecting data and measuring production.

The collection of data took several months, and the results were as follows: The older women not only equaled but surpassed the younger women in production. Using 100 percent as the standard production for skilled workers, the average production of older workers was 112 percent, whereas the production of the younger group was 95 percent.

The figures on turnover and absenteeism also favored the older workers. And so did measurements of ability to learn new skills. Thus, on the basis of criteria selected by the staff itself, the older women proved more than equal to the younger ones.

Even though the results were in sharp contrast to the findings they had expected, the fact that the findings were their own made them trustworthy to the group. Faced with a contradiction between their findings and their long-held attitudes—in short, their prejudices—they chose in this case to act on their findings. An individual regards facts he himself has discovered in an altogether different way from those presented to him by other people.

The battle, however, was only half won. It remained to inform and (as it turned out) to convince all the members of the supervisory staff who had not taken part in the project. These men and women remained rigid in their opposition to employing older people.

Before the second phase of the project was undertaken, a small experiment was tried. A member of the study group selected a supervisor who managed an assembly line that consisted of seventy workers, eight of whom were older workers. "How is Mrs. X getting along?" the supervisor was asked casually. The woman replied that Mrs. X, an older worker, was one of the mainstays of her group. She had similar glowing statements about the other seven older workers in her department.

Then it was suggested that since the older workers seemed to be doing so well, the employment office might send down a few older workers to fill vacant places in her department. But the supervisor rejected the suggestion out of hand. Older people learn more slowly, she explained. They were also absent more often and they didn't really produce as much as the younger ones. Her good older workers were exceptions to the rule, but you couldn't be lucky all the time.

The vigor of the supervisor's prejudice convinced the study group that the supervisors could not be won over as individuals; the whole group had to be reeducated. At ensuing meetings of the supervisory staff, the findings about older women were presented and people talked about why everybody wanted to believe that older women were poor risks for employment. After a time the group began to compare its prejudices with the facts. It was not a rapid process, but the meetings did produce some new insights that slowly broke down old stereotypes. Group decisions were reached recommending that all departments make a serious effort to train older workers to see if they could equal the performance of the older women already in the plant. In this way the hiring of older workers gradually became accepted. Twenty years later most of these same employees were still with the company and were exceeding the standards of most other plants in the nation. This does not deter visiting engineers from occasionally commenting, "A beautiful plant but too many old ladies around."

One of the most serious managerial problems at the plant during the years of Lewin's association with us was the resistance of production workers to changes in methods and job tasks even though these were required by competitive conditions, new engineering methods, and change in consumer demands. When it came time to change product styles—something that happened several times a year—workers complained bitterly about being transferred from old jobs they knew well to new jobs that required unlearning and relearning. Interviews showed that the morale of transferred groups dropped very low; many individuals were despondent to the point of tears. There was evidence of frustration, of loss of hope of ever regaining the former level of production, of feelings of failure and a very low level of ambition. All of this, it seemed, could be attributed to "loss of face" resulting from the sharp contrast between their previous elevated status in terms of production and their present reduced status of having to learn everything all over again.

A number of earlier investigations suggested that the strong resistance to transfers, and the slow relearning process, were primarily problems of motivation. An experiment was planned to test whether or not participation would help overcome the resistance to change.

Three groups were formed, but for the purposes of a brief summary, we will refer to only two. The first, which was the control group, would not participate in the transfer process any more than usual. They were merely told that changes were being made and the production manager explained, as usual, the new mode of work, the new job assignments, and new piecework rates.

The second group—the participative group—was asked to meet with the management and was given a complete explanation of why the change was mandatory. The employees were told frankly that business had fallen off. They were told that unless new orders could be attracted by less expensive models there might well be layoffs. They were shown the simplified and less costly model that was being proposed. They were asked to discuss cost reduction and job methods as a joint problem of the management and the workers. It was stated this way: "We don't want to sacrifice quality, and we don't want you to lose income. What ideas do you have about this?"

The workers responded with a good many practical and useful suggestions on both counts. Along with the management they discussed new models, new ways of working, and new production rates. They also asked for another meeting for further discussion. Management and all the operators sat together until all the issues were agreed upon. Decisions were reached by consensus; there was no formal vote.

The results were extremely pleasing to those of us who had felt that joint problem solving would work well. Production by Group I, the nonparticipative group, dropped by 35 percent after the changeover and did not improve for a month afterwards. The employees were markedly hostile to the company and restricted output accordingly. We learned later that they had made an explicit agreement to "get even" with management. Within two weeks after the change, 9 percent of the operators had quit. Others filed grievances about the pay rates, although the rates, in fact, were a little too high. Morale was expectedly bad. At the end of six weeks the group was dissolved and its members assigned to other work stations.

The participative group, on the other hand, learned the new mode of work remarkably fast. By the second day they were back to their former level of production, and after three weeks they had raised their production level 14 percent higher than ever before. Their relationship with their supervisor was friendly and cooperative. Not one operator quit and no grievances were filed with the union.

Two and a half months later it was possible to confirm even more dramatically the value of the participative method. The members of the earlier nonparticipative group, which had been broken up, were brought together when another new order had to be filled. This time, however, the management followed the procedures that had been used for the participative group. The result was that now the same people who before had conspired to "get even" with the company and hold down production did the reverse. Their productivity recovered rapidly after the changeover. They attained a new and much higher level of output. There was no manifestation of hostility and there were no quits. It was clear that the lowered resistance to change was proportional to the amount of participation, and that the rate of turnover and aggression was inversely proportional to the amount of participation. Figure 1 contrasts the two groups graphically.

Figure 1. Output by two groups of workers after job change.

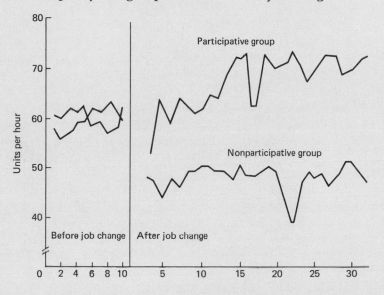

About five years later the participative method underwent a more extensive test. The company had long discussed but never started a profit sharing plan for supervisors. Now the supervisors were told that management was ready to share with them all reductions in the current cost of production, which had risen considerably above the plant's standard cost.

The supervisors were asked to work out the details of a suitable plan and present it to management, bearing in mind such questions as these: When should the bonus payments be made—weekly, monthly, or annually? (The longer the time lag between the time the profit is earned and the time it is paid, the less the incentive. Yet profit or cost savings cannot always be quickly determined.) Who should be included in the plan? (Not all supervisory staff had direct influence on production costs.) What yardstick could be set up to relate the effort a department head put out to the bonus he might get for it? (Because conditions varied among departments, it would be harder for some supervisors to cut costs or raise production than for others.)

It was recognized that a plan that directly rewarded supervisors for the showing of their particular departments might not be fair. The product one department produced might, for example, be easier to sell than something made in another department. High sales might tell little about the quality of the department's supervision. Moreover, if units competed among themselves there would be a tendency for plantwide cooperation to break down.

The management felt strongly that a plan developed by the staff would have a better chance of working than anything decided for them. First of all, the plan would be the result of their own decisions based on their own deliberations. Moreover, the staff would have a clearer understanding of how important their role was in keeping costs down. Their discussions would drive home the point that their efforts directly and specifically influenced the profit and loss of each day's operations.

The profit-sharing plan was to be based solely on savings in production cost rather than on total profits. Obviously, it would be unfair to penalize people in production departments because of possible failures elsewhere, perhaps on the part of the sales or purchasing departments, or in the front office.

Discussions among the staff people brought up problems that had not occurred to management. What should be done, for example, about a foreman who might be taken sick and who would be away from his job and receiving sick benefits? Should he get a bonus for the period of his absence? The group decided that profit should be shared only on the basis of services actually rendered. A sick foreman would share only if he were on the job at least part of the week for which profits were calculated.

The staff group set up what was called a Cost Control Council to meet every two weeks to review cost figures and search for new ways to keep costs down. The council was small enough to act effectively, and subcommittees did much of the preparatory work. These subcommittees met before the meeting of the full council and sent a representative with a report of findings to the full council meeting.

There were early snags, many of them parliamentary in nature. But these were smoothed out. Technical problems were eased, too, with the help of experts. The supervisors were shown how to read the forms and reports that would give them an insight into how turnover, absenteeism, and other such factors raised costs. Then the council decided to concentrate on how to cut down delays in production caused by mechanical failures, and how to reduce training time by giving more personal attention to learners. The council and its subcommittees also looked for ways to control the work flow and the work quality, as well as ways of promoting better communication among departments, from design to shipping. An effort was made to discover better work methods and work-area layouts. To cut down the absentee rate, the council started a program of personal interviews upon the return of any absent employee, designed to find out why he or she could not come to work more regularly and whether there was any way the supervisor could help.

Management knew that dramatic savings could be made if everything worked well, and these would provide rewards more than large enough to reinforce the cost-cutting incentive. But nobody expected anything like the actual results that followed the introduction of the new plan.

After four months, the figures showed a 58 percent decrease in make-up to standard pay (to workers who were not earning the minimum wage), a 53 percent drop in employee turnover, a 12 percent drop in absenteeism, and a 9 percent rise in production throughout the plant. (See Table 1.)

Table 1. Effect of supervisory profit-sharing plan.

ITEM	AVERAGE RATE FOUR MONTHS PRECEDING PLAN	AVERAGE RATE FOUR MONTHS AFTER PLAN	PERCENT OF IMPROVEMENT
Turnover	8.2	4.4	53
Absenteeism	6.1	5.4	12
Make-up pay	31.0	13.0	58
Average hourly production	56.5	61.7	9

If it were not for the fact that similar methods have produced similar results many times since, one might regard such an astonishing success in the same way the supervisor on the line regarded her older workers— as merely exceptional. Nonetheless, the project demonstrated that people on a middle supervisory level will respond with enthusiasm to a chance to participate in decision making and to take on more responsibility. There is practically no foreseeable limit to what can be accomplished in every area of industry if that is kept in mind. It is simply another piece of hard evidence that most supervisory employees have far more leadership potential than they are usually given credit for by management.

In 1958, about ten years after the successful experiments I have described, the company undertook a major modernization program that affected every one of its 1,000 employees and called for no fewer than 1,300 method changes and an equivalent number of pay-rate changes.

Labor costs were rising, and new mechanized manufacturing equipment was needed if the company was to maintain its competitive edge. In addition to a reduction in direct costs, there were other savings that would come from the use of new equipment. These included a reduction in the amount of inventory, more flexibility in the production lines, shorter in-process time, better quality control. All the engineering changes could have been accomplished in two or three months.

Why we took a year instead—and saved the company money despite the delay—is the point of what follows.

The routine way of making such plant transformations was to install the hardware, impose the new methods, and let the workers get used to the newness of things as fast as they could. The dislocations, the frustrations, the anger, and the humiliation that went along with everything being upset and disrupted were regarded by most managements as simply inevitable.

In making the decision to reengineer its production lines, Harwood management had no intention of lowering individual operators' earning opportunities. But the piece rate would be lowered, because the job was to take less time. Consequently, the planned changes carried inherent danger. Consider the impact of a rumor flashing through the plant: "A speed-up is planned!" "They're going to cut everybody's rates!" Management might explain desperately that while there would be lower rates, the jobs would also take less time. Mere words, interpreted as: "They admit they're cutting rates!" And the issue would be joined.

To avoid such an outcome, a large-scale participation program was planned with the help of Dr. French, who was then at the University of Michigan. All employees would get a complete explanation of the necessity for the planned changes and would be invited to collaborate with management in solving the technical, mechanical, and human problems that would arise.

It was clear that the streamlining of the production lines and the changes in methods would succeed only if the employees wanted them to. Therefore, the plan was for key staff members, such as the plant manager, the chief industrial engineer, the director of personnel, and the various department heads to work closely with each group of workers whose tasks and orientation were being changed.

It was impossible, of course, to take these staff people entirely away from their daily work and assign them solely to helping groups of workers all over the plant to work out new plans and procedures. Instead, the installation of the new equipment and the associated new methods was spaced over a period of one year. Job changes were introduced only as fast as the workers who had already participated in the change-over process showed full understanding and mastery of their new jobs.

This was no easy matter for the workers, their supervisors, or the key staff people. On the part of the key staffers, as a matter of fact, there was an enormous extra load of work. Nobody should make the mistake of thinking that participative methods make things any easier for managers; to the contrary, they challenge managers to the fullest. It is far easier to issue an order and expect it to be obeyed than to manage in a participative way to gain the cooperation and enthusiasm of workers. It is much easier to install an entirely new production system, and then complain about how long the workers take to reach standard production, than it is to participate with the workers in a way that calms changeover anxiety, reduces distrust, and increases communication.

In a change of such magnitude, and with the application of the new work aids still untested on many jobs, it is impossible to provide workers with an exact forecast of what they will confront. The development of new methods is so complex that the industrial engineers themselves are hazy about what to expect. Some workers will encounter genuine difficulties with the new systems; others will look for and find problems where none exist. Some workers will be better off and not admit it; others will come out about as before and complain that they are worse off. But over all—provided management has been honest, done its arithmetic fairly, and spoken openly—the participative method is likely to more than make up for its inherent delays. In our case, there was a galaxy of problems of every sort, both technical and psychological. But they were solved as they arose, and never allowed to fester. Informal discussions were held throughout the changeover year. As the new methods were mastered modifications were made. Sometimes these changes were at the suggestion of management. More often than not, these time- and work-saving modifications were prompted by the workers themselves.

Improperly handled, changeovers of this magnitude cause endless grief and have resulted in lowered productivity, large-scale quitting, excessive absenteeism, floods of grievances, crippling strikes. Yet the Harwood plant emerged with most of its workforce and most of its high morale still intact. Productivity was generally higher than it had been before the program. Turnover and absenteeism were unaffected. Only one worker quit directly because of the change. The success of the program enabled the company to retain its share of the market, improve its profit, preserve its reputation for high quality and on-time performance, and strengthen the trust and confidence of its employees.

Four years later, in 1962, when Harwood acquired its largest competitor, there was an unexpected opportunity to test again, on an even broader scale, our company's approach to participative management theory and practice. What we learned is the subject of the next chapter.

ALFRED J. MARROW / STANLEY E. SEASHORE
DAVID G. BOWERS

Managing Major Change

From the standpoint of behavioral science, we were very lucky. It is rare for conditions to be so right for behavioral scientists who want to study and compare two contrasting ways of managing an organization.

Harwood acquired its leading competitor, the Weldon Manufacturing Company, in 1962. It was a typical business acquisition. Harwood management believed that the two companies combined could operate with greater efficiency and lower costs. Executives understood that when you buy a business you are taking a high risk, no matter how good your information may be. The seller does not simply open up his books and his operations to a potential buyer—especially if that buyer happens to be his leading competitor. The buyer must therefore size things up the best he can and consider long-range alternatives in case unexpected problems should arise.

On the available facts, the merger appeared to be a perfectly logical one. Harwood planned no major changes in Weldon's products, which were much like its own. Nor were changes planned in Weldon's merchandising or manufacturing operations. Each firm employed about 1,000 people; their main plants were each about thirty years old; they put the same raw materials through similar manufacturing processes, on much the same kind of machinery, and sold them at competitive prices in similar and overlapping markets.

It had been agreed that Weldon's entire staff was to be retained. The company's two owner–managers would become salaried managers, but otherwise would go on as before. While efficiencies were to be introduced wherever indicated for increased productivity and profits, the companies were to continue to operate separately and maintain separate identities.

Not long after the merger it became clear to Harwood's management that, despite all the similarities, there was an irreconcilable conflict between the managerial systems of the two companies. As a result, it was impossible to carry out the original plan to keep Weldon as an independent operating company.

Whereas Harwood emphasized and encouraged participative methods in dealing with its problems, Weldon operated under the traditional authoritarian system. Harwood's executives could credit their management approach with creating job satisfaction among their employees and themselves; Weldon, on the other hand, was plagued by low morale among its workers and among many of its executives. While Harwood showed outstanding success in the areas where it counts—profits and productivity—Weldon was struggling with high costs and was getting a low or nonexistent return on its investment.

Careful study confirmed that except for the difference in management approach, the two companies were very much the same. The obvious course was to introduce the Harwood participative approach into Weldon as quickly and smoothly as possible, with the minimum human and financial cost. If Harwood's system could work in Weldon it was probable the merger would be a profitable one after all. If transplanting the system failed, there would be a serious financial loss.

Harwood called in a number of consultants. One, Dr. Rensis Likert of the University of Michigan's Institute of Social Research, was asked to provide a research team to measure and interpret the attitudes and behavior of the Weldon employees during the period of change. The researchers would have the opportunity to observe events as they took place, to record what was done and what happened. Dr. Likert was enthusiastic and agreed that a research team should be assigned immediately so that measurements of the bad existing situation could be made before the change. Professor Stanley Seashore and Dr. David Bowers of the Institute agreed to work on the study.

It was agreed, too, that similar information for control and cross-reference purposes would be gathered at Harwood's main plant in Virginia. Seashore and Bowers were given free access to the records of both companies; special records would be prepared where necessary. Interviews were available with any and all employees as needed. The researchers, in short, had carte blanche.

The project got under way in August 1962, a few weeks after the discussion with Dr. Likert and about seven months after the purchase of Weldon.

A second team of behavioral scientists was brought in by the Harwood management to act as the "change agent." These men were to guide the change in leadership style, strive to increase managerial competence, improve interpersonal relations, train supervisors and executives in the principles of participative management, and serve as instructors in human relations for the entire staff. Two groups of consulting engineers were also employed to introduce the needed technological improvements. The entire operation was supervised by senior executives of Harwood.

The foundation was thus laid for an unusual collaboration of practitioners—behavioral scientists and engineers—to introduce changes aimed at increasing efficiency and helping employees at every level.

The challenge facing Harwood was to reshape the Weldon organization without risking its complete disruption. The job had to be done quickly to avoid the loss of customers and to halt the ongoing financial drain. Nobody expected the task to be easy.

Harwood's executives felt—with good reason, as it turned out—that the hardest task would be to change the practices of the Weldon managerial staff from autocratic to participative. Weldon managers were not a team; they had to be developed into one. They had to learn how to share responsibility and to exercise power in what, for them, would be a strange, baffling, and infuriating new managerial framework. At the same time, new technology would be installed in their plants and work methods would be changed.

Among the first steps taken by the research team from the University of Michigan was a survey of the factory employees at Weldon and of the Harwood employees in the Virginia plant. This provided comparative information about the attitudes of the employees toward their company. In four of the five areas investigated, the number of employees expressing a high level of satisfaction was significantly greater at the Harwood Virginia plant than at the Weldon plant.

It is hard to overstate the dissatisfaction at Weldon. A related survey discovered that nearly 50 percent of Weldon's employees were thinking about quitting the company; at Harwood* the figure was only 17 percent. When rated by their subordinates on personal merit and ability to help workers get their jobs done well, Harwood's supervisors scored better in every respect than Weldon's. Finally, the results showed that more people exercised effective and purposeful influence over decisions at Harwood than at Weldon.

A graphic means of assessing the way a total organization operated had been developed by Dr. Likert. He conceived of four main types of organizations whose management methods ranged across a scale from "exploitative-authoritative" (System 1) to "participative" (System 4). In between were "benevolent-authoritative" (System 2) and "consultative" (System 3). The ratings were based on the extent to which an organization displayed these six attributes:

Positive motivations
Openness of communication
Rate and scope of interaction activities
Decision-making processes
Methods of setting goals and evaluating progress
Distribution of control

* The company name Harwood is used here to designate the employees in the Marion, Virginia, plant.

In condensed form, Figure 1 compares the conditions in the Weldon and Harwood organizations according to rating made by the top executives, managers, and supervisors of each of the plants. These ratings were confirmed by the members of the research team. (A full description of this rating method can be found in *New Patterns of Management* by Rensis Likert.

Figure 1. Operating characteristics 1962.

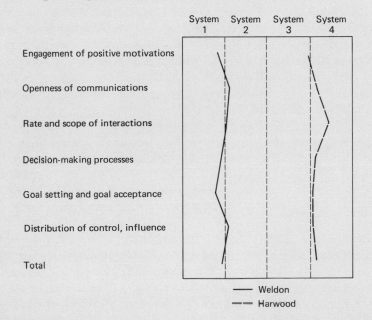

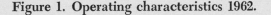

The profile for the Weldon organization runs along the borderline between System 1, the exploitative-authoritative system, and System 2, benevolent-authoritative. Harwood's profile ran well into System 4, the participative. A few examples from the rating form will illustrate the difference measured between the two organizations.

☐ Weldon people, including those at the top level, said information flowing upward tended to get restricted and filtered—in short, garbled. Harwood people said that upward-moving information was likely to be accurate.

☐ Weldon people said that their relationships within the company were often tarnished by condescending supervisors and by fear and caution on the part of lower-level workers. Harwood people said that their relationships were trustful and confident on all levels.

☐ Weldon people said that almost all company goals were set by directive, usually without any wide discussion. Harwood people said that goals were set after discussion with subordinates or, on some matters, by means of group decision.

☐ Weldon people said there was an informal organization within the organization that covertly opposed the goals of the company. Harwood people said that there was an informal organization within the company, too, but most of the time it supported the goals of the company.

The dismaying results of the employee attitude survey were fed back to the Weldon staff and other employees. There was no indication in the summary as to what the solution might be. These were to be worked out jointly between supervisors and their subordinates.

The difference between Weldon and Harwood could hardly have been more complete. For the year 1962, before efforts to change Weldon began to have a significant impact, Harwood was superior to Weldon in every area that was investigated. Some examples are shown in Table 1.

Table 1. Comparison of organizational performance, Weldon and Harwood, 12 months, 1962 (percent).

AREA OF PERFORMANCE	WELDON	HARWOOD
Return on investment	−15	17
Production efficiency	−11	6
Average earnings above minimum	None	17
Make-up pay to reach minimum	12	2
Average monthly absenteeism	6	3
Average monthly turnover	10	75

At 6 percent, Weldon's monthly rate of absenteeism was twice as high as Harwood's 3 percent. Absenteeism caused serious daily disruption at Weldon. In a plant of 1,000, an average of sixty absentees meant that many days began in uncertainty and confusion while empty places were located and filled.

Weldon's monthly rate of turnover was 10 percent—fourteen times higher than Harwood's .75 percent. Consequently, supervisors did not have dependable manpower resources, and much of the time invested in training employees and in gauging individual aptitude was lost.

Weldon's make-up pay, which brings the piecework earnings of employees with substandard output up to the plant minimum wage, amounted to 12 percent of its payroll, while Harwood's was 2 percent. In other words, for each $1 million of payroll Weldon was laying out $120,000 for nonproductive labor.

Harwood's piece-rate workers had average earnings that were 17 percent higher than the standard. This reflected their higher production. Though piece rates were comparable, only a few Weldon workers earned more than the guaranteed minimum wage.

Harwood's overall production efficiency was rated as 106 percent of standard (a conservative estimate). That is, the average Harwood worker exceeded the production standard established for him by 6 percent. This compared to 89 percent—11 percent below standard—at Weldon. Harwood was getting one-fifth more than "standard" production in relation to fixed overhead costs that were the same regardless of output. By contrast, Weldon was getting about one-tenth less than could reasonably be expected.

Finally, while Harwood was earning a 17 percent profit on invested capital, Weldon was showing annual losses equal to 15 percent of its capital.

The evaluation presented such a dismal picture of Weldon that the research team feared that the survival of Weldon was very much in question. The Harwood executives, who were not about to see their acquisition fold up, took note of the weaknesses, but at the same time never lost sight of Weldon's strengths. With their experience, and their broader perspective, Harwood's management people realized that locating weakness is vital when you are looking for places to make changes. But the strengths must be found also, since strength is the starting point for rebuilding any organization.

Weldon's strengths included a plant actually producing products of good quality in large volume, a roster of desirable customers, and a fair number of firm orders in hand to be filled. Moreover, the Weldon organization, for all its weaknesses, still included a large number of people with personal qualities of goodwill, energy, technical competence, readiness to undertake a program of change, and a great deal of interest in the outcome of the whole affair; Weldon, after all, was their livelihood.

Harwood had no choice. To protect its investment in Weldon it had to find ways to encourage the Weldon people to work at their best. But there were some large questions. Could the habits and attitudes of Weldon people be unfrozen enough for useful change to come about? Could change occur without disrupting the entire organization and causing wholesale quitting and sabotage of the program for change? How could the supervisory staff, which was as suspicious and anxious as the rest of the workforce, be persuaded to take on the risks and responsibilities that lay ahead? Most important, would participation and trust be acceptable to people who had spent their working lives in an opposite environment?

Efforts to change Weldon from a System 1 company to a System 4 company went on without letup until the end of 1964, a period of almost thirty months. The program had three elements: First, Harwood moved to ease the anxiety of the working staff at Weldon. Second, a major physical improvement program at the Weldon plant gave workers confidence that Weldon was not going to be allowed to decay. Third, the management system and the patterns of interpersonal relationship throughout the Weldon organization were gradually changed.

From the start, the consultants, the new owners, and their representatives made every effort to apply the participative System 4 principles in their dealings with Weldon people. A number of strategies, including sensitivity training, were introduced in an effort to break down the old habits of distrust, secrecy, and noncooperation and to develop instead openness and trust. The entire Weldon organization, from the plant manager down to the production workers, was involved in team building and problem-solving sessions. The purpose was to make group participation a normal Weldon procedure. Finally, there was a concerted effort to spread responsibility and influence downward in the organization so that each worker could have some significant part in the management of his own work and in the work of those associated with him.

The process was gradual. Revolutionizing managerial methods takes time. Shifts toward participation and shared responsibility may well provoke the most damaging kind of skepticism from workers who are accustomed to traditional bureaucratic ways. There is always a good deal of anxiety and confusion at first. Employees cannot be overwhelmed with too many new practices. Where they have been conditioned to blind obedience and ruled with a heavy hand for long periods, they may interpret sudden freedom as a sign of weakness in management.

This had been well dramatized five years before in Harwood's plant in Puerto Rico. The manager there had actively encouraged employees to participate in problem-solving meetings. But soon afterward there was a sharp increase in employee turnover. An investigation revealed that the workers had decided that if management was so "ignorant" that it had to consult employees, the company was badly run and would soon fail. So they quit to look for jobs with companies that were "well managed" and told their employees what to do.

People who for years have been denied involvement and influence also lack the skills required for effective participation. They are either timid or too aggressive. Only slow and careful reeducation can change deeply ingrained relationships.

When the program was seven months along, it became clear that although there was no worsening of the tense situation that existed among Weldon supervisors and managers, it was getting better very slowly indeed. There was still a great deal of discontent and uncertainty, and the lower-level workers could sense it. It held down morale, production, and profits. The problems nagged on despite staff meetings at which disagreements were discussed with a candor that astonished some of the Weldon people. For the first time supervisors and managers were given the fullest information about all matters—absenteeism, job-change rates, discipline, future plans—and were consulted about ways of dealing with the problems. It is possible that these factors alone would in time have brought about a change of behavior at Weldon. But the financial drain was too great to permit the process of change simply to crawl. Faster improvement was essential.

One of the consultants, Dr. Gilbert David, proposed a series of extended "confrontation meetings" for staff members at which sensitivity training methods would be used in an attempt to accelerate the working out of antagonisms and the development of collaboration. The plan was as follows:

□ The initial meetings would be limited to top managers. After that, the program would probably be extended to all supervisors and managers.

□ All meetings would be based on "family groups"—that is, people who normally were related in their work and might therefore bring their regular work roles and relationships to the sessions. This is the kind of group which probably experiences the greatest difficulties in sensitivity training, since the participants may well be very reluctant to talk frankly with their superiors, or with colleagues with whom they have ongoing relations. This risk, however, seemed worth taking.

□ Staff members were advised that their attendance was expected. Though it is generally preferable to give people the option of coming to such sessions, it was felt there was too much antagonism and apprehension for attendance to be voluntary. There was considerable effort to bring about a receptive attitude; the program was discussed fully in staff meetings and each participant was interviewed by the consultant in advance.

□ Comparatively brief sessions of two to four days were planned, rather than the more leisurely and extended sessions commonly used in sensitivity training. The pressures of work precluded keeping key managers away from the organization for a longer time.

□ Provision was made for follow-up interviews after the main sessions.

□ Sessions would be held at locations away from the Weldon office or plant, with facilities for living in.

□ All sessions would have the same psychologist in attendance; Harwood executives or their representatives would attend only if asked by the Weldon group.

The first group selected for training was composed of the five department heads in Weldon's New York office. They were mostly concerned with marketing administration and coordination of sales and production. Significantly, their superior, one of the former owner–managers of the company, refused to attend the training sessions.

The training session was intense, continuing from the evening of the first day through noon of the fourth day with breaks only for meals, brief recreation, and sleep. The "program" was at first unstructured. This is a conventional procedure in sensitivity training. The first evening's discussion got under way with a rather neutral opening device: a problem census. But in this case, there were enough deep and frustrating problems to provoke, more quickly than usual, strong and emotional expressions of concern. By the next day, the participants had begun to express themselves to each other quite directly and frankly, something they avoided in their daily work. As the discussions went on it became easier for them to accept criticism without slashing back. Ultimately the session "unfroze" a flood of long-suppressed hostilities, anxieties, old attitudes, values, and feelings the managers had about each other and about business problems.

You will simply have to imagine the relief that came with getting things out into the open. From the second day on, the discussion was spontaneous, uninhibited, and free of most of the old defensive politeness, superficiality, and concealment. These men were now susceptible to much more objective self-analysis. There were tense moments. Years of suspicion, distrust, and antagonism do not just melt away magically with a few days of sensitivity training. But the issues were out on the table, and most were aired without too much acrimony.

There was, however, one major problem with which the participants were unable to deal—the absent former owner–manager. It was clear that this man's behavior profoundly affected their own. Nonetheless, once it became clear that they had no choice but to discuss him, even if it was "behind his back" in a sense, they went ahead and did so. A great emotional dam burst when that decision was reached, and torrents of complaint and criticism poured forth. Since the group included the absent man's son and son-in-law, the situation was dramatic.

The consensus that emerged was beyond doubt. The only way to establish more cooperative relations among the top Weldon staff was to gain the cooperation of the absent man. He had to agree to work with them as a team, instead of playing each one against the other in a fashion that produced the continual turmoil on which he seemed to thrive. He would have to grant them greater freedom to act; he would have to share information; he would have to modify his jealously held role as the sole decision maker.

The participants asked that the absent superior, together with the two top executives of the Harwood organization, meet in conference with them to discuss the issues openly. The Harwood owners agreed, and a plan was made to meet a week later at an out-of-town retreat. But the absent man again refused to attend. The Harwood people urged him to cooperate. Reluctantly, grudgingly, he agreed to come only for a single evening session. He would leave early the next morning.

The five staff men spent the first day of the planned two-day session reviewing the issues they wanted to discuss with their superior. The five were nervous about the whole affair, but they had no doubt that what they were doing was necessary. That evening the confrontation came.

With courage they had never shown before, the staff men spoke of misunderstandings that arose because the superior always met with them individually instead of as a group. They pointed out errors that had been made because of poor communication. They recounted delays that had resulted in considerable extra costs because none of the staff could make final decisions within their area of responsibility without first obtaining the superior's approval.

The scene must be imagined and absorbed: the son, the son-in-law, the three others, the new owners, the former owner. One thing seemed apparent: the former owner was not about to change. As he saw things, he had spent a lifetime in a dog-eat-dog business and he knew all the tricks. He had managed by keeping everybody off balance, by breeding suspicion, sowing distrust, letting the others squabble among themselves so that they would never turn on him. Now they had suddenly conspiratorially, treasonously grouped against him, the very thing he had worked to prevent for all those years. There was both sadness and finality to the scene. The man was defensive at first, then aggressive, and at last very angry.

After many hours of discussion that lasted past midnight, all retired. The next morning the former owner made his final statement. He had no intention, he said with barely repressed anger, of changing his methods. The management practices at the Weldon office would continue on Monday morning just as they had always been. He then got up and left the room. Although it only became clear a little later, this confrontation effectively signaled his departure from the company.

Before long, the new owners and the five staff men changed the pattern of organization so that authority and responsibility were distributed among the Weldon people. They were pleased with the outcome and with each other. The new mood of helpfulness and understanding on the job even carried over to their social contacts. Two of the Weldon managers, who had not spoken to each other outside the office for a year, exchanged visits to each other's homes.

The next group for training was composed of the six top staff members from the plant, including the plant manager. These men had been working long hours under considerable strain because of the upheaval caused by the numerous technological changes and the internal disorganization. This group met for four days about a month after the first group had met.

The session started badly. Some members of the group had resisted the notion of participating and would have declined had they felt free to do so. Furthermore, the training location turned out to be badly suited to the needs of the group and had to be changed after they had assembled. But once the meetings developed momentum, the group worked with considerable success. The pattern was similar to that adopted by the earlier group, beginning with a problem census and moving on to more personal matters of their own relationships and work arrangements, and then to a candid assessment and analysis of their own behavior and the ways they would wish to change.

It emerged that the problems of this group were to some extent focused not on the absent owner–manager, but on the production manager, who was present. The session helped him to learn a great deal about the inadvertent effects of his behavior, and his colleagues in turn came to see his problems and point of view. Subsequently, his changed behavior became a subject for widespread comment at the plant, and a source of satisfaction to himself.

Another notable development in this session was the beginning of positive relationships with the New York office, which came about because one of those present was the plant representative of the corporate controller's office. This "agent" of New York was, for the first time, welcomed into the fellowship of the production–management group and was able to resolve some misunderstandings and suspicions.

The participants were deeply moved by the experience. Several described it later as a reassessment of a lifetime of values and beliefs. They had a new feeling of confidence in dealing with each other, and greater awareness of their own impact on others. They felt they had learned something about the exercise of authority, about group rivalries and the struggle for power, and about new ways to create an atmosphere in which conflicts could be resolved.

About three months later, each of the participants was interviewed. The comments of all were favorable. For example:

I feel my job is much easier . . . things don't upset me as much as they did before. I get more work done . . . I'm not so tense. Before I went to the sensitivity sessions my ulcers had been kicking up. Knock wood, I haven't had a single painful attack since.

I am devoting all my energy to my job instead of half doing it and half fighting others. I don't feel as though someone is looking over my shoulder and cooking up trouble.

I have been given more authority than I had before. There definitely has also been a change in my subordinates. I guess because I have changed toward them, they act differently toward me.

There is a tremendous improvement in my relationship with the New York people. There is a willingness on their part to try to understand, and if they don't understand, they are willing to say, "I don't understand," instead of always criticizing us.

There is a greater effort to cooperate within this group as well as with the New York organization. There is a new feeling of teamwork. We seem to have as many differences, but we straighten them out with less irritation.

Among the comments on the training session itself were these:

> When we first got settled around the table everyone was thinking, "What is going to happen now?" I guess we were just scared. By the time we left on Sunday, everyone felt at ease with one another. We all felt we had received tremendous help. This was a valuable experience for me.

> I think each and every one got a different meaning out of it. It's hard to tell another person how you actually feel. It has helped me in my work and in my family.

> You get to see yourself as other people see you. If you don't know that, you can't do anything to change your ways. So I am much more understanding.

The plant manager and his top staff were asked whether they wanted similar training for others in their organization and, if so, to suggest how it might be handled. Their recommendations led to additional sessions, similar to those held earlier, for groups of supervisors, assistant supervisors, and senior staff people.

On the whole, participants found the sessions much more helpful than disturbing, and in some cases their subordinates, who had not attended, remarked that they had noted positive changes in their superiors' behavior. For example:

> There is a remarkable change in the plant managers. They have a different attitude toward practically everything. My boss in particular is much calmer, even when something goes wrong. He used to blow his top even when things were normal.

> They are much easier to talk to. Before, I couldn't talk to certain people too well. They would get angry or sarcastic. Now they seem much calmer and don't get mad as often, even when something goes wrong.

The relationships of the supervisors to each other and to the hourly worker came under special scrutiny from the start, because the situation was bad. The supervisors were technically competent, they worked hard, and they had many skilled people to work with. Still, there were chronic failures of coordination among different work groups. These led to avoidable errors, hostility, absenteeism, high turnover, low individual performance, and a general sense of uneasiness and confusion. The new owners assumed from the start that the primary fault lay in the authoritarian methods that had grown up over the years.

The new management and the various consultants knew what was needed if production goals were to be met. First, the supervisors would have to gain a new concept of their leadership role—and this included a conscious and purposeful fresh look at their power relationships with their superiors, peers, and subordinates. Second, changes in relationships and practices would have to be made by supervisors and their subordinates in problem-solving confrontations.

The program designed to rebuild relationships and practices was directed by Robert Pearse. Spread over eighteen months, the steps taken were as follows:

1. The attention of supervisors and managers was drawn to the critical role of shop-floor relationships in aiding or impeding production.
2. Policy changes forced disruption of the old pattern, thus requiring that a new one be formed.
3. Reviews of progress and reports on successful solution of the first problems tackled were provided.
4. The use of consultative and participative problem-solving methods and the training of supervisors in applying them were begun in relatively isolated situations and only later spread throughout the entire plant.

One of the main objectives of the program change was to find ways, particularly at the shop-floor level, to draw employees into freer communication about work problems. A series of problem-solving meetings helped build trust. Both supervisors and operators attempted in the group sessions to air their common work disagreements and to develop joint solutions for them.

During and after this series of problem-solving meetings, positive responses were reported. "What a welcome change," exclaimed one employee. "This is something Weldon never did before. You have a chance to tell them what you think and you feel you're part of the company. In the past they told you want to do and you did it."

The idea of involving production-line workers in problem-solving sessions aroused some early skepticism. One worker asked: "You mean they are really going to let us talk about what is going on even if we think they are doing things wrong?" The slow realization by workers that their ideas were accepted and treated with respect represented a genuine breakthrough. The policy of discussing interpersonal as well as production problems was beginning to pay dividends. Hourly employees saw their own recommendations being implemented by their supervisors, and team spirit and pride began to develop. Individuals and teams gradually accepted responsibility for improving their own work results.

The process of change was painful at one time or another for everybody involved—and in Weldon's case, that included everybody in the company. For top management people it was frustrating to hold themselves in check while comparatively unskilled subordinates wrestled with tasks that the managers were used to doing easily, quickly, and effectively.

To those further down the ladder, the contacts with higher levels of the company brought uncomfortable moments. The observers and consultants were at first perceived as threatening new agents of company manipulation.

The stress on the managers was terrific. Change of this magnitude puts the heaviest kind of physical and emotional burdens upon the supervisory staff, especially at the beginning when they must spearhead the change program while at the same time keeping up with daily production under the restraints of the old system. Demands on their time become extreme: fifteen-hour days were common, with weekend and take-home work besides. There were times when some people risked physical exhaustion. But during this trying period only one senior member of the Weldon plant management left the organization.

The program really took hold in 1963. By the end of that year, the main period of rapid change in practices and performance was over. Since then, the rate of change in Weldon's overall organizational function has been at a normal level.

By 1964 the main economic goals of the program had essentially been achieved, as Table 2 shows. Weldon's negative return on investment in fiscal 1962 was transformed into a healthy, profitable 17 percent return during fiscal 1964.

What makes such a sharp change in return rate possible is that apparel manufacturing is a "labor-intensive" industry. Capital is relatively modest

Table 2. Indicators of organization efficiency in production, Harwood and Weldon, 1962 and 1964 (percent).

	WELDON		HARWOOD	
AREA OF PERFORMANCE	1962	1964	1962	1964
Return on capital invested	−15	+17	+17	+21
Make-up pay	12	4	2	2
Production efficiency	−11	+14	6	16
Earnings above minimum (piece-rate and other incentive employees only)	None	16	17	22
Operator turnover rates (monthly basis)	10	4	¾	¾
Absences from work (daily rate, production employees only)	6	3	3	3

in relation to the total value added to raw materials. Nevertheless, the improvement is striking and most satisfying. As the figures for this index show, Weldon did almost as well in 1964 as Harwood, which earned a 21 percent return. Production efficiency also rose markedly. In the fall of 1962, Weldon was rated by the engineers at 11 percent below standard output for all production employees combined. Harwood's estimated efficiency was 6 percent above standards for that year.

In other words, on an average for the entire year 1962, the performance of Weldon's piece-rate employees against their individual job standard was 89 percent, or 11 percentage points below standard. By early 1964, the Weldon efficiency had risen to 114 percent.

One of the high costs incurred by Weldon during 1962 and earlier took the form of make-up payments to supplement pay actually earned by pieceworkers in order to satisfy the minimum wage requirement. These supplemental payments during 1962 were a 12 percent addition to payroll. This reflected the large number of Weldon operators who were performing at levels below standard. During 1964, the make-up pay was cut to just 4 percent. During the same period, Harwood remained stable at 2 percent make-up pay.

Another indicator of the production efficiency of the total organization is the rate of operator earnings for above-standard performance. While make-up pay for less than standard output is a direct loss to the company, the extra pay for above-standard output represents a gain. The company benefits from additional production at little additional cost. In 1962, Weldon had few employees earning more than the guaranteed minimum. In 1964, however, plant earnings were 16 percent above the guaranteed minimum.

Weldon's operator quit rate was 10 percent per month during 1962. This rate decreased to less than half that during 1964. Weldon's absenteeism declined from a daily average of 6 percent to 3 percent; Harwood remained steady at about 3 percent, a level some in the industry regard as an optimum. Weldon's rate of manufacturing defects (those caught and corrected within the plant) was reduced by 39 percent. This improvement was clearly not a result of slipshod or declining quality inspection standards; during the same period the rate of customer returns also dropped—*by 57 percent.*

There is yet another category of criteria by which Weldon may be judged: Do its employees view their organization with greater confidence and optimism? Do they get more personal satisfaction from their work?

During the period of the Weldon change program, the attitude of Weldon employees, as measured by a Likert attitude survey, became more favorable toward the pay system. Substantial changes were also recorded in their perception of how hard they were working and in their personal plans for staying or leaving. In 1962, about half the Weldon employees said they were definitely planning to leave or would do so if the right opportunity came along. By 1964, a very substantial majority was planning to stay on indefinitely.

From the results of the survey, and from personal observations, it does seem that basic gains in satisfactions, motivations, and positive feelings may be harder to achieve than output increases and cost reduction. Such psychological gains may well come about over a long span of time. Employees are very conservative about the personal meaning of policy and work-system changes until they prove enduring.

The key effort to describe changes in Weldon's philosophy and practice of management was carried out with the aid of the Likert rating procedure described near the start of this chapter. As modified for use in the Weldon-Harwood study, the procedure rated forty-three aspects of organizational functioning. You may recall that in 1962, Weldon was a clear System 1 company. The 1964 results for Weldon, based on reports by all top plant managers, supervisors, and assistant supervisors, are shown in Figure 2. The ratings indicate that Weldon had shifted to System 3, the "consultative" model.

Figure 2. Weldon's progress toward participative management.

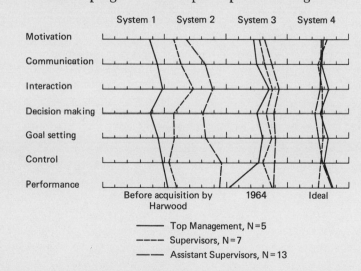

There was remarkable agreement among the Weldon staff. Regardless of rank, they wished to progress further to System 4, the fully participative system. Some allowance must be made for the fact that these ratings were constructed when there was considerable effort to advocate System 4 principles at Weldon. Nonetheless, the ratings indicate a clear acceptance of participation as an ideal.

The research team and the new Weldon owners knew that changes in the management system at Weldon might be only temporary. Perhaps, when the consultants left, there would be a reversion to the old management system. Therefore the Weldon managers and supervisors were asked two years later (in 1966) to repeat the rating procedure. Figure 3 indicates that the changes in Weldon's management system appeared to be lasting.

Figure 3. Weldon's 1966 profile of organizational characteristics.

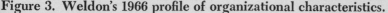

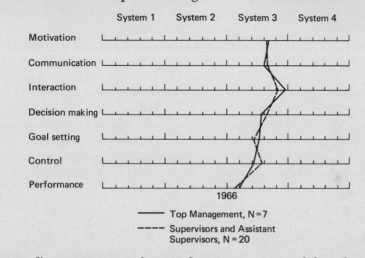

Harwood's program to change the management philosophy of the Weldon organization succeeded. Weldon did indeed change, and in the ways intended. Personnel relations, productivity, and profits all had been radically—and rapidly—improved.

STANLEY E. SEASHORE / DAVID G. BOWERS

Does Organizational Change Last?

A question often asked is whether organizational changes that have been planned, successfully introduced, and confirmed by measurements over a relatively short span of time can survive as permanent features. Does an organization so changed continue the new direction and pace of change? Does it become stabilized? Or does it revert to its earlier condition?

In mid-1969, four and a half years after the end of the intensive change program at Weldon, we invited ourselves back to the plant for a follow-up measurement of the state of the company. The evidence we assembled suggests that Weldon has made additional progress toward the goals which were envisioned by the owners and managers in 1962, and envisioned somewhat later by supervisors and production employees as well. This outcome invites speculation about the psychological and social forces at work there.

We confess a momentary regret that there was not an opposite outcome; we are rather better equipped with ideas about organizational stability and regression than with explanations for continuing development. For example, before the Weldon data became available, we were gearing up to make some remarks about the "Hawthorne effect"—concerned with the superficiality and ephemerality of organizational and behavioral changes induced under conditions of external attention and pressure. Similarly, we were prepared to offer wise comment about cultural forces, habits, and the natural predilection of managers for nonparticipative methods. These, we thought, would help explain a reversion to the prevailing conditions in organizations. We were prepared to assert that in the absence of contrary environmental forces, a company would fall back to some more primitive form of organizational life.

Clearly, in the case of Weldon, we needed to appeal to other ideas than these. One possible explanation for the continued momentum of change was that the heavy investment of external talent, money, and effort that characterized the original change period at Weldon was continued during the subsequent years. We were assured, however, that this was not the case. Some continuing use of external consultants has been made, but no more than is considered normal and permanent. Further improvements have been introduced in the work system and production facilities, but also at no more than a permanently sustainable rate. There has been a continuation of certain policies and activities introduced as part of the original change program, but these are regarded as normal operating procedure and not as special change efforts. Economic conditions have been favorable to the firm, but they were also favorable before the change of ownership in 1962.

The original change program sought to bring about mutually reinforcing changes in psychological, organizational, and technological areas. A central idea was to make only those structural changes in the organization that were appropriate to the way work was actually accomplished and that accorded with reasonable assumptions about the values and motives of individual employees. Thus, the revitalized piece-rate system was understood to be viable only if sustained by a structure that allowed high earnings, assured instant supervisory response to low earnings, and supported production employees in becoming skilled in the new work assigned.

In short, the program was based on a view of the factory as a total system in which all elements are interdependent. The interdependence of elements tends to preserve and to enhance the central characteristics of the system, and consequently to prevent retrogression.

Another reason for the persistence of change at Weldon may be that the original program of change put employees at all levels in the habit of considering the effect of their actions on other parts of the organization. This is speculative. We have no ready way to assess the extent to which Weldon people deliberately and self-consciously examine the potential side effects of the many policy and operating decisions, usually technical or economic in origin, that arise daily. But one of the fragmenting features of many organizations is the tendency to isolate problems, to treat them as if they could be best resolved without reference to their broader context. An organization habituated at all levels to think about, discuss, and weigh the full range of elements in the system might well have unusual capacities for self-development.

But the best explanation of how Weldon has perpetuated and even extended change under conditions of limited continuing external influence may lie after all in the inherent worth of the participative organizational model. It might just be that people who have experienced a taste of it get hooked, know what they want, and lend their effort to preserving it.

EDWARD E. LAWLER III / CORTLANDT CAMMANN

What Makes a Work Group Successful?

In 1970, the chairman of Harwood Companies came to us with a most unusual request: Why, he wanted to know, was one of their work units so extraordinarily productive? Usually when firms seek out behavioral science researchers it is because they are having problems. Consequently, specialists in the field of organization behavior usually analyze groups or institutions that are not working right. A lot can be learned from observing groups that are having troubles, but it is refreshing and very useful to study successful groups, too. Only in this way can hard evidence be obtained on what distinguishes effective from ineffective groups.*

The work group singled out was the warehousing, order packing, and shipping unit in one of Harwood's Virginia plants. At the time, the unit consisted of eleven employees and a supervisor. All lived in rural Virginia. Their mean age was thirty-seven. Only six of them had high school diplomas. Their average length of time in the group was fifteen years, and their average service in the company seventeen years. All were married, and most had children.

The department assembles the products manufactured in several of the company's nearby plants, stores them until needed, fills customer orders as they come in, and ships them out. Though the work does not require a high level of skill, it can be physically tiring. Alertness is required, as the inventory contains more than 3,000 separate styles and sizes. There are several thousand separate accounts, and requirements for quantities, sizes, and colors vary widely from order to order. During some periods of the year the men can put in a great deal of overtime if they wish. At other times the workload is relatively light.

Our first task was to determine whether this group was, in fact, as productive and effective as management said it was. We quickly dis-

* The authors would like to thank Dr. Alfred J. Marrow for making this study possible.

122

covered, from the records and from interviews, that the group had not always been thought of so highly. Indeed, between 1950 and 1958, its productivity was abysmal. In those years as many as twenty-one men worked in the department during seasonal peaks. Because of clerical chaos, many of the orders that reached the shipping department were for products that were out of stock. Floors were cluttered with partially filled orders.

Understandably, turnover, absenteeism, and grievances were high. Annual turnover ranged from 20 to 50 percent. Personal relationships in the department were marked by arguing and fighting rather than by teamwork. Each man had a specific job, and since the flow of orders from customers was not controlled, it frequently happened that some of the men were extremely busy while others had little to do. The attitude was every man for himself.

The shipping department surpervisor was beset by difficulties. It was his job to maintain the rate of shipment, to accept responsibility for the accuracy of shipments, and to oversee the workforce. In carrying out these responsibilities, he had to work under the direction of the plant manager, the production manager, and five men connected with sales in the New York office. He found himself pulled in many directions at the same time, and he was never able to perform to the satisfaction of all his bosses.

In 1958, an inventory and order control system was introduced, and the layout of the plant was changed. Soon after these changes were instituted the supervisor was transferred, and his assistant became the new supervisor. The role of the supervisor was changed. He no longer received instructions directly from New York. Since a new computer had begun to produce "clean orders," his role was primarily to organize and maintain the force necessary to ship the orders that came to him each day. All instructions and changes in the daily routine of shipping came from the plant customer relations office and from a plant staff member who was assigned responsibility in this area.

At about the same time, a bonus plan was proposed to the work group by management. This included a sharing by the company and the group of any reductions in cost from the previous year. After thoroughly discussing the proposal with management, the group unanimously agreed to accept the plan. Several days later group members requested that their number be cut from seventeen to eleven. The six who left were placed in other jobs within the company, and the size of the group has remained at about eleven ever since. With the exception of some minor improvements in the packaging of the merchandise, there have been no significant technological changes since 1958. Thus the productivity figures for the years from 1958 to the present are comparable.

During this period the shipping department's output has climbed steeply. Data on average productivity per man-hour are presented in

Figure 1 and show a gradual increase from 1958 to 1967, and a sharp rise since then. Over all, the average worker was turning out twice as much in 1970 as he was in 1958, even though there were no changes in technology or equipment.

Figure 1. Change in average productivity, July 1958–June 1970.

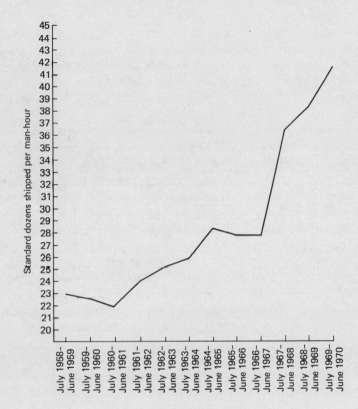

Two other measures of this unit's effectiveness were available. During the twelve years from June 1958 to June 1970, only three people chose to quit the group. This represents a voluntary turnover of under 2 percent per year, compared with a turnover for the entire plant of 25 percent per year. Also, from June 1969 to June 1970, the only year for which it was calculated, absenteeism was less than one percent of the total possible man-days, compared with 5 percent for the total work population. So, not only has this become a decidedly productive group—it is one in which people seem to want to participate.

Any group's productivity is influenced by a variety of forces, not all of which by any means are related to technology. Some forces—for example, poor equipment, group pressures to restrict output—hold production down, while others serve to push it up—individual motivation, new equipment, group norms *favoring* increased output.

Researchers have found five factors that strongly influence group productivity: technology, intrinsic motivation, extrinsic motivation, group norms about cooperation and productivity, and the abilities of the group members. To discover why the productivity of the Virginia shipping department was higher than that of other groups, we needed to learn how each of these five factors was affecting it. This was accomplished in a comparative study.

The first group to be compared with the shipping department was also in the Virginia plant. It performed a different kind of work (cutting and spreading fabric) and was considered to be about average in efficiency.

The second group chosen for comparison was the shipping department in another factory in another state. This department was chosen because it did the same kind of work, operated under a similar pay plan, was part of the same corporation, but had lower productivity. The researchers had to accept management's assessment of relative productivity, since the actual figures were not comparable. Turnover and absenteeism were much higher in this department than in either of the Virginia groups. The average seniority was 5.2 years, in contrast to 15 years and 18 years in the Virginia groups.

While the study focused on both similarities and differences among the three groups, the differences naturally were of most interest to us, because they were the characteristics more likely to explain the Virginia shipping department's better record. Some of the characteristics it *shares* with other groups probably do contribute to its productivity; but the comparative analysis is unlikely to pinpoint those.

We began our research informally by interviewing several workers in the Virginia shipping department. On the basis of these interviews, a "structured" interview was prepared and a questionnaire developed to measure group norms, intrinsic (that is, self-generated) motivation, and extrinsic (externally induced) motivation. All members of the three work groups completed the questionnaire. Interviews were conducted with all members of the Virginia shipping unit and with six members of the other shipping department.

There were no significant differences in technology between the Virginia shipping group and the other shipping group. Unusual physical or mental abilities were also ruled out in accounting for the record of the Virginia group. Any physically fit man with average intelligence can perform shipping-department tasks. We had no reason to doubt that the employees in all the company's shipping departments possessed the requisite ability.

By elimination, we were left with the probability that the clue was to be found in psychological factors. Specifically, it seemed likely to rest in the Virginia group's desire to produce at a high level and in the kind of personal relationships and group pressures, or norms, that existed.

What a group accepts as normal in matters such as productivity and cooperation can have a strong impact on its performance. A number of studies have shown that when groups adopt anti-productivity norms, individual members tend to restrict their output. It is also true that when groups develop pro-productivity norms, production tends to rise.

Our questionnaire and interview data clearly indicated that the Virginia shipping department had developed pro- rather than anti-productivity norms. This is undoubtedly *one* of the main reasons its output was so high. However, its norms about productivity were not significantly different from those of the comparison groups. Therefore the pro-productivity norms alone could not explain why it surpassed the other groups.

When groups perform tasks that require cooperative effort, productivity is influenced by their norms about teamwork. The work of the shipping department demands mutual help. Boxes and cartons are passed from one person to another, a process that must go smoothly. All the groups studied tended to have norms strongly favoring cooperation. But these norms, and in particular the feeling of team spirit, were strongest in the Virginia shipping department group, as illustrated by the following comments made by its members:

> *We all try to work as one team. It's a good bunch of boys to work with.*

> *We have a lot of fun . . . nobody gets mad.*

> *They're all nice fellows. They work well together.*

Two of the workers used the analogy of the family to describe the atmosphere of the group. On the other hand, the shipping group in the other plant described itself in different terms:

> *There could be a lot better cooperation. Sometimes the fellows get to work together and other times they just don't.*

> *They don't work together . . . not a hundred percent like they should.*

The clearly superior team spirit of the Virginia group appeared to be at least partially responsible for its greater efficiency.

The norms of the Virginia department seemed ideal from many points of view. Members were promanagement, supported and encouraged high productivity, and favored cooperation. How do such norms develop?

Supervisory style, trust of management, and the reward system all contribute to the making of high-spirited morale. In the Virginia group, these three factors seem to have combined to encourage high productivity.

The Harwood management has been using a participative approach for a number of years and appears to have won the trust of its employees, who told us:

I think they would look out for my interest.

They [the top plant management] will speak to you if they see you outside the plant. Now I think that goes a long way with people working for them. Something like that means a lot to me. I'd go out of my way if I could do anything for a person like that.

Other employees stressed that management had never harmed them and had always shown concern for them. They also trust Harwood not to do what so many companies do: change the incentive plan when the employees start to earn more.

The Virginia shippers were much more satisfied with their supervisor than were the members of the other two groups.

I haven't got anything I can say against him—taken all the way 'round he is a good supervisor.

I don't believe they have any better here at the plant. He's a good fellow.

This supervisor didn't push the men; he didn't supervise them closely. He told them what had to be done and expected that it would be accomplished. As he himself described it, he would rather lead than push. He was prepared to exert influence if something was not getting done, but he wouldn't ride the men about it.

In the shipping department of the other plant, the employees complained that their supervisor was at first too strict, later too lenient. He is gone now. The new supervisor was promoted from the work group and has yet to prove himself. Some of the men lack confidence in him. Some say he supervises too closely. These differences in leadership style seem to contribute to the better team spirit in Virginia.

The kind of incentive plan used in the Virginia plant supported the development of favorable norms. When this plan was started in 1958, job classifications were abolished. All members of the group were free to perform all tasks, so the workload could be distributed evenly. This encouraged cooperation. Almost certainly, part of the increase in productivity since 1958 has resulted from the increased ability of the work group to use its labor where it could be most effective.

At the same time the job classifications were tossed out, a group incentive bonus was introduced to tie the individual worker's pay to his group's performance. The plan created a "reward situation" where it was to the advantage of each member to keep his fellow workers on their toes.

Provided that workers trust management and have a participatory relationship with their supervisors, group plans generally tend to encourage favorable norms about productivity. This seems to be precisely what happened in the Virginia shipping group.

It has often been observed that some people work hard, under any conditions, because of their values about work. Jobholders who are committed to the Protestant work ethic, and who strongly believe in self-control, are said to have high intrinsic motivation. High intrinsic motivation may be a factor in the superior productivity of the Virginia shipping department. Measures of this variable were included in the questionnaire and the employees did tend to score high.

Intrinsic motivation is reinforced when a good fit occurs between the needs of the worker and the characteristics of his job so that good performance leads to inner rewards, such as a feeling of competence. Lawler and Hackman argue that this occurs when workers who value such intrinsic rewards hold jobs that provide them with feedback, autonomy, and wholly meaningful tasks.

An analysis of the shipping jobs suggests that they are capable of generating some intrinsic motivation. Feedback and autonomy are high, but opportunities to work on challenging, meaningful tasks are limited. Interestingly, on our questionnaire measure the Virginia group had higher intrinsic motivation scores than the other groups. This seems to stem from a feeling that they have more autonomy than the other groups. It does not appear that the higher degree of autonomy they report is owing to any basic difference in the nature of the job itself. Rather it seems due to the different styles used by the supervisors. It is an interesting example of how the supervisor can have an important influence on his subordinates' perceptions of the nature of their jobs. Again in part, the higher motivation of the shipping group can apparently be explained by a greater intrinsic motivation.

Any external reward can be a source of motivation if it is valued by the employees and if earning it is seen as being related to performance.

The external reward most frequently used is money; indeed, incentive plans that tied dollar reward to superior performance were used by all the groups studied. The employees in all the groups valued money very highly and clearly saw a connection between their pay and their performance.

The Virginia shipping department, however, differed from the others in one important respect: The workers saw a much closer connection between their productivity and their pay than did the members of the other groups. The Virginia shippers felt that they could actually figure out what their earnings would be in a given week and clearly understood the basis on which they were paid. The other shipping group workers could not clearly grasp how their pay was determined. Both the questionnaire and the interview data suggested that they were unsure about the calculations. Their plan was more complicated; it is not surprising that they were unable to understand it.

Lawler and Hackman have shown that when employees participate in the design of a pay plan it is likely to be more successful because they understand it better and are more committed to making it work effectively. The Virginia shipping group had participated in the development of its plan. Members had been given a voice in drawing it up, and they had a chance to accept or reject it. In the other shipping department, this procedure was not followed; the employees clearly had less comprehension of their incentive plan and were less committed to it.

One other piece of evidence strongly indicates that dollar reward is a strong motivation in the Virginia work group. Until June 1967, the incentive system included a ceiling on the bonus that the men could receive. This ceiling was removed in the summer of 1967. Figure 1 shows the obvious results: Average productivity rose about 30 percent, and the higher level of output has been consistently maintained since then. This rise seems to be attributable almost entirely to the nature of the pay system. Accordingly, a strong case can be made that a major reason for the Virginia group's higher productivity is the unique pay incentive system.

Why is the Virginia shipping department highly productive? The answer now seems clear. The men who work in it have high intrinsic and extrinsic motivation, and have group norms that promote cooperation and productivity. The high motivation and positive group norms have been encouraged by a number of favorable conditions. These include good supervision, trust of management, an acceptable pay system, and work that allows some autonomy. The other groups studied had generally positive norms and reasonably high motivation. However, these factors simply did not interact to create the strong forces for productivity that developed in the Virginia group.

The reasons for this seem to lie in two important factors: First, the pay system in the Virginia shipping department makes a clear connection between pay and performance, and the employees are committed to it. Second, the supervisor in the Virginia group generally uses a participative style and is respected by his men. These elements were missing in the other groups, and because of it they turned out less work.

One way to determine the validity of our diagnosis would be to try to change the other groups. Specifically, the pay plan and type of super-vision could be revised in the other shipping department—and, indeed, the management is planning to try this. If our analysis is correct, the change should result in better performance there. The kind of compara-tive study we have done can produce valuable indications about why a group is productive, but final proof can come only from experiments in which changes are introduced.

part three

Releasing Human Potential

The Right Man
in the Right Job

The day is in view when managers will need precise answers to questions that few organizations are attempting to deal with scientifically at present. For example:

☐ What is the level of competence within the organization today?

☐ Who are the men with growth potential, and just how high are they likely to go?

☐ How well have we balanced the talents and skills needed for current operations with those that will be needed ten or twenty years from now?

Tomorrow's management will be expected to predict with some accuracy each man's potential within an organization; to spot the "comers" early so they can be encouraged with rapid promotions; to discern among apparently equal production workers the ones most likely to succeed as supervisors—in short, to choose the right man for the right job, right from the beginning. As today's companies expand under the press of swift technological change, the present mismatching of men and jobs, when multiplied several times over, would spell disaster.

Conventional decisions based on past performance too often result in the promotion to the forefront of an organization of men whose technological skills far outweigh their leadership qualities. More often still, the ranks of middle management are swollen with overpromoted men.

In the absence of more precise evaluative techniques, promotions have been based on spurious data and hedged about with compromise. Age, or length of service, has been allowed to become the deciding factor in a choice between two men. Strictly imposed requirements, relating to education, job background, specialty, or age, are rationalized as "objective" whether they are realistic or not; college degrees or preliminary work experience are often required when unnecessary or irrelevant. Frequently, as a safeguard, even the most capable employees are upgraded only step by step, each promotion bringing only a slight increase in responsibility and not "too large" a raise. It's been an expensive game. The company loses the value of the unrealized contribution of the able young man who is held back and stands a chance of losing him altogether in the end.

The situation promises only to grow worse. As organizations grow in size, top management will grow even further away from managers at the lower levels, losing daily contact with them. They will need to rely more and more on the immediate supervisor's judgment in regard to promotions, even though these lower level managers are the very men whose judgment they already tend to hold suspect.

Without professional help, mistakes in assessing personnel will continue to proliferate. Men who shouldn't be promoted will be, and will then be left to flounder at their own "level of incompetence," blocking the way for others. As in the past, the mediocre may be pushed ahead, the talented carelessly overlooked. Either way, it's painful—a waste of dollars and of human resources.

Recently, however, new scientific techniques have been developed that may bring an end to the mismatching of men and jobs. Many large firms—AT&T, Standard Oil of New Jersey, J. C. Penney, and Sears Roebuck among them—have discovered ways to bring more objectivity and accuracy to the business of appraisal.

The new assessment techniques make use of simulated situations, often played out in special centers, that recreate managerial problems with astonishing realism and attention to detail.

The new methods have proved effective. Twenty thousand candidates have gone through AT&T's assessment centers, and the corporation finds that as many as 50 percent of those selected for promotion under the new evaluation method earn the rating of "above average" in their new jobs, a much higher proportion than among those chosen by the old procedures. Humble discovered it had been spotting only a fourth of the new employees who were potential top executives.

Since the new techniques have been adopted, men have been put on faster tracks to leadership positions, and many have been switched to more suitable careers. None of the companies relies exclusively on the new techniques. But these methods have added precision to the process of evaluation and have increased the likelihood of getting the right man for the job. More and more large companies, and particularly expanding ones, with new jobs to fill, are turning to them.

The successful programs have one thing in common. They are all tailor-made, one to a company. The qualities sought or measured are the ones needed in a particular job at a real company, not those of an ideal executive or manager. What's good for Sears may not be good for General Motors. Creating such specialized evaluative instruments involves disciplined work, of course, and this may be where the new techniques differ most from the old, which relied in the end on playing it by ear. But it is also where their greatest promise lies.

A. J. M.

How a Scientific
Assessment Center Works

J. C. Penney Company

Deciding whom to promote to management from the rank and file is a classic difficulty. Companies have learned from bitter experience that the best salesman or the finest mechanic does not necessarily make the best supervisor.

In an "assessment center," however, under controlled conditions, promising young men can be observed in action and evaluated objectively, both for specific job capabilities and for more general ability as managers. From an assessment report, superiors can get an excellent "gut" feel for whether a man will fit into the organization in the future, where he will do best, and how he ought to adapt and develop himself for the challenges he will meet as he moves up the management ladder.

The assessment center technique has shown itself to be a more reliable indicator of future success than any other tool yet devised. It also brings many valuable fringe benefits to the company that uses it. In this chapter we will explain how the technique works, why it is superior to others, and the steps a company should go through in developing a center of its own.

The use of assessment centers at the J. C. Penney Company began in the fall of 1968 when William Beckett came to the management development staff with a problem. Beckett headed Penney's Product Service Division, which was in the process of a huge expansion. The division's size was scheduled to double, and then redouble, over the next three to five years. This expansion was to come largely from establishing free-standing Product Service Centers from which servicemen in panel trucks would go to customers' homes in a metropolitan area. Beckett's problem was how to choose managers for these centers.

"Is there a test you can give my technical men to evaluate their management potential?" he asked.

He was told that no such test had been published. Moreover, materials were not available to develop a test in-house because of a lack of time and the small number of managers then in such jobs at Penney. As an alternative, it was suggested that the Product Service Division might set up an assessment center for that purpose.

At that time the use of centers for identifying management potential was quite new. Not many professionals were familiar with the procedure, and fewer than ten companies had centers in operation. Yet research reports from several of these indicated the method had considerable validity.

The term assessment center does not necessarily refer to a physical facility. It describes an evaluative method that brings together many techniques, including situational exercises, interviews, business games, tests, discussion groups, and a variety of simulations in an effort to elicit patterns of behavior previously identified as important to success in a given management position. A number of trained managers, who are usually not the candidates' own supervisors, observe their performance. They later pool their observations to make recommendations. The assessment center differs from other appraisal techniques or procedures in that a number of candidates are processed at the same time, simulations are used to expose key behaviors, teams of trained management assessors make the evaluations, and the procedures are conducted off the job.

The Product Service Division's assessment center was designed to identify employees with managerial aptitude and to determine the training needed to prepare them for the jobs. Six management assessors met in a nearby motel to observe twelve participants for two and a half days while they went through a variety of exercises designed to bring out behavior previously defined as important to success. Participants were service technicians or field representatives who had some management responsibilities and were thought by their supervisors to be ready for advancement to a managerial position. Assessors were specially trained product service executives two or more levels above the participants. The exercises included were typical of those included in most centers.

The Manufacturing Company Game. In teams of four, candidates must organize and operate a "company" to manufacture toys. Each team is given starting capital, parts lists, and models of the toys to be assembled. Teams must determine the most effective allocation of their resources, the relative profit margin of each toy (considering purchasing, manufacturing, and selling costs), and how best to organize to accomplish the task. The team buys parts, assembles toys, and sells them. The goal is to maximize profits.

Prices of the raw materials and finished products change for each of the three 20-minute periods comprising the game. This forces the members of the team to replan and allows the observers to make repeated observations of their planning, organizing, and controlling skills, their behavior in a stressful situation, their leadership qualities, and their adaptability to change.

The Background Interview. The personal and business background of each participant is explored in a one-and-a-half-hour interview with an assessor. Indications of motivation, work standards, initiative, interest in self-development, and goal-orientation and planning are sought. The background interview also affords assessors data which may help explain the candidates' performance in other exercises.

The Irate Customer. Participants are told to expect a phone call in their rooms and they are to answer the call as a product service manager. When the call comes, it is from a very irate customer (an assessor reading a carefully prepared script) who seeks immediate satisfaction of a number of complaints. Assessors evaluate the participant's ability to handle a stressful and unexpected situation. Is he polite and sympathetic while directing the conversation toward a resolution of the problem? Is he able to calm the customer and at the same time obtain the information needed to make a correct decision?

The In-Basket. This exercise confronts the candidate with a pile of letters, notes, requests, and problems, such as might be found in a service center manager's in-basket. The participant is given background information on the service center, the employees, and the former manager's activities. He is instructed to function as the manager. Within the allotted time of three and a quarter hours, the participant must decide which items have priority over others, organize the material, plan, delegate, make decisions, and seek information. In other words, he must do the many things that effective managers do every day. Later he will be interviewed by an assessor who has studied the in-basket. This provides the participant with an opportunity to explain his actions and decisions and allows the assessor to clear up any questions about the meaning of certain actions.

A Simulated Appraisal. The candidate conducts an appraisal of performance with a "service center technician," who is role-played by a college student specially trained for the task. The participant must first complete an appraisal form and prepare for the meeting, then conduct the interview.

He is given directions for planning and holding an appraisal interview, an appraisal form, and the personnel file of the person with whom he must hold the conversation. He has an entire evening to read the instructions, fill out the form, and prepare a plan for conducting the meeting in the right way. The participant is rated on both his preparation of the appraisal form and his handling of the interview.

The Job Applicant. Acting as a service center manager, the participant interviews an applicant for the job of service center technician. The participant is given half an hour to study the applicant's filled-in application form and résumé before the interview. A student acts as the appli-cant. After the interview, the participant presents an oral evaluation of the applicant and makes a recommendation on hiring. The assessor discusses the interview with the participant, typically questioning why he omitted certain questions and why he discussed the material he did.

Trouble in El Paso. Participants are given background information about the operations of a mythical service center in El Paso and are instructed to function as members of a consulting team sent in by the zone service manager. Their task is to advise the zone manager in writing how to deal with the center's staffing problems. Each participant is evaluated on his effectiveness in the group discussion and his ability to understand the problems and determine appropriate action.

The Small-Business Financial Analysis. As an evening assignment, each candidate is given descriptive and financial information about a small business. He is instructed to act as a management consultant; to analyze the material provided and prepare answers to questions posed by the business's owner about ways of increasing profit, adding personnel, and whether to open a new branch. The "consultant's" task is to prepare a five-minute oral presentation of his recommendations. He delivers them the next day to the "owners," who are actually the assessors. After the oral reports, the participants in groups discuss the finances of the busi-ness for one hour. They are seeking the best single solution to the owner's questions. This exercise includes several areas of evaluation: What is the candidate's ability to cope with financial data? How well does he plan and organize? The observers rate the candidate's decisiveness, im-pact, and facility at making an oral presentation. In addition, his role as a member of a group discussion is assessed.

"Cases." Brief histories of four disciplinary cases are presented to participants. They must resolve each case and make a recommendation in writing within one hour. Participants are evaluated both in terms of their group participation and by the quality of their arguments.

All those taking part are exposed to all exercises, but not necessarily in the same order. Because there are only half as many assessors as participants, it is necessary to juggle the schedule around so that all candidates are busy at all times. For instance, while half are receiving their background interview, the other half are taking tests which do not involve assessors.

The six management assessors are systematically assigned so that can-didates are observed by different assessors in the various exercises. Every assessor sees every participant at least once. After candidates have re-turned to their jobs, assessors spend up to two and a half more days sharing their observations, reaching decisions, and making recommenda-tions. Up to two hours are spent discussing each man.

These discussions open with a report from the assessor who conducted the background interview. He summarizes the candidate's past history, highlighting the experiences that seem to relate to the aspects of behavioral dimensions to be rated. The background report establishes the base against which subsequent observations are interpreted. For example, poor performance in the applicant interview simulation would be interpreted one way with a candidate who had never before conducted such an interview, but quite differently with a man experienced at it from past jobs. Once the candidate's background is explained, the assessors report to one another on his performance in each of the exercises in which he participated.

After each category of exercise, the assessors stop to consider what they have learned. They look at how the behavior fits together. Is there a pattern, or a lack of one? No judgment is made as to the meaning of the observed behavior until the final report is heard. Assessors are told to observe, record, and report only actual behavior, such as "wrote out detailed instructions for each subordinate in the in-basket exercise." They are told not to make interpretations ("Jones was a 'Theory X' manager") or judgments ("he delegated improperly").

Only after all the evidence is in do the assessors discuss its implications. They compare and contrast observations obtained in different exercises and make projections as to how the participant would perform if faced with similar problems in a real-life situation.

Each of the traits previously established as important to success is discussed individually and a judgment made. The discussion closes with rating the participant's overall potential. The following scale is used:

1. Should remain in present job.
2. Limited potential for product service manager position but could do well in lower level managerial position.
3. Average potential.
4. Above-average potential.
5. Has potential to be a regional or national manager of Product Service Division.

A rating of 1 does not mean a candidate is fired. It simply means he is seen as having more strengths in technical areas than in managerial ones. His poor performance in the assessment center has no necessary effect on his current job situation, where it must be assumed that his performance is good or he would not have been nominated to come to the center. A high rating, on the other hand, can have considerable positive effect, particularly if the individual's talents were previously unappreciated. It is not uncommon for major job promotion or development assignment to follow a favorable report from the assessment center.

The assessors' responsibility does not end when a candidate is rated. Development plans are discussed next. Because assessors are completely familiar with alternative development routes, company mores, various local training environments, and projected expansions and reorganizations, the discussion is often quite specific. If a participant is considered to have above-average potential as a manager, and the assessors feel he will be ready for it in five years, they will outline a complete development plan for him to ensure his having the breadth of background needed for success. Self-development priorities for the participant are also considered. Finally, the assessors decide how the center's findings can best be communicated to the candidate and his supervisor.

An assessor is assigned the task of taking notes during the discussion and preparing the report. Guidelines and examples are provided to help in the preparation. The reports are written the following week, when the assessors are back at their regular jobs. Often the reports are circulated to the other assessors for their comments before being sent out. A typical report is three or four pages long.

Written reports on each candidate go to the national manager of the Product Service Division and to the appropriate regional manager. They use it as a supplement to other information about the employee in making decisions about his career.

The participant himself gets an oral report. This is provided with great care by specially trained regional representatives who have had experience as assessors. The focus of the conference is on developmental challenges and on setting goals to meet them—not on personal factors difficult to change. Depending on the nature of the report, the participant's immediate supervisor may or may not be invited to the conference. If the candidate is considered promotable and the supervisor is needed to help him develop, both are usually invited. But if areas of poor performance not amenable to development predominate, reports are given separately. The supervisor always gets a general report, but there is no disposition to provide information that will only serve to bias his observation of the employee in the future. After all, that same supervisor nominated the participant in the first place as an outstanding performer with high potential.

The feedback to supervisors concerning their ability to spot management potential is an additional benefit of the program. Most become better at the task as they get reports on candidates they have nominated. But not all. One supervisor was extremely distressed about his low batting average. At one point he refused to send anyone else, claiming that the procedures could not be accurate. He was then invited to be an assessor, and after one week at a center he needed no further proof. He became enthusiastic about the assessment procedure, and his ability to spot potential among his own subordinates increased markedly.

In the eyes of management, the Product Service Division assessment center was an immediate success. Executives were convinced that they were getting a new level of information that was invaluable in making selection and placement decisions. The evident logic of the center's method and exercises was its basic weapon for winning management support. But anecdotal evidence of the center's value quickly accumulated too. In the first center, a person previously thought to have great potential received an extremely low evaluation. Management was shocked, but since the man was already in line for a managerial position, he was promoted despite the adverse report. Fortunately for the method—but unfortunately for the company—the exact weaknesses predicted by the center showed up on the job within three months and the man had to be relieved. Almost simultaneously, two participants discovered to be high in potential received early promotions and performed outstandingly.

The initial assessment center program did not last long enough to collect statistically significant data establishing its validity. Unfortunately, the assessment reports on early participants made it apparent that very little management potential existed among the service center technicians. Very few candidates with outstanding potential were identified—far too few to meet projected needs. As a result of these findings, the division decided to adopt a completely new approach to filling the product service manager positions. Rather than trying to develop managerial potential in technicians, it would select managers from other parts of the company and give them the technical training needed. Without the assessment center this fundamentally important decision might never have been made.

Because of this contribution, Penney management decided to apply the assessment center technique to two additional problem areas. The company now uses centers to help identify promising candidates for entry-level management positions in its New York headquarters and to find replacements for middle-level store managers who are under consideration for further advancement.

Though statistical validation of Penney's assessment centers must wait until a sufficient number of the people evaluated have progressed further, considerable evidence of the validity of assessment centers per se has accumulated elsewhere. Research in four large companies (American Telephone and Telegraph, IBM, Sears, Roebuck and Co., and Standard Oil of Ohio) has established validity in two ways.

The first method has been to compare the job performance of supervisors promoted partly on the basis of assessment center recommendations with that of people promoted without such aid; the groups compared commonly consist of 100 supervisors promoted immediately prior to the installation of an assessment center and an equal number promoted after evaluation at the center. The other principal validation technique has been to compare the performance of those who received high ratings at the assessment center with those who received low ratings.

Both methods have established that assessment centers are often two to three times as accurate as normal appraisal and selection methods. Of the fifty-three reported studies, all but one have found assessment center ratings a significant aid in promotion decisions.

One of the strongest proofs of the effectiveness of assessment centers comes from the American Telephone and Telegraph Management Progress Study reported in this book. This study has established assessment centers as highly accurate predictors of subsequent performance.

Assessment centers seem to be most dependable in situations where normal appraisals work least well. Although it is difficult as yet to generalize from the research, assessment centers seem to be most helpful when:

□ There is considerable *difference* between the job requirements of the candidate's current or past positions and the requirements of the job for which he is being considered. In these circumstances, the man's past performance offers relatively few clues as to how well he will do in the future.

□ The job requirements can be accurately specified. The more specifically the behavior required by the job is delineated, the easier it is to develop exercises to bring out this behavior.

□ There are considerable differences in the types of jobs the various candidates currently hold. When men are in markedly different jobs, it is very difficult to compare their potentials for yet another kind of position. By putting candidates through comparative exercises, the assessment center makes possible such comparisons.

□ There is no common standard of acceptable performance and potential by supervisors. The rating forms are being filled out by different people and may more accurately reflect differences in the raters than in the candidates.

The accuracy of assessment center ratings depends on both the exercises employed and the skill of the assessors. The exercises provide an opportunity to evaluate candidates under constant conditions, so comparative judgments can more readily be made. Each candidate has an equal opportunity to display his talent. Moreover, the exercises are designed to bring out the skills and ability needed for the prospective position.

With regard to the skill of assessors, it may seem strange that the very managers who may have been criticized for their lack of skill in evaluating on-the-job performance can make successful assessors. One explanation is that they are *trained* as assessors before serving. But the assessor has several other advantages. Because he does not know the candidate, he may be less emotionally involved. He is protected from the many interruptions of a normal working environment and can give his full attention to observing behavior. Finally, the specific behavior that he is to evaluate has been made known to him.

Organizations that have used assessment centers have found that the centers can provide benefits quite apart from their main purpose of identifying managerial potential. The most obvious of these fringe benefits is participant training. Even when training is not a stated objective of an assessment center, it does take place. Completing an in-basket and participating in group discussions and management games are by nature training exercises, even if there is no immediate feedback of results. Indeed, these exercises served as training methods long before they were used in assessment centers.

In most centers considerable performance feedback is provided during the assessment program. A good example is the assessment center program of the Autolite Division of the Ford Motor Company. Participants watch videotapes of their performance in group activities and take part in professionally led critiques on how they did. After the in-basket exercise, they meet in small groups to share and mutually evaluate their decisions and actions.

Participation at an assessment center usually has a positive effect on the participants' attitudes toward their organization. The center offers them a chance to demonstrate their ability under fair, realistic conditions. They see their participation as a way to "show what they have" to top managers of the company.

Participants also obtain a more realistic idea of the nature of the positions for which they are being considered. In a few cases, candidates have withdrawn voluntarily after going through an in-basket exercise because they had not realized the amount of paperwork involved in a manager's job.

Because the exercises are carefully designed, they may bring about subtle changes in candidates' attitudes. For example, the "El Paso" staffing exercise previously described leads to the conclusion that the only acceptable solution is for management to increase overtime. By participation in this exercise, the candidates, who are technicians, should better appreciate management's reasons if they are ever asked to work overtime when they return to their current jobs. Similarly, a popular leaderless group-discussion situation has participants play the role of supervisors recommending subordinates for promotion. This exercise shows participants the difficulty of making promotional decisions; it also forces them to think about the numerous characteristics that must be considered.

Another valuable contribution of a center of this sort is assessor training. The instruction of an assessor prior to his assignment is quite similar to some "involvement-oriented" management training programs. Assessors take part in management games, in-basket exercises, and group discussions. These are followed by discussions of their performance. Even more important is actual experience as an assessor. In a normal work situation, managers rarely have the opportunity to spend uninterrupted hours observing behavior and then comparing observations with others. One assessor, who was also the chief operating officer of his company, remarked rather exuberantly that if he had had the interviewing skills twenty years ago that he got from being an assessor, the company would be earning twice its present return on investment.

No company operates assessment centers solely to identify training needs. But many companies do use the center's reports partly for that purpose. It is possible to summarize the individual training and development needs of many candidates and then to determine common needs. This information can be used to develop training and development strategies and priorities.

All these fringe benefits of assessment centers indicate what may be a crucial advantage of the assessment center method over other means for recognizing managerial talent. When a company uses psychological tests, or sends candidates to a psychologist for evaluation, it is in reality weakening itself, because its executives become less dependent on themselves and more dependent on the skills of outsiders. But applying the assessment center method strengthens a company because executives *develop their own skills and hence become more independent.*

When corporate executives hear about assessment centers for the first time, questions naturally arise. Here are some of the most common, with the answers suggested by current experience:

What happens to the employees who are not chosen to attend? No statistical studies have been conducted, but the effect of not being chosen seems to depend on how the center has been set up. There are still enough examples of men promoted without going through a center to give other such men hope. Nevertheless, in certain companies assessment centers have achieved a reputation as steps in the upward progress of young executives. Just as an ambitious man may feel he must go through T-group or grid training, he feels he must be assessed. In these situations, considerable anxiety can be developed among those not chosen. As passage through an assessment center has become more of a prerequisite to management responsibility, some companies have taken a closer look at their selection procedures. More often now, self-nomination is being used. Organizations announce the schedule of assessment centers and allow anyone interested to attend on a "first come, first served" basis. At the very least, this protects companies against missing likely candidates who are being held back for one reason or another by their immediate supervisors.

What happens to people who perform badly at a center? Most of them are well aware of their performance, but whether they take what might seem the logical course and start looking around for other jobs is unclear. Research at three companies says no, while research at one says definitely yes.

Most organizations go to great lengths to stress that the assessment center is only one portion of the assessment process—a supplement to regular appraisal and other methods. They stress that the participant has an opportunity on the job to disprove any negative insights gained from assessment.

An increase in turnover among participants who are evaluated as having little potential may be interpreted in different ways. To a limited degree, this turnover may be seen by some companies as beneficial in clearing out deadwood. But where candidates represent a sizable investment in terms of company experience or technical know-how, an increase in turnover may be a disaster. Penney's experience has been that the key lies in the feedback of assessment center results. If this is accomplished in a professional manner, pointing out alternative development routes and possible developmental programs, negative effects can be held to a minimum.

Do centers create "crown princes" and "golden boys"? They can, if the organization allows special treatment for successful participants. It is natural for the outstanding participants in centers to win promotions. This is simply putting the company's money where it will return the greatest dividends. But a high rating should not result in special treatment while the candidate remains in his present job. The morale of other members of his work group is sure to sag if an individual is seen as being allowed to do less work because he is the "number one boy."

Is the stress involved harmful to some participants? Some men will have a difficult time holding up in any stress-producing situation. The ability to handle stress is a characteristic to be evaluated in most assessment centers. But center administrators are very careful to provide enough opportunities for tension release and to keep the stress low enough to minimize ill effects.

Most companies have had no trouble at all. One had only two slightly emotional experiences out of 400 participants: two men broke into tears during interviews. Another company had only two problems out of 450: one man cried, and one got drunk.

How much do centers cost? Centers operated by Penney range from the cost of a few lunches to $2,000 per twelve participants, exclusive of salary but including travel, accommodations, materials, and the like. The key to keeping expenses down is the use of commercially available exercises and facilities on company property. Assessment center costs should be appropriate to the importance of the information obtained. A center for selecting middle managers will tend to last longer and be more expensive than a center for selecting management trainees.

Can smaller companies use centers? Emphatically yes. Companies with as few as 1,000 employees have successfully applied the method. It need cost a small company no more nor less to assess twelve people han it costs J. C. Penny. Economies do come from amortizing the levelopment costs of the center. A company that plans to assess several undred people a year can afford to spend a great deal of money on levelopment, because its per-head cost will be relatively small, while he same expense for a small company would be too high. The solution or most smaller companies is to use commercially available exercises nd other methods to keep down costs. Special training of assessors nay be needed to compensate for the fact that they may already know ome of the participants. Another problem for smaller companies has een getting the number of assessors needed. Who will run the plant? aturday and Sunday centers have been tried by some companies as a way around this problem.

How does operating an assessment center compare with using tradiional psychological evaluation? Sending an applicant or employee for esting and interviewing by a psychologist may be much cheaper, and s certainly much more convenient, than operating an assessment center. But the center has an advantage in that exercises elicit *actual* behavior, vhich is far more meaningful than descriptions of what a participant as done or might do. Many candidates know in their minds the right hing to do, yet in an actual situation they regularly do the opposite.

Will assessment centers increase the trend toward conformity in busiess? Some people do worry that assessment center procedures are creatng managers in the mirror-image of the assessors instead of producing he creative, imaginative managers needed for the future. A conclusive nswer to this charge will come only through long-term studies, using riteria that reflect actual organizational effectiveness. However, a study t IBM by W. E. Dodd and A. I. Kraut, reported under the title "Will nanagement assessment centers insure selection of the same old types?" heds some light on this question. It was found that participants in ssessment centers were more ambitious and less conformist (as meaured by tests given three years previously for other purposes) than hose not selected to attend.

Are assessment centers fair to women and minority groups? In studies t a number of companies no significant differences correlated to race ave been found in performance on individual exercises.

Practically no research has been done on whether women perform lifferently from men on center exercises, though many women have articipated in centers.

As companies gain experience with assessment centers, new applications uggest themselves. One unconventional use of centers has been as an id to selecting salesmen. Like so many assessment center innovations, his was pioneered by researchers from AT&T. They assessed the sales ptitude of seventy-eight candidates, but withheld the reports from mangement. The men were trained and placed in jobs. Six months later, the performance of each of the seventy-eight was rated by trained ob servers who accompanied them on their calls. A significant correlatio was obtained between assessment center evaluations and performanc Table 1 shows the extent of this relationship.

Table 1. Validity study of assessment of sales representatives.

	NUMBER OF CANDIDATES		
FINDINGS	ORIGINAL ASSESSMENT	FIELD REVIEW	VALIDITY OF ASSESSMENT, %
More than acceptable	9	9	100
Acceptable	32	19	60
Less than acceptable	16	7	44
Unacceptable	21	2	10

Several other companies have subsequently established assessmen centers for selecting salesmen or diagnosing sales problems that coul be eased by improved personnel management. Companies hiring sales men from the outside must carefully coordinate visits by applicant in order to get together the four or six people needed to hold a cente Companies hiring and promoting from within usually have an easier tas in getting the minimum number of candidates together.

Another new development is the multi-company assessment cente For many companies, the assessment center method would not be ap propriate even if the costs were manageable. Particularly at higher jo levels, they may not have enough candidates to warrant setting up center. These companies can establish multi-company centers, to whic a number of companies send one or two candidates to be appraise Three of these centers have been conducted on an experimental basi apparently with good results. One center used psychologists and othe professionals as assessors; another asked companies that sent candidate to contribute a management representative to the panel. The latter seem preferable because it ensures that someone in the company will hav the training and orientation to the proceedings needed to interpret th assessment center report.

The development of any successful center, whether by a single compan or several, includes a number of essential steps. The main ones ar discussed here.

Establishment of Objectives

In the center developed by Penney's Product Service Division, the origi nal objectives were to identify technically trained employees who pos sessed aptitude for managerial positions and to determine what further training would be needed to prepare them for the new job. Stated goals in other Penney assessment centers include deepening the participant's insight on behalf of his future development and placement and determining his role in organizational development.

Determining What Aspects of Behavior to Assess

A center's success depends upon the proper choice of tests and exercises. These stimulate and bring to the surface the behavior to be observed. Thus, there must be a definition of the specific behavior one wants to observe. This can be formulated by having group discussions with key managers familiar with the position or positions for which the candidates are to be rated. Managers should be invited to describe the behavior of successful and unsuccessful people in these jobs, and should be asked such questions as "How do you evaluate people for this position?" and "What are the tasks to be performed?"

After a list has been compiled and agreed upon, another meeting should be held to determine which of these characteristics or dimensions can be assessed adequately in a person's current job. After eliminating these from the list, the dimensions that remain become the focus of the assessment center program. Questionnaires can be developed to broaden the involvement of management in making these crucial decisions. Figure 1 presents a list of common dimensions used in assessment.

Selection of Participants

Although one of the reasons for using the assessment center technique is to get around some of the prejudices inherent in supervisory judgment, the supervisor's opinion remains the sole criterion for nomination to most assessment centers. Ways around this possible bias include self-nomination by participants, or the automatic assessment of participants as they reach certain levels in the company. When assessment is used to define development needs, it is often possible to assess an entire organizational level, thereby eliminating all selection problems.

Selection of Assessors

Typically, assessors are line managers two or three levels above the persons being observed. They will be the ones responsible for recommending promotion and must therefore know the requirements of the open positions. A major point of controversy among operators of assessment centers is the desirability of using professional psychologists. Those in favor emphasize the belief that psychologists can recognize behavior not obvious to the untrained eye. While the argument is plausible, it has yet to be proved in an assessment center situation in which professionals are compared with trained observers from line management. Three studies have found no significant differences.

Figure 1. Common dimensions of managerial success.

IMPACT Ability to create a good first impression, to command attention and respect, to show an air of confidence, and to achieve personal recognition.

ENERGY Ability to be self-starting and to achieve a high activity level.

ORAL COMMUNICATION SKILL Effectiveness of expression in individual or group situations.

ORAL PRESENTATION SKILL Ability to make a persuasive, clear presentation of ideas or facts.

WRITTEN COMMUNICATION SKILL Ability to express ideas clearly in writing in good grammatical form.

CREATIVITY Ability to come up with imaginative solutions in business situations.

RANGE OF INTERESTS Having breadth and diversity of interests, concern with personal and organizational environment, and a desire to actively participate in events.

STRESS TOLERANCE Stability of performance under pressure and opposition.

MOTIVATION The importance of work in personal satisfaction and the desire to achieve at work.

WORK STANDARDS The desire to do a good job for its own sake.

LEADERSHIP Effectiveness in bringing a group to accomplish a task, and in getting ideas accepted.

SALESMANSHIP Ability to organize and present material in a convincing manner.

SENSITIVITY Skill in perceiving and reacting sensitively to the needs of others.

LISTENING SKILL Ability to pick out important information in oral communications.

RISK-TAKING Extent to which calculated risks are taken based on sound judgment.

INITIATIVE Active efforts to influence events rather than passive acceptance.

INDEPENDENCE Action based on own convictions rather than a desire to please others.

PLANNING AND ORGANIZING Effectiveness in planning and organizing own activities and those of a group.

MANAGEMENT CONTROL Appreciation of needs for controls and maintenance of control over processes.

USE OF DELEGATION Ability to effectively use subordinates and to understand where a decision can best be made.

PROBLEM ANALYSIS Effectiveness in seeking out pertinent data and determining the source of the problem.

JUDGMENT Ability to reach logical conclusions based on the evidence at hand.

DECISIVENESS Readiness to make decisions or to render judgment.

The superiority of psychologists over *untrained* line assessors is, however, well established. It is for this reason that psychologists are often used in pilot programs, where the training of assessors would be impractical. Psychologists are also used occasionally for assessing higher levels of company management. At these levels, it is much harder to get and train managers who do not work with the candidates. The objective, independent psychologist is regarded as the fairest evaluator.

With a few major exceptions, companies tend to establish a pool of trained assessors. Each person so trained is drawn from the pool to serve once or twice a year. Some companies ask assessors to serve only once. AT&T, which assigns assessors for six-month terms, and center administrators for one year, does not conform to the more general practices.

Selection of Exercises
Because the dimensions listed in Figure 1 are commonly recognized by most companies, exercises that bring them out are used at many centers. Exercises found to be predictive of these behavior dimensions are shown in Figure 2. Thus, almost all centers have an in-basket, a leaderless group discussion, and a management game. Although the exercises may be similar, the specific content may be quite different depending on the educational background and job-rank of the participant.

The Use of Tests
Standard intelligence, reading, arithmetic, and personality tests have all been found to increase the accuracy of certain assessments, but should be given only under the direction of a psychologist.

Great care must be taken in communicating the results to assessors lest the results bias their first-hand observations of candidates. It is good practice to withhold test findings until the very end of the assessment discussion of the candidate. Even then, test results are best communicated in broad categorizations such as "superior," "average," or "below average." Numbers or percentiles can be too easily misinterpreted.

Development of Forms and Procedures
The clearest evidence of the professionalism of an assessment center is probably visible in the sophistication of the forms provided assessors to record their observations. Of course, the purpose of the form is to distill the assessor's report on a particular exercise. Some forms encourage a detailed description of all pertinent behavior; others provide only for a series of 1 to 5 ratings on key variables. Well-developed forms will guide the assessor in making his observations and aid in structuring his report. Commercially available exercises include pretested assessor forms and other necessary material.

Assessor Training
Among the companies operating assessment centers, there is a noticeable variation in the emphasis placed on training the assessors. Some companies give new assessors as little as one hour of training, really just

Figure 2. Guide for selection of exercises.

Check marks indicate those categories of exercises which usually bring out a particular dimension. A circle around the check mark show an exercise that is particularly good at bringing out the dimension.

Common Dimensions of Managerial Success / Categories of Exercises	1 Interview	2 Management Games	3 In-Basket and Interview	4 Leaderless Group Discussion (Assigned)	5 Leaderless Group Discussion (Nonassigned)	6 Fact Finding and Decision Making	7 Analysis Presentation (If group discussion see also column 5)	8 Interview Simulation
1. Impact	(√)	√	(√)	√	√	√	√	√
2. Energy	(√)	√	(√)	√	√	√	√	√
3. Oral communication skill	√	√	√	√	√	√	√	√
4. Oral presentation skill				(√)		√	(√)	
5. Written communication skill	√		(√)				(√)	
6. Creativity	√		√	√				
7. Range of interest	(√)							
8. Stress tolerance		√		√	√	(√)	√	
9. Motivation	(√)							
10. Work standards	(√)							
11. Leadership	√	(√)		(√)	(√)			
12. Salesmanship				(√)	√	√	(√)	(√)
13. Sensitivity	√	√	(√)	√	√	√	√	(√)
14. Listening skill		√		√	√	(√)		√
15. Flexibility		√		(√)	√	(√)	√	(√)
16. Tenacity	√	√		√	√	(√)	√	√
17. Risk taking	√	(√)	√		√			
18. Initiative	√	√	√	√	√			
19. Independence	(√)	√		√	√	√		
20. Planning and organizing	√	√	(√)				√	√
21. Management control	√		(√)					
22. Use of delegation	√		(√)					
23. Problem analysis	√	√	√	√	(√)	(√)	√	√
24. Judgment	√	√	(√)	√	√	(√)	(√)	
25. Decisiveness		√	(√)		(√)	(√)		

a bare orientation to the procedure. Others spend three weeks preparing them.

It can be argued that the task of an assessor is essentially no different from the tasks most managers have to face in their jobs. The manager must interview people, observe groups, and evaluate presentations—all tasks similar to those required of an assessor. Why then give the assessor further training?

Well, for one thing, because a man has been doing something long doesn't mean he's been doing it well. Companies report marked improvements in the reliability of ratings after the training of assessors. Nonprofessional assessors need to be shown what to look for in observing group discussions and individual presentations. Otherwise they may focus on surface characteristics.

Time factors, and a desire to rotate as many assessors as possible through the system, most often dictate the amount of assessor training given. Centers that establish a pool of assessors who may be used several times—and companies like AT&T, where assessors serve for an extended period—devote considerable care and energy to instructing them. Assessors who serve only one program are usually less well trained.

In the usual training situation, the apprentice assessor sits through the entire center procedure as a nonvoting observer. Another method, used particularly when a center is first being introduced, is to conduct a three- to five-day assessor training program where the novices practice observing behavior, interviewing, and so on. Having the assessors go through exercises as candidates is not training; it is orientation. Although necessary, it is not enough to prepare an assessor. Practice, feedback, and the opportunity to re-observe are necessary for real learning.

This outline of the steps required to get a center going should leave no doubt that doing so is a complex, even arduous, enterprise. But the effort can be eminently worthwhile. It has become clear, both from day-to-day experience and from formal research, that assessment centers can single out potential managerial talent more fairly and reliably than any other method currently in use.

DOUGLAS W. BRAY / DONALD L. GRANT
RICHARD J. CAMPBELL

Studying Careers
and Assessing Ability

American Telephone and
Telegraph Company

Nowhere have scientific efforts to find out what distinguishes good managers from bad—and to assess candidates accordingly—been pursued longer or more energetically than in the Bell System. The reasons are quite apparent. The system is immense and complex. It has more than one million employees. Some ninety million telephones are used by our subscribers in all states. In recent years, *approximately 7,500 new managers have been appointed annually*. Many are beginning a management career with us that will span thirty years. Since these managers will be responsible for providing service, frequently in hard-pressed urban areas, the system has a great stake in them.

In the post-World War II years, especially during the 1950s, the Bell System made large investments in management development programs. These ranged from three- or four-day, in-house courses taken by thousands of people, through special summer-college experiences for smaller numbers, to the well-known University of Pennsylvania course in which perhaps twenty men at a time spent an entire academic year in liberal arts study. This program in particular made frequent use of behavioral scientists as instructors.

Robert K. Greenleaf of American Telephone and Telegraph (the parent of the Bell System) directed much of this activity. He was aware that there had been little research on human development in the middle years of life. This being so, there appeared a gross imbalance in devoting so much effort to training junior managers while allocating so little to gathering the fundamental knowledge still needed.

He proposed a "lives in progress" study of men in management, and got top-echelon support for it. Douglas W. Bray was employed to design and carry out the research.

The aim of this "Management Progress Study," which started in 1956,

154

was very general: to learn more about the characteristics and growth of young men as they become, or try to become, middle and upper managers of a large business enterprise. The original focus of the research was on development—*possible changes in motivation as managers grow older*, for instance—rather than on selection. No promises were made as to specific results deriving from the study; the company was warned that at least five years might elapse before any findings could be expected.

The basic plan was to follow men closely through their careers from as early a point as possible. The hope was that it would eventually be feasible to draw definite conclusions about changes in their personal characteristics, managerial ability, achievement motivation, life satisfaction, and so on. Once the change measures were obtained, analyses would be made of the correlation between these changes and the facts of each man's career: What was the sequence of his job assignments, the nature of the supervision he had received, his rate of advancement? The objective was to establish links between his tasks, his job environment, and his development.

For example, it might be found that those with certain types of assignments improved in leadership over time, whereas those with different types showed no leadership improvement. If findings of this nature were obtained, and could then be applied to the thousands of managers in the System, the payoff would be enormous.

The study design called for measurements at various stages of the subjects' lives. The subjects would have to undergo many tests and interviews, and even special medical examinations. The most efficient plan, it became clear, was to group all the measurement activities except the medical examination in an "assessment center."

The center was set up. Each subject, as one of a group of twelve, went through the center at the time of his inclusion in the study. The assessment lasted for three and a half days. It included interviews, objective and projective tests, a paper-work administrative problem, a leaderless group discussion, and a short business game. The staff carrying on this work was comprised of six Ph.D. psychologists, two highly rated Bell System middle managers, and one or two subdoctoral graduate students in psychology. They administered and reported on each assessment technique and, after all data were pooled at a staff meeting, each subject was rated on twenty-five variables and a narrative summary of his performance was prepared.

Annual follow-up procedures began one year after this. One of these was an intensive interview covering the year just passed. Although primary emphasis was given to job experiences and attitudes, all areas of the subjects' lives were explored.

The second part of the annual follow-up was the collection of information about the subject and his work environment from the associated telephone company in which he was employed. This information was gathered from company records and from extensive interviews with personnel supervisors and managers who had directly supervised the subject.

While these annual interviews were invaluable in keeping track of each man's career, they were not enough to detect changes in many of the variables originally measured. So, eight years after the first appraisal, each of the original subjects who was still available was put through another assessment center patterned closely after the first. Some tests were, in fact, administered in identical form.

Of the 422 subjects drawn from six Bell System telephone companies, about two-thirds were college graduates. Because the center's professional staff was available only during the summer months, and only twelve men could be seen each week, it took from 1956 to 1960 to appraise them all.

The noncollege men represented a sampling of those who had reached supervisory posts early; none was more than thirty-two years old, and each apparently had a good chance of competing with college recruits for middle-management jobs.

The first test group was made up of 146 new college recruits for two telephone companies. These men had been hired under a rule that both the recruiter and the person doing the final hiring had to be convinced that the applicant should have the potential to reach at least the bottom step of middle-management—the so-called "district level." This is the third in a seven-step management ladder from first-level supervisor to president. It entails considerable responsibility. For example, one district plant manager, located in a major city, is responsible for servicing 152,000 residence and business telephones. (This involves the installation and repair of complex equipment as well as individual telephone sets on the customers' premises.)

This district manager's organization also services nine central offices and tool-switching machines. There are 390 people in his organization, including 46 lower-level supervisors. The recruiter, in reaching his decision, was influenced not only by his own judgment of the applicant, but also by certain criteria known to correlate with later performance, such as rank in graduating class and extracurricular achievement.

Selection research was not the primary goal of the Management Progress Study; nevertheless the assessment staff rated the middle-management potential of each recruit as the final step in evaluating his personal characteristics. The assessment staff's judgment was that less than half these 146 recruits had such potential.

At this point, the researchers had to face a choice. They could have decided to be narrowly scientific and keep their opinions to themselves. On the other hand, speaking out—the course they chose—entailed the risk that management might retort that most of them had no business experience and that they had better wait to see how their predictions came out before sounding any alarms.

As it happened, management responded positively. Key operating managers studied the reports based on the test scores of the 146 new employees and on their performance in small group and administrative situations. The reports suggested that there was clearly room for improvement in the process of employing college graduate applicants. As a result, greater stress was placed on making campus recruit the full-time job of better-trained company representatives. Attention to such indices as rank in graduating class was reemphasized. Pre-employment mental ability testing was instituted. Since then, college employment practices have been under continual review.

The early follow-up interviews with the same 146 college recruits brought about an important change in the program for new management trainees. In the old program, which was run on lines common to many large businesses, the new man spent months—sometimes as much as two years—merely touring the organization and learning, or at least observing, many basic jobs. After that, he arrived at a low-level, and often not too demanding, supervisory assignment. The follow-up interviews revealed that no more than half the recruits were satisfied with their early job experiences and that their attitudes had changed drastically. The rosy expectations they held at the time they were hired had faded away.

During the early 1960s, the Bell System was losing approximately one-third of its college recruits during their first five years of employment. The estimated cost of these early separations for the telephone companies was $5 million annually, a figure that included salary, recruiting, and training costs.

Data collected from company sources revealed that the training program also had flaws from management's point of view. Because the recruits had not been given difficult assignments, the company still had little idea of their potential. Appraisals of them during the first two years were generally unreliable and overly favorable.

These findings led to vigorous remedial action. A new program required each new college recruit to report directly to a selected middle manager, who was responsible for developing assignments designed to challenge the graduate's ability. The manager was expected to create a climate encouraging growth so that, by the end of one year, it could be determined whether his charge had the ability to advance to middle management in a short period of time. Each manager was given a week's special training to prepare him for this additional task.

Though put into operation long before any truly conclusive scientific evidence was available, these new programs for recruiting and training college graduates were quickly seen as highly valuable early byproducts of the Management Progress Study. Indeed, their success was such that the study tool that had first indicated the need for them—the assessment center—soon threatened to divert attention completely from the rest of the study.

The assessment center had been put together as an aid to research. It was to study a group of men at various points in their careers. There was no intention, at first, of using assessment center methods as a selection procedure for promotions. However, key managers in the telephone companies were concerned about picking the right people for the job of foreman (the first-line management job) from among those in such lower-rung positions as telephone installer and switchman. Many department heads were convinced that managers were not making the best selections. Managerial errors in this regard were hardly surprising. It is quite difficult to make accurate judgments of the management ability of rank-and-file employees. A supervisor has little opportunity to observe his men actually performing managerial tasks. How can he possibly determine a craftsman's leadership skills if he has never seen him in a situation calling for a display of them? Promoting the best craftsman is not the best way to select a foreman. Too often it results in the loss of a good craftsman, and the addition of a problem supervisor to the managerial ranks.

One company, Michigan Bell, recognized that the assessment center might be a helpful selection tool. But there were obstacles. The Management Program Study assessment center had been designed for a specific area of research and would have to be altered to accommodate any new functions. No data were available to establish the validity of assessment in selecting people for promotion from nonmanagerial ranks, nor would the long-term study produce such findings for several years. In addition, the research center was staffed by professionals, primarily psychologists, whereas the proposed selection center would be staffed by telephone company managers.

Nonprofessionals were not qualified or trained to use some of the more complex techniques, such as personality tests. Hence, the first step taken was to include a telephone manager on the staff during the third year of the Management Progress Study. He performed well, making it clear that *professional* training was not a necessary prerequisite for functioning as an assessor; the first major hurdle was passed.

In adapting the assessment program at the research center for suitable use at Michigan Bell, all techniques which obviously required professional training, such as personality tests, were eliminated. The list of variables to be rated was reduced to a manageable twenty. The techniques retained were: (1) an individual simulation (the in-basket, in which the subject deals with the paper work of a management job); (2) group simulations (a leaderless group discussion and a short business game); (3) a personal interview, including a personal history form; (4) several paper-and-pencil ability tests, and (5) a Q sort (in which the subject sorts cards containing statements of behavior and attitudes as he believes they apply to himself).

It must be emphasized that the *selection*-oriented assessment centers with which a good part of this chapter will be concerned, such as the one at Michigan Bell, are completely separate from the Management Progress Study. These are service programs in which psychological measurements of employees *are passed along to the company.* None of the data produced in these centers are included in the Management Progress Study. The study continues to use the assessment center technique for its own purpose, but all observations of individuals are held strictly confidential.

The Michigan Bell center was staffed by six second-level managers and directed by a third-level manager. The rationale for using second-level men was that they themselves had held first-level (lowest-level) jobs. They also supervised men in such positions. The staff had no prior experience with assessment techniques, so they were given three weeks of intensive training under a psychologist. Emphasis was placed on the underlying concepts, developing understanding of the qualities to be rated, techniques for observation, rating principles, and communication of impressions and judgments. The training techniques included lectures, role playing, observation of practice candidates, and preparation and critique of reports. The course concluded with a full week devoted to the evaluation of a practice group of twelve candidates.

The center began operating in 1958. At the outset, the operation was limited to one department. Line executives were informed that they would continue nominating men for advancement, but that now these candidates would be assessed, and the results used along with other available information in decisions about promotion. Line management retained final authority; but the assessments of strengths and weaknesses were expected to play a strong part.

A follow-up study of this project was made by Michigan Bell in 1960. It compared those moved up by traditional methods just prior to the start of the program with those advanced on the basis of the more "scientific" assessments. Evaluations of each man's performance on his first-level job, as well as of his potential for further progress, were obtained from interviews with the subject's second- and third-level supervisors. The results showed that approximately two-thirds of those assessed were rated "better than satisfactory" in performance, as compared with approximately one-third of those promoted by traditional procedures.

Parallel findings were also obtained for potential for advancement beyond the first level: two-thirds of the assessed group were considered to have substantial promise, as compared with one-third of those selected by less rigorous methods. The finding that twice as many men with potential for promotion beyond the foreman level could be selected with the aid of assessment was very important from the company's point of view. The major source of second-level managers in the telephone companies is workers who have been raised from the nonmanagement ranks. If the foreman level becomes clogged with nonpromotable super-craftsmen, serious staffing problems can result.

Because it was a study of an ongoing program, this follow-up did not contain all the controls we might have wished for in a tight research study. But the results at Michigan Bell confirmed the judgment of line managers. They had observed the assessment program and were convinced that better people were being chosen. The Michigan center is still in operation.

Michigan Bell was not the only telephone company aware of a need to improve the caliber of supervision at lower levels. The assessment center approach to the selection of managers began to spread to other companies in the Bell System in the early 1960s. Most of the growth occurred without any explicit endorsement by the top echelon of AT&T. Other companies learned of the Michigan center, investigated, and adopted the program on their own initiative.

The program grew in another direction, too. The first centers processed only male candidates, simply because the tests were conducted for technical employees in the plant. But in 1962, some associated companies began to establish assessment centers for the traffic and commercial departments, where mostly women are employed. By 1965 nearly all the associated companies had assessment centers for selection of first-level managers in several departments. In 1969 there were sixty-five such centers operating in the Bell System, almost all on a full-time basis. The program has been heavily supported. By the end of 1969, nearly 60,000 employees had been appraised and 1,275 management people had served on assessment staffs.

At the conclusion of each appraisal, the candidate is given an overall rating reflecting his potential for managerial responsibilities. Candidates are rated acceptable, questionable, or not acceptable. Although distributions vary somewhat by location and year, the typical finding is that one-third are rated as belonging to each group.

Those rated questionable and not acceptable are not automatically removed from further consideration for management. Each case is handled individually. The candidate and his supervisors, after hearing from the assessment staff, meet to discuss the assessment results and their implications. Developmental plans may be established. In addition, management may determine that the individual will be promoted to fill a specific management position for which he has outstanding technical qualifications and where his managerial weaknesses will not be an important factor.

The reactions of the candidates to this process vary. Some drop the idea of becoming a manager and may set as their goal the attainment of a top-rated craft position. Others continue to aspire to management and may begin self-development efforts to overcome weaknesses.

Another follow-up study of how accurately the centers were predicting individual success or failure was made in 1965, encompassing over 500 male employees in four telephone companies. The findings supported those of the earlier study at Michigan Bell. As a result, it was recommended that (1) all candidates assessed as "acceptable" should be promoted as soon as appropriate openings are available; (2) those assessed as "questionable" should be carefully reviewed and advanced if further development occurs or if there are other strong positive indications; and (3) no one rated "not acceptable" should be promoted unless very strong evidence exists that the candidate was incorrectly assessed or can definitely overcome the weakness observed at the center.

The line organization has largely followed these recommendations. Almost all "acceptable" candidates are promoted, about one-half of those rated "questionable" are promoted, and only a small percentage of those rated "not acceptable" eventually make their way higher.

The program has been in operation for more than a decade. It has had substantial impact on the selection and appraisal of lower-level supervisors. Technical competence and length of service are not the dominant factors they once were in the selection of foremen. Younger employees are being sent to the centers and promoted. This is possible because the centers have screened out some 20,000 candidates who did not promise to be good supervisory material. More importantly, more than 15,000 persons have been identified as having good potential for the second level of management—a critical staffing area for the telephone companies.

The assessment center has been adapted successfully in the Bell System for purposes other than picking first-level managers. A wide variety of candidates have been screened for positions that have varied from the fifth level of management (department head) to the nonsupervisory position of salesman. A typical fifth-level manager has responsibility for an entire department in an area of the company. The area may cover an entire state and an organization of several thousand workers. The salesman, or communications consultant, on the other hand, has no supervisory responsibilities and works primarily with business customers. Of course, the assessment techniques and the psychological qualities to be judged are quite different in each instance. But the same basic approach is used.

In one such application, started in the early 1960s, a large associated company, Southern Bell Telephone and Telegraph, asked the AT&T staff to assist it in developing an assessment program for men already in middle management. Candidates for this center came from positions similar to that of the district plant manager (described earlier) and the next higher level of supervision, division manager. Many of these candidates aspired to the top rung of middle management, the fifth-level department head position.

The procedure now in operation at the Southern and South Central Bell Companies (into which Southern Bell split) is similar to that used earlier. Personality tests are included, and the staff is a mixture of professionals and fourth- and fifth-level telephone managers from other associated companies. The simulations are patterned after those used in the Management Progress Study, but the content is designed to be more appropriate for experienced managers.

In an interview a few weeks later, a staff psychologist furnishes each candidate with a picture of his strengths and weaknesses as seen by the assessment staff. The psychologist begins with a description of the qualities that have been evaluated. He then reads the reports covering the candidate's performance on each test. Finally, the candidate hears his ratings on each quality.

Up to this point, the psychologist's task is to let the man understand how he has been evaluated and what information has been used to formulate the ratings. Once the candidate has had the opportunity to ask questions, the discussion switches to developmental issues raised by the assessment. When the feedback concludes, the man knows what has been reported to the company about him and has valuable information to assist him in planning his own development.

More than 250 men have been evaluated in this program under the direction of John J. Hopkins of South Central Bell. Test results have been implemented judiciously, but they have played a definite part in decisions about the men who have been rated. For example, the center has identified some employees who had been well thought of, but who had not previously been recognized as having the outstanding potential revealed during assessment. In other instances, some hidden but important weaknesses were uncovered.

The New York Telephone Company has made a more recent application of this approach, focusing on the second level of management. Three departments—traffic, commercial, and accounting—had a shortage of candidates for second-level management, while others, such as plant and engineering, had more first-level men with potential than they had openings. Previous attempts had been made to relieve this imbalance by promotion across departmental lines, but the results had often been disappointing. An assessment center program was initiated, and it has worked.

While great contributions to operations have come from the selection-oriented assessment centers run by the associated companies, the most interesting general conclusions on the nature of managerial ability continue to flow from the original research-oriented center used in the Management Progress Study. On the basis of our extensive experience with the 422 subjects of the study, we have been able to identify seven areas into which the individual characteristics essential to managerial success can be grouped. They are:

Administrative Skills. A high-potential candidate plans and organizes his work effectively, is willing to make decisions, and arrives at high-quality decisions.

Interpersonal Skills. He makes a forceful and likable initial impression on others, presents effective oral reports, gets people to perform appropriately by displaying leadership, and readily modifies his behavior to reach a valued objective.

Intellectual Ability. He learns easily and has a wide range of interests.

Emotional Stability. He maintains effective work performance under uncertain or unstructured conditions and in the face of unusual pressures.

Work Motivation. He finds satisfactions from work more important than from other areas of life and wants to do a good job even if a lesser one is acceptable to his superiors.

Career Orientation. He wants to be promoted significantly earlier than his peers, is unwilling to defer rewards for a long time, and is not very concerned about having a secure job.

Dependence on Others. He is not greatly concerned with gaining the approval of his superiors or peers and is unwilling to change his life's goals.

Assessment staffs do not, of course, give equal emphasis to each of these groupings in arriving at an overall evaluation. The staffs primarily stress administrative skills, interpersonal skills, and emotional stability. Intermediate consideration is given to work motivation, career orientation, and intellectual ability. The least emphasis is placed on his dependence on others. However, all seven clusters of characteristics contribute significantly to an appraisal.

In making their judgments, the assessors also pay greater heed to some techniques than to others. The group exercises and the in-basket exercise have most influence, while the paper-and-pencil personality questionnaires have the least. Analysis shows that:

☐ Judgments of administrative skills are determined most strongly by performance on the in-basket test.

☐ Evaluations of interpersonal skills depend most heavily on behavior as seen in group exercises, such as business games and leaderless discussions.

☐ Ratings of intellectual ability are quite directly influenced by scores on paper-and-pencil ability tests.

☐ Judgments of emotional stability are most dependent on performance in the group exercise and the in-basket.

☐ Work motivation is seen most clearly in the projective tests of personality and the interview, with additional contributions from the simulations.

☐ Career orientation is strongly apparent in the projective personality tests and interview reports. It is in connection with this characteristic that the personality questionnaires make their only significant contribution to assessment judgments.

☐ Judgments of dependency on others rest heavily on the projective personality tests.

The staff reviews all this evidence. The next step, once again a matter of judgment, is to combine these ratings into a total picture for appraisal. In the Management Progress Study, this evaluation took the form of an answer to the question: "Will he, or will he not, reach middle management (third level) within ten years?" The staff's predictions, and all other assessment data, have always been kept completely confidential. They have had no influence on the subjects' careers.

Eight years after their initial assessment, the management levels of all participants remaining with the Bell System were obtained from their companies and compared with the original projections of the assessment staff. The results are shown separately for college graduates and non-college managers in Table 1. The results for the college recruits are based on 123 college graduates in the Management Progress Study who were initially employed by four telephone companies. Of those rated "will reach third level" by the assessment staff at the original evaluation, almost two-thirds had reached the third level within eight years. Of those given lower potential ratings at assessment ("will not reach third level"), only one-third had attained third level in the subsequent eight years.

Table 1. Comparison of staff predictions with progress in management

| | MANAGEMENT LEVEL EIGHT YEARS LATER | | | |
STAFF PREDICTIONS	THIRD LEVEL OR HIGHER	SECOND LEVEL	FIRST LEVEL	TOTAL
College recruits				
Will reach third level	64%	36%	—	100%
Will not reach third level	32	68	—	100
Non-college managers				
Will reach third level	39	61	—	100
Will not reach third level	9	41	50	100

The results for the non-college managers were based on 144 men in the Management Progress Study who had been promoted up from the ranks into the lower levels of supervision. These men were initially employed in three companies. The agreement between assessment ratings and progress over the subsequent eight years is again striking. Thirty-nine percent of those rated "will reach third level" actually made it within eight years, as compared to only nine percent of the group rated lower in potential at assessment.

These findings demonstrate that personal characteristics, observable even on the first day of employment, underlie later success. They show that these characteristics can be identified through scientific procedures. To be sure, the correlation between the assessment staff's evaluations of potential and the managers' subsequent achievement was less than perfect. Variations could occur because progress within management is not exclusively dependent on the individual's own qualities. External factors might include the availability of opportunities for advancement, the challenge of job assignments, the skillfulness of supervision. But to some extent, of course, the variations may reflect a need for refinements in the assessment center process. Such refinements are made whenever the need becomes apparent.

The findings lend support to the use of such time-consuming techniques as in-basket and group exercises. These methods tap important abilities (administrative and interpersonal skills) which other techniques miss or suggest only indirectly. It is also apparent that other techniques (paper-and-pencil ability tests, interviews, and projective instruments) yield valuable information on such personal characteristics as intellectual abilities and motivation.

The Management Progress Study is now in its fifteenth year. A comprehensive body of information has been assembled, perhaps the most complete set of data over time that exists on any large group of young men during the early phase of their managerial careers. A great deal has already been learned, but the study has only now reached the stage where the most important research issues are ready for analysis. The four general areas of expected results are (1) the relationship of personal qualities to ultimate managerial performances and progress, (2) changes in personal qualities over the years, (3) the causes and results of such changes, and (4) the effects of business policies and practices on personal growth and progress.

A man's personal characteristics at the time he joins a company exert a strong influence on the course of his career, but, naturally, this is only part of the story. Personal attributes tend to change to some extent; careers are also determined by unexpected opportunities. Thus the reassessment, conducted eight years after the original assay, revealed changes in the management-potential ratings of approximately one-third of the group. Some of those who had been rated as having middle-management potential were dropped to lower ratings; others were moved upward.

A review of their case histories confirmed that the early careers of young managers are a time of turmoil, learning, and adjustment. Some of the biggest shifts are in attitude and motivation. At the outset, the men in the study had very positive attitudes toward their jobs, their company, and their career expectations. But these attitudes were found to slump during the eight-year period. After a considerable amount of practical experience, the men had become more realistic, sometimes even pessimistic, in their outlook.

Measures of each subject's concern about his work were obtained at the annual interviews. Job involvement clearly increased over the eight-year period, with the biggest increases occurring during the first two years at work. The trend is presented in Figure 1. The college recruits thus developed greater job and career involvement while they were undergoing a difficult adjustment period and a revision of expectations.

Figure 1. Occupational involvement of college recruits over first eight years of their careers.

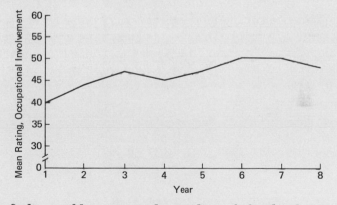

These findings add to our understanding of the development of the young business manager, but they do not provide clear guidelines as to how a company might influence job involvement. An analysis of the relationship between these changes and variations in the working environment is needed.

One environmental variable that has been given considerable attention in the study is *job challenge*. A number of preliminary analyses and a 1966 study by Berlew and Hall indicated the probable importance of this variable. Measures of job challenge were therefore obtained through a review of the various tasks performed by each man over the eight-year period. On the basis of this information, the men were divided into three categories of job challenge—high, medium, and low—

representing the challenge present in the positions held during those first eight years.

The relationship between challenge and job involvement is presented in Figure 2. It can be seen that the two are definitely related. *Those in the low challenge category showed little change in job involvement, while those in highly challenging jobs demonstrated considerable gains in involvement.*

Figure 2. Occupational involvement of college recruits experiencing different degrees of job challenge.

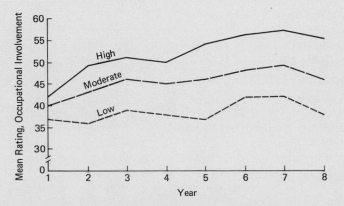

Another fruitful area under study is the real reason for termination of employment. The ultimate response an individual can make to his early experiences in management, if he finds them disappointing, is to leave the company. Approximately 40 percent of the college recruits in the study left the Bell System within eight years, somewhat less than the average loss rate experienced by other large employers. However, even this rate is too high and calls for investigation.

All those who quit have been interviewed at least once since leaving the Bell System. A study of 100 of these men revealed that about half had been encouraged to resign, indicating that they had failed in at least this attempt at a managerial career. The other half had left voluntarily, although they were good performers who could have progressed in the System. A majority of these former employees cited uninteresting or unchallenging assignments as a prime cause for their decision.

Changes in attitudes, expectations, and job involvement are but a few of the issues under study. Much remains to be analyzed before more comprehensive and firm conclusions can be reached. But the early results are encouraging. The study promises to increase greatly our knowledge of the young business manager and his development over a period of time.

By 1971, fifteen years had passed since the first subject made his way into an assessment center. The continued underwriting of a project of this scope by corporate management is noteworthy and unique. It may therefore be worthwhile to review some of the reasons for the study's continued acceptance.

Ongoing management support for a long research effort is much more likely when concrete applications emerge from time to time. Rather early in our program, the study led to sweeping changes in practice—changes management found to be decidedly for the better. Improvements in the selection and training of college recruits and the various applications of the assessment process were foremost among these.

The Management Progress Study was ambitious in its conception. It was expected to take an indefinite number of years, to use the labor of many professionals and telephone managers, and to demand a fair amount of time from the subjects. Attention was to be focused on the total company environment, including job challenge, departmental climate, nature of supervision, and so forth, rather than just on the psychological characteristics of the subjects and special medical examinations. Consequently, it was possible for the study to make substantial recommendations about recruitment, selection, placement, and development.

From the start, the director of the study had the good fortune to report to a department head who had ready access to the top-echelon corporation executives. This meant that the more important findings of the study, as well as its recommendations for action, had a good chance of being considered at high levels. Some early results were reported at Bell System conferences less than two years after the start, and were applied in practice almost as quickly.

These applications would not have been made had the researchers insisted on withholding opinions or advice until they had rigorous scientific proof of their convictions. They might, for example, have declined to say that they thought a significant number of the college recruits of the late 1950s were poor selections until they had waited eight to ten years to prove the validity of their assessment methods. If they had delayed, many years of fruitful application would have been lost and it is questionable whether management support for the Management Progress Study would have continued.

It seems likely that the use of assessment techniques and concepts will continue to grow and expand. At the present time a dozen or so organizations, including General Electric, Sears, Roebuck, and Standard Oil of Ohio, have assessment programs derived from those pioneered in the Bell System. One federal agency, the Internal Revenue Service, has implemented a similar program.

Although more large organizations can be expected to use assessment, perhaps the greatest prospect for growth is in small and medium-size companies, where the need for standardized assessment procedures is strongest. A number of such organizations have expressed interest in the method, but the complexities and cost of the program have curbed their enthusiasm.

Assessment *is* feasible for smaller companies. What has been missing is a cadre of assessment specialists who can design and administer programs for smaller companies and conduct the necessary research. Of late, a few consultants have begun to specialize in assessment methods. One new company has developed a complete line of assessment techniques for off-the-shelf purchase.

The Management Progress Study will continue to provide research findings on the effectiveness of assessment. When the analysis of the second round is completed, we will know more about the stability of personal characteristics over a long period of time. These findings will have obvious bearing on the design of career development programs. It is extremely important that we determine which characteristics are most susceptible to change, so that developmental efforts will be focused in the areas that promise to be the most productive. As mentioned, we also hope to learn how changes in the working environment affect personal traits. These are the most challenging issues for the researchers. They should also be the most rewarding for our subjects—the managers themselves—and for the associated companies that share the responsibility for their growth and development.

WILLIAM C. MERCER

What We Ask of Behavioral Scientists

American Telephone and
Telegraph Company

For many years the Bell System has been making use of behavioral science in various ways. In addition to recent knowledge developed elsewhere, our researchers have made original contributions of their own. One of their major efforts—the assessment of management ability—is detailed in the foregoing chapter.

We look for even more problem-solving help from behavioral science in the years ahead. Here are some of the areas of our personnel practice that seem to me, as an operating executive, to be among the most in need of attention from the psychologists working in the field of organization behavior.

Individualized Training and Development

Large organizations employ a truly imposing range of human talents. The typical company hires people who vary in terms of educational attainment, all the way from the high school dropout to the Ph.D. We take account of these wide differences initially, of course, by placing new employees in different levels of jobs.

In the telephone business, for example, a recent college graduate will likely be assigned to a management development program; the high school dropout might start on the frame. Wherever the employee starts, he will need some technical training to advance from his starting assignment. Large organizations characteristically provide much training, although rather illogically they often offer it after promotion, rather than before.

The problem for the behavioral scientist is to devise more flexible teaching methods that will prepare the beginner for successful performance in a higher job.

One person hired to be an information operator, for example, may be new to the city and require special training in local geography. Another may need practice in understanding unfamiliar accents. Traditional training programs are often inflexible, and they offer the same curriculum to all trainees, regardless of differences in background and aptitude. This is true whether one looks at the training of operators or at a "planning and organizing" course for junior managers. Some trainees spend longer than they need to in their course and get bored. Others fail because they leave without all the skill and knowledge the training was supposed to impart.

Training methods that take account of individual differences are even more desirable now that industry is hiring large numbers of disadvantaged employees. Our old standard training packages are not suited to these workers, who, in any case, have as wide a spectrum of needs as any other group. We should know a lot more about the disadvantaged than we do now, and we need deep research into the methods by which they can be helped to be successful employees. The conventional methods too often fail.

The goal of completely individualized training can only be approximated. It is not feasible to offer training exactly suited to each person's unique pattern of background, aptitudes, and motivation. But we can go a lot further than we have.

Channels for Reassignment

The talents of many employees will be underutilized if there are not free-flowing channels for reassignment and advancement through which they can move to jobs of greater skill and responsibility. In most businesses there is, of course, a flow from the entry levels of semiskilled jobs up to the high-skill levels. Such advancement, however, usually takes the course of least resistance: the worker progresses only within one specialty. If that line of progress is blocked, there is often no mechanism for transfer into another area where opportunities for promotion exist. A foreman supervising telephone installation and repair work, for example, would rarely be considered for promotion to another department as a commercial manager even though a thorough evaluation might reveal good potential for that job.

Many managers actively resist the transfer of one of their dependable workers because they fear that the replacement they get won't be as good as the man they lose.

Although a business cannot tolerate the expense of continual job shifting, transfer possibilities should be made much easier than they are now. To lessen the resistance to transfer among units, scientific studies should be made of the range of jobs a business has to offer and the development of mobility patterns that would cover the basic training needs for a variety of jobs. Such a study might include a review of the extent and cost of additional training for possible transfers. It might also be expected to come up with a greater variety of possibilities for development and growth, to benefit both the worker and the business.

Personnel Assessment

For channels of advancement to be used productively, it is necessary to have a complete and accurate picture of the abilities, potential, and motivation of each employee. This is as true of the skilled craftsman as it is of the college graduate management trainee. For the craftsman, we must learn just what deficiencies exist, if any, as against the demands for a supervisory job. Then the most suitable training can be provided. In the case of the beginner who we hope has the potential to rise to the level of middle manager, we need to know his relative strengths in areas which are of central importance in managing—face-to-face leadership, planning and organizing his work and the work of others, readiness to be decisive.

Accurate evaluations are needed to ensure that latent talent is quickly spotted. We cannot afford to lose track of people in the routine of day-to-day operations. Too often, however, we sit back and wait for ability to show itself—even in circumstances that may keep it from coming to the surface.

Failure to select the best-qualified man or woman when a job opening presents itself can obviously keep a business from achieving optimum profits. Moreover, poor selections are a source of disillusionment to those passed over and to those who are to be supervised by the one mischosen.

Accurate identification of manpower needs in terms of education, skills, management potential, and the like is necessary if the whole system of employment, training, and advancement is to be in balance with company needs. For example, if more people of high potential and motivation are hired than can be fully utilized within a reasonable length of time, there will be excess costs in turnover and poor morale. A common problem has been the overhiring of college graduates, who get backed up at the lowest levels of management. The company is hurt in two ways. Not only are the college graduates dissatisfied and frustrated, but they stagnate in positions that would afford excellent opportunities for the employee working his way up from the ranks. If, on the other hand, underhiring takes place, a conflict develops between units eager to grab any possible candidate and those holding back promotable men because no qualified replacements are available.

Truly comprehensive manpower planning is not easy. It involves estimates of attrition and growth as well as other variables such as the present workforce's potential for filling future job requirements. In addition, the planning of manpower needs must be reviewed constantly to adjust for changes in the rate of growth, the impact of new technology, and other unknown factors.

What we ask of behavioral scientists is the development of manpower-planning models which will enable operating units to make accurate projections. The models should ideally be straightforward enough to be usable by operating executives. Most businesses rarely know how fully they are using their human resources. True, they become aware from time to time that all is not well.

Turnover rates rise ominously; the supply of candidates for lower-level management jobs dries up; rank-and-file employees raise a chorus of complaint that the company is hiring new people to fill the better jobs for which they deem themselves qualified.

But signals that something is wrong often come only when a crisis is near. What would help is a manpower accounting system to record at least a rough measure of how well people are moving along. Such a system would show the number of people promoted to higher-rated jobs both inside and outside the work group, the amount of training for advancement undertaken and completed, and so on. It would also show the number of people with long service who have not had promotions or further training.

Possibly a dollar value might be placed on human resources so that the costs of attrition, retraining, and recruiting could be juxtaposed to normal operating statistics. The regular appearance of personnel utilization figures, whether expressed in monetary equivalents or not, would give management a useful tool. Hopefully, it would pinpoint responsibility for weaknesses in the system and lead to their improvement before they reach harmful proportions.

Making Jobs Flexible

In a pyramidal organization there cannot be infinite opportunities to move ahead. A sizable percentage of the force will top out at a modest level. Unfortunately, this has often meant that chances for any greater responsibility or even a change of job come to an early end. The dead-end problem can possibly be solved by finding new ways of letting a job expand in response to the worker's ability and motivation.

This is especially difficult at the low-skill level where many jobs are determined by the way the equipment is engineered. The assembly-line worker who tightens a single bolt is an instance. In our own company, promising job-enrichment studies have shown that many jobs need not be as simplified as they are. Boring jobs have been frozen into the system only because of the often misguided belief that job simplification makes for greater efficiency. We now have evidence that many low-skill jobs can be enriched so that the employee has responsibility for more than one fragment of an operation, more freedom to apportion his own efforts to the parts of the job, and more knowledge of the results of his own work.

Although some job restructuring can be done centrally, in all probability really effective change must come from the immediate supervisor.

Knowing on-the-spot conditions, he can match job-growth possibilities to individual employees, not all of whom will be able or even willing to accept greater challenge and responsibility. Granting increased responsibility to employees means that the supervisor gives up some degree of detailed control. Thus, many supervisors will have to change their approach. Instead of trying to make jobs so defined that they become boring, supervisors will have to think about how they can give subordinates more scope and responsibility than they had previously assumed.

Better Forms of Organization

The rigidities of organizational structure are among the forces making job enrichment difficult. Each job is defined as having certain functions. Indeed, we often set these definitions down in great detail for purposes of job evaluation or to let the employee know exactly what is expected of him. Although there are sound reasons for doing this, the chances of the job's growing with the person who performs it are hampered by such specifications. As the employee reaches out for more responsibility, he finds himself doing tasks assigned to someone else, or even to his boss.

One answer to this dilemma may be to let boxed-in workers serve on interdepartmental task forces. A group made up, for example, of representatives from the marketing, sales, research, and engineering departments could discuss, study, and attack problems from several directions. Task forces enable staff members to get involved with larger problems than their regular assignments have allowed and, at times, to fill leadership roles more influential than their level in the company usually permits.

Task forces do entail problems, however. If they are not a full-time assignment, the participant must apportion time between his work on the task force and his regular duties. In addition, supervisors, who are ordinarily responsible for deciding salary raises and promotion, may have no opportunity to appraise their subordinates' performance while serving outside the department on a task force. If task forces are used frequently, we may have to modify methods of supervision. We must also be alert lest the attractiveness of the task-force approach blind us to our basic need to change existing organizational structures.

There are many other ways in which behavioral science can contribute to organization improvement. How many levels of management does a particular company need? Is it better to have a foreman responsible for both technical and managerial matters, or should he merely manage and be supported by technical experts? Can we make supervisors into better managers by giving them more responsibility? How can performance be evaluated if a worker is a member of several different task forces? How can the anxiety associated with change in an organization be reduced and the readiness to participate in such change increased? These are just a few of the questions that urgently call for new answers.

Stimulation of Teamwork and Communication

If substantial progress were made in all these areas of personnel practice, organizations would run more smoothly than they do. The focus of day-to-day activities remains on production, however, not on group processes. Although it avails little for a group to be continually preoccupied with how its members are working together if they are not doing much work, the emphasis on production can also be self-defeating.

Too often the members of a group do not have a shared perception of their joint goals. Some members of a staff group may believe their role is merely to provide assistance when asked; others may view the group as an aggressive force for change. Group members may not understand their part in achieving goals. They may have no idea whether the goals are being reached, or lack methods for overcoming obstacles that may arise in moving toward them.

What we seek from behavioral science are the means by which groups can develop a clear picture of their goals in relation to the total goals of the company, while remaining attentive to how the group is functioning as a unit. Methods for improving organizational development, interpersonal relationships, team building, and so on must not be so time-consuming that groups will be reluctant to use them. In addition, we must learn how to make both upward and downward communication freer and more accurate.

Management should not relax merely because it has launched a program in this or any other personnel area. There must be a monitoring mechanism to provide feedback on how well groups are functioning and how effectively communication is taking place. It is well known that the natural processes of upward communication often result in atypically favorable viewpoints reaching higher management. Equally unfortunate is the distortion of top management's pronouncements on the way down. "Let's be a little careful on expenses" may become "Don't spend another dime." Although surveys and interviews are useful monitoring methods, other techniques for observing the actual interaction within a managerial group and for tracing the flow of communication in a hierarchy would be of great help.

Attitude Change

If the abilities and potential of every employee were thoroughly assessed, if individualized training were available, and if channels for advancement were fully open, we would be greatly benefited. Yet experience shows that some groups of employees do not share equally in even the opportunities that are already available.

In recent years business has finally come to realize its obligations to minority groups. And at present the underutilization of women in the workforce is being brought home to us. From time to time special steps must be taken to ensure that the personnel system works equally well for all. It is not enough for a company to have a stated policy of equality for all employees. There are thousands of executives with decision-making powers in large companies, and there are many possibilities for them to rationalize their prejudices. Instead of assuming that management's intent is clear, we must change attitudes all down the line. There are many ways of doing this. Behavioral science could indicate which ways are the most effective and which are practicable in a business context.

Some Additional Observations

Human institutions are imperfect, and there is no large organization known to us that has not fallen significantly short of ideal practice in the areas of management touched upon here. Obstacles to perfect practice in large companies, particularly under today's conditions, are formidable indeed. No management, however enlightened and decisive, could possibly do everything right. The responsibility for progress rests on management nevertheless. Management must be willing to divert part of its attention from operations and apply some of its best thought to developing the human resources of the enterprise.

Business management has not taken full advantage of what behavioral scientists have to offer. Some large companies make little conscious use of behavioral science. Others employ behavioral scientists but deal with them ineffectively.

Behavioral scientists, on the other hand, do not make their maximum contribution merely by refining techniques or by limiting themselves to researchable problems rather than major operating challenges. They should take an active role not merely in identifying problems and analyzing causes but in devising and pushing corrective measures.

Businessmen must dedicate themselves to improving practices and procedures. Those commitments will fall short of maximum effectiveness, however, unless they utilize the findings already available from behavioral science and support the additional research still urgently needed. Only when the forces of business and behavioral science are pragmatically joined will we come closer to the goal of fully realizing the potential of every employee.

DELMAR L. LANDEN / HOWARD C. CARLSON

New Strategies for Motivating Employees

General Motors Corporation

As industry's problems of manpower utilization have continued to grow, so has the need to better understand the complexity of employee motivation. It has become crucial to find ways of realizing the full potential of people at work. This chapter attempts a general review of the problem of industrial motivation, describes the major strategies available for understanding and increasing job satisfaction, and briefly describes some of the programs now under way in General Motors.

What It Is

Motivation is not a simple or fixed human quality that can be turned on and off with some sort of key. Unfortunately, there exists no single technique, no universal approach to take with all employees.

Motivation has both short- and long-range aspects. A hungry person has a short-range need, one that seeks fairly immediate satisfaction, which directs behavior toward a relevant goal. Eating a meal achieves that goal. The hunger need is thus satisfied and no longer operates as a motivational force. Other needs do not lose their potency after satisfaction, but persist and even increase in strength over time. The need for recognition may not diminish when some satisfaction has been achieved. Getting some recognition may simply whet the appetite for more.

A need rarely exists in isolation. Several different needs can operate simultaneously, and some may be in conflict with others. Different needs may exist at different levels of potency and the relative importance of motives within any person may fluctuate depending upon the individual's perception of people and circumstances surrounding him.

Managers generally define motivation by the extent to which behavior is directed toward the goals of the enterprise—a "motivated" worker directs his behavior toward accomplishing the manager's objectives.

Motivation is identified with compliance. Employees who do what they are told are rewarded; those who do not are punished either by the withholding of rewards or by disciplinary action. The most common kind of reward is economic—pay, promotions, fringe benefits. The view is still current that people work almost exclusively to get money. Thus it is believed if you pay people more they will work harder! Or, conversely, people will work harder so they can get more money.

The theory seems logical, but how is it working today? The typical unskilled hourly employee in the motor industry earns about $4.25 per hour. He receives in addition a large number of benefits which add substantially to his standard of living and provide him with a good measure of security.

Despite all these economic inducements, most companies have experienced alarming increases in hourly turnover, absenteeism, grievances, and discipline cases in the past five years.

Some companies experience turnover rates of 40 to 50 percent of newly hired hourly employees. Most of the turnover is in the form of voluntary quits, taking place largely in the first months of employment. Some plants must hire ten people to show a net gain of one. Asked if he was not in need of a decent paying job, one departing worker answered, "I need the bread bad, but not that bad."

In one large company, as many as 20 percent of the employees do not come to work on certain Friday nights. A young employee, with little seniority, has been known to sacrifice about $35 in pay and risk firing to attend a high school basketball game.

In a five-year period, turnover rose 70 percent, grievances 40 percent, discipline cases 45 percent. One employee sent home for a three-day disciplinary layoff at a personal cost to him of about $100 requested that the foreman make the layoff five days instead of three. He wanted to go fishing. Another employee with a particularly bad attendance record, when asked why he worked only four days a week, unabashedly responded, "Because I can't live on what I make in three!"

If money were the sole answer, surely the absenteeism rate would be less of a problem today. In 1970, most General Motors hourly employees lost about three months' pay during an eighty-day strike. But absenteeism a year later persisted at the prestrike level of 5.5 percent.

These problems of absenteeism and turnover bring into question traditional notions about employee motivation. When managers are asked about the causes of these problems, one answer frequently given is that the workers involved are *not motivated*. It should be clear, by now, that these people *are* motivated—they are motivated not to come to work! Other more powerful needs than work are fulfilled by not coming to work. Employees are avoiding what they see as an unsatisfying or meaningless job. They are attracted, at the same time, to what they perceive as a more rewarding set of circumstances off the job.

These more rewarding circumstances are not likely to be economic n nature. If an employee is away from work to fulfill some need, it s likely that such a need can only be satisfied through some forms of reward that are not monetary but are purely psychological, like greater esteem, recognition, self-respect. Additional money cannot "buy back" the absent employee. If he is trying to find a psychological reward he cannot get in his job, money seldom works as a substitute.

Growing Alienation of the Worker

Much has been written in recent years about the growing alienation of he worker. Many businessmen don't believe it. Their position is that American workers have the world's highest pay and living standard, plus more conveniences or luxuries than any similar group in the history of mankind, and are overindulged. They point out that these economic gains for the worker have been accompanied not by appreciation but by less productivity, poorer workmanship, greater absenteeism, higher turnover, little or no company loyalty, and a growing disrespect for authority.

Are American workers really alienated or is this a myth perpetrated by journalists and other "informed" observers? Answering this question takes a bit of soul-searching. Do workers feel that they are a very unimportant part of their company? If the answer is yes, then many industrial workers are indeed alienated. Do workers generally believe they are unable to influence their working environment? If the answer is yes, then many are indeed alienated. Are workers less able to identify with their work, to see what they have produced, to take pride in their contribution? If the answer is yes, then feelings of alienation are very prominent among many industrial employees.

Research carried out by Frederick Herzberg of Case Western Reserve University suggests that motivation is two dimensional: things which make people unhappy are not the same as those which make people happy. Herzberg's "two-factor theory of motivation" has one set of conditions called "hygiene factors." These conditions relate to the physical and psychological surroundings in which people work and include such factors as working conditions, supervision, benefit plans, and pay. The other set of conditions is called "motivators." These include responsibility, advancement, recognition, variety, and growth.

One conclusion from this theory is that if a person's job does not possess motivating elements—recognition, responsibility, advancement, growth, and the like—then that person *cannot* be motivated. This conclusion follows from a conviction by Herzberg and others that motivation is an internalized force. It is self-generating, self-controlling, and self-rewarding—and not as subject to external control as traditional management and organizational practices would have it.

As Herzberg sees it, in order to motivate people, you must provide them with work that is meaningful, so that the individual *knows* he is doing something worthwhile. The sources of motivation are within the job and within the working environment, which should be stimulating, healthy, and supportive.

What impels a person to act is largely dependent upon what need or needs are unsatisfied. Thus, motivation is a dynamic and ever-growing psychological phenomenon. The late Abraham Maslow has contributed most to this understanding of motivation. He also helped to establish the principle that motivation (and hence behavior) is triggered by unsatisfied needs.

Maslow asserts that needs are hierarchically arranged in order of strength from lower- to higher-order ones. Physiological and safety needs are primary and provide the foundation for the higher-order needs When the primary needs are adequately met, and only then, people are able to concern themselves with higher ones, such as being an accepted member of a group they want to be part of. If they succeed in this need, others appear. They may then develop a need for greater individual identity, self-esteem, self-respect—and seek answers to the question of "Who am I?" If work is meaningless and mundane, and the managerial practices bureaucratic and authoritarian, then a person has great difficulty in building an image of himself as an adult with a sense of pride and personal worth.

Human beings, if they are to remain emotionally healthy, must always be growing psychologically. For many, that growth occurs through their work and the challenges it provides. If the challenges are not there neither are the feelings of accomplishment and self-fulfillment.

Another view of employee motivation was formulated by Douglas McGregor in his book *The Human Side of Enterprise*. McGregor conceptualized his ideas as Theories X and Y to contrast the assumptions about human nature that underlie the authoritarian and participative systems of management. McGregor considered that conventional management policies ran counter to what psychologists know about human nature. Those management policies that don't work, he said, fail because they are based on false assumptions about what people are like and how they must be managed. These assumptions, representing the authoritarian viewpoint, McGregor labeled Theory X. For contrast he offered Theory Y, which drew on the current scientific research into motivation and recognized the interdependence of workers and the men who manage them.

The main assumptions behind Theory X are that by nature most people don't like to work, have to be pressured into it, and would rather be told what to do than think for themselves. These assumptions are still widely held today; many managers take them for granted.

Theory Y, by contrast, assumes that most people are neutral about work to begin with. Whether they like it or not depends on their experience with it. Pressure isn't always needed to get people to work. Other approaches can often be at least as effective, without the harmful side effects that pressure often brings. Under the right circumstances, people do not avoid responsibility—they seek it. When they are involved in setting their own goals, whether for material or psychic reward, they will pursue them as strongly as if outside pressure were applied.

Theory X managers assume that workers have tacitly agreed to accept a system of controls in return for wages, and that controls are essential to keep workers up to standard and to prevent chaos. McGregor claims instead that, when properly motivated, people are more cooperative and effective without controls. Freed from the annoyance of overvigilant watchdogs, they can devote their energies to the task at hand, and usually produce more. Self-discipline is the spur. It accomplishes more, and at less cost to management. Most adults, McGregor says, behave as adults when given the chance.

Theory Y does not deny the need for authority. But there are many forms of controls, and not all are appropriate at all times. Under Theory Y, there are still restrictions, but they are largely self-restrictions. The aim is not an unregulated workforce but a self-regulated one, based on voluntary cooperation through self-interest. When the possibility of personal growth is coupled with financial gain, as it is under Theory Y, a powerful motivator is released. The job is seen as the avenue to greater competence, better self-discipline, and a sense of accomplishment. Where Theory X subordinates the goals of the individual to the goals of the organization, Theory Y integrates the two.

Rensis Likert has extended McGregor's Theories X and Y into a four-way division he calls Systems 1, 2, 3, and 4; System 1 is characterized by extreme authoritarianism and System 4 is the most participative. Likert studied many high-producing units and a number of low-producing ones. He concluded that their productivity depended on how their supervisors operated. Some supervisors were production centered, others employee centered. The employee-centered supervisor, who behaved more as a helper than an overseer, got the higher productivity. A boss of this type considers the responsibility for the work to be the workers'; after giving them the needed information, material, and supplies to get on with their work, he stays pretty much out of their way.

Likert agrees with McGregor that workers can be trusted to show self-discipline and organize their work effectively without being pressured. He is also convinced that when employees are allowed to assume responsibility for their own work, their pride offsets any tendencies they might have to take it easy. The supervisor who affords his operators a high degree of self-management usually gets greater production.

When the members of a work group are encouraged to participate in their own management, and when their advice and expertise are sought, then their individual goals become linked to the goals of the company. Thus, to Likert, the role of the supervisor is not that of the enforcer or controller, but that of the expediter, the helper, and—the ego supporter.

Chris Argyris of Harvard also looked at the impact of the organization on the individual. He found that the usual organizational structure itself, along with its leadership and system of controls, inhibited the growth of mature individuals. The typical organization, Argyris said, is primarily for men who are willing to remain childlike. The structure is tight, allowing little leeway for choice or flexibility in adapting the rules to fit the circumstances. Workers are expected to do what they are told and leave the thinking to supervisors, whose capacities they may privately question.

The new employee soon learns that he is expected to be passive and submissive, to do as he is told, to leave the thinking to others. In the name of efficiency, millions of workers are required to shut off their brainpower, not infrequently to be detriment of efficiency.

Concentrating power and decision making in a relatively few hands at the top, Argyris claims, inevitably fosters apathy and inflexibility among the many hands further down. This is unhealthy for the men below and for the organization as a whole. The organization will function at its best, Argyris believes, only if it meets the needs of both those it works for and those who work for it.

The tightly controlled environment which once seemed so logical has turned out to be self-defeating. Work needn't be frustrating or bring out the worst in men. When decision making is dispersed appropriately through the ranks, when men are encouraged to use their minds and participate in the choices that affect them, and when managers gain a better understanding of the real dynamics of motivation, then organizations will become more productive.

A growing trend in industry seeks to provide more satisfaction to employees by enlarging jobs, enriching job content, and giving employees more control over their work. This movement was born of the recognition that traditional practices of job design have begun to backfire in these days of better education, greater leisure, and higher aspirations. Simplification of a job easily learned, or a dull repetitive operation, has not brought the advantages it was supposed to. Instead, it has brought a sense of meaninglessness and boredom to employees. It removed challenge and any sense of individual commitment to production goals.

Here are new approaches to job design which are beginning to be used, either singly or in combination:

☐ *Job rotation.* The employee is moved through a series of related tasks or operations.

☐ *Job enlargement.* Tasks that normally would be done by several employees are combined in a sequence of tasks performed by a single employee.

☐ *Job enrichment.* The level of difficulty or complexity of the job is increased and the employee assumes some responsibility for planning and controlling his job.

Each of these approaches seeks to build greater *meaning* into jobs, a missing element in the job-simplification designs of the past.

To enhance employee motivation, many companies are also taking another look at the strategy of matching people and jobs. Here are a few of the ways in which successful job matching is being accomplished:

☐ *Job stylizing.* Although many employees may have the same job title (for example, production foreman), actual job content may vary from person to person. All foremen do not possess common strengths or job interests. We now provide for a variety of job models which afford a best fit between the individual and his job in the organization.

☐ *Job–man measurement.* The needs of individuals and the potential of different jobs to satisfy needs should be measured. Technology intended to make this possible is now under development at General Motors.

☐ *Task progression.* With the increasing need to provide expanded training opportunities for women and minority group employees, job performance levels must be more precisely defined and linked sequentially in a pattern of job progression. Here again, a best fit assures steady job progression and optimal employee motivation.

Another strategy is team building, which seeks to increase a group's motivation to do its work well. A group is first introduced to a process of self-examination. Through the use of survey data feedback, experience-based learning exercises, and the help of an outside team-building specialist, group members became increasingly aware of their interdependency. Gradually, the group acquires a capability for self-diagnosis, self-evaluation, and self-correction. Even partial accomplishment of this team-building objective brings about a major improvement in the group's performance.

There are a number of ways in which human organizations can be more constructively "wired together." Functions, reporting relationships, priorities, and reward systems can be changed. Manufacturing processes can be designed around social systems (rather than the reverse). Organizational development strategies can be planned to remove obstacles that limit groups from functioning as effective teams.

The major strategies of motivation have evolved from a great deal of independent study and research. Over the last decade there has been sufficient application and evaluation of these strategies that their validity or usefulness should no longer be in question. However, many managers in every company are still skeptical. Such skepticism cannot be ignored or minimized, because managerial commitment is essential to efforts to improve employee motivation.

Many managers view traditional motivational techniques—reward and punishment—as hallmarks of the "tough" manager. They see the more current notions as being "soft"—not fitting their image of a "true" executive. Furthermore, applying newer and more effective techniques may require some fundamental changes in organizational structure, work-group relationships, union and management relations, supervisory practices, plant layout, and reward systems.

Many managers believe the ultimate tool for achieving success, progress, or survival is power. They are also convinced that power is finite—there is just so much of it. This is a faulty notion and managers must be made aware that it is faulty if we are to achieve increased employee motivation.

The sharing and multiplication of power requires a high degree of self-confidence, an ability to be moderately objective about one's assets and limitations, a capacity to diagnose the managerial leadership requirements of a particular situation, and the flexibility and skill to meet requirements of that situation.

Managers must take greater risks. They must be willing to strive for long-range improvements, accepting perhaps some difficult intermediate periods. Organizations, like human beings, don't move from good to bad or bad to good overnight. Enduring improvement takes, among other things, time. Some managers are not willing to accept this fact.

Most managers have the freedom and resources to do much more than they are now doing to bring about improved employee motivation. However, they may be reluctant to do so because they are not convinced that change is needed, or that top executives want them to change. Put directly, they are not motivated to change.

Motivated people are people who share responsibility, make decisions, take risks, and seek growth and recognition through their own work and through their organization. To do all this they must have power, defined in terms of the ability to influence conditions, decisions, goals, and priorities. When managers accept this concept of power, they soon learn that they multiply their influence—thus making power infinite.

Despite some skepticism within the organization, a number of new and distinctive approaches to better employee motivation are being applied at GM. These efforts, though recent and somewhat isolated, represent a vital commitment of our corporation. There is a conscious effort to avoid basing all efforts on any single philosophy or any single approach. In most instances, employee motivation programs have been accompanied by a research plan that provides for a systematic determination of what programs should be used and how they should be implemented. The research designs also provide objective measurement and evaluation of the effects or outcomes of these programs. Progress through research is thus intended to be the hallmark of our motivational program. Here are some examples of what we have been doing:

☐ In 1967, a joint study by AC Spark Plug and the GM Employee Research Section sought to determine the content of the foreman's job at AC and to find ways of making foremen more effective. One of the things learned was that it is difficult to isolate a job from the organization and try to change it without also affecting the content of other related jobs and levels of responsibility.

☐ In 1969, Saginaw Steering Gear embarked on a program to learn more about how first-line supervisors allocated their time, how much of their job was discretionary, and how the job could be made more effective. The study showed a need to improve jobs by means of an overall organization development program.

☐ Beginning in 1969, the GM Air Transport Section initiated a series of job-enrichment activities in cooperation with Employee Research. Thirty-three airplane mechanics met weekly with their supervisor to arrive at joint decisions about such matters as work flow, job duties, and supervisory practices. Because of the success of this initial effort, plans are in motion to extend the program to the Avionics Division and the maintenance shop.

☐ In the United Delco parts-distribution department, supervisory and nonsupervisory employees have recently begun a series of meetings in preparation for job enrichment. These meetings seek to examine, with the aid of an Employee Research representative, attitudes toward departmental goals and work-flow designs.

☐ Approximately two years ago, Pontiac Motor Division initiated a program to create more cooperative working relationships among foremen in one manufacturing operation. Because of the program's success, similar team-building activities have been introduced elsewhere in the division and at all levels of supervision. It is generally felt that communications, problem solving, intergroup cooperation, and general morale have all noticeably improved.

☐ Employee Research, General Motors Institute, and Manufacturing Development have worked jointly with the Oldsmobile Division in an effort to reduce absenteeism in car-and-engine assembly plants. One approach involved establishing employee task forces, each led by a foreman, to determine the causes of absenteeism and recommend possible solutions. Perhaps most significant was the experience of management and hourly employees in exploring a new working relationship based on shared responsibility and mutual acceptance of ideas. Absenteeism has dropped in the experimental plants to a level below that for all of Oldsmobile and for Fisher Body Assembly, which is located in the same city.

☐ Another study at Oldsmobile dealt with the problem of inspection error. A problem-analysis team was established, composed of hourly inspectors and repairmen, foremen, and other personnel. As in the previous study, the utilization of hourly wage earners as problem solvers proved highly effective. Their personal knowledge contributed to the clarification of the problem, and they collected additional facts when it became necessary. They showed a high degree of interest in attacking and resolving a problem that was frustrating management's attempts to build a defect-free automobile. At least partially because of this project, a 50 percent improvement in the quality of electrical assemblies occurred.

☐ Since the fall of 1969, GM has been cooperating with the Institute for Social Research (ISR) of the University of Michigan in an organization development program. The program is designed to identify the kinds of organizational variables that differentiate plants or smaller units known to be operating at different performance levels, and to use the knowledge gained to diagnose problems, derive solutions, and institute managerial practices to sustain the process of organizational improvement. The program is also intended to develop ways to share what is learned with other GM units.

All the principles and strategies described earlier in this chapter are embodied in various forms in this plant program. An initial survey among all salaried employees in each of these plants showed specific ways in which the management and functioning style of an organization are related to operating performance. Among the many variables examined was employee motivation as reflected in the way people perceive the effects of various forms of leadership, climate, and work-group relationships. The survey findings clearly indicated a need for heightened motivation at each of the plant sites. The long-range program designed to bring about changes in these organizations is now entering its third year. Results to date have been very encouraging.

One result of the GM-ISR Organization Development Program is the establishment in the General Motors Assembly Division (GMAD) of a new function, organizational analysis and development. Each of the plants is following a similar plan: Two people are selected as full-time organization development coordinators. Each receives highly specialized training. The plant manager, the personnel director, and the coordinator participate as a team in a concentrated training program covering the principles and techniques of organizational improvement. Each plant communicates throughout its operations the objectives and principles of this new effort and each location is encouraged to apply the principles and techniques of OD and to make use of available resources in whatever ways are most appropriate to its operations.

It is clear that the task of creating a more highly motivated workforce is complex. It is *not* something that can be done with poster displays, campaigns, and across-the-board programs. It is a long-term process. It requires not only tremendous effort, but imagination and deep commitment. Motivating workers is not a special assignment for a group of specialists; it is an integral part of every manager's job. It is not something that can be actively engaged in by only a few plants, but must become a matter of policy, of priority, of principle for the entire corporation.

The problem of employee motivation is still regarded as a core issue in the future of General Motors. As such, it is being dealt with by more and ever-broader programs throughout the corporation. GM employees are attempting in all manner of ways to communicate their intense need to become more involved in their work and in their organizations.

Management is now recognizing this fact and taking steps to permit everyone to become a vital contributor to the success of the corporation. With all of these efforts and programs, however, we are probably only beginning to ripple the surface of a deep reservoir of untapped human potential among GM employees.

Contemporary organizations require new managerial principles and actions. A handful of people—managers—can no longer effectively shape and control the direction and destiny of large or even small companies. As change accelerates and becomes more complex, decisions must be made where the problems are, by the people closest to the problems.

It is unnecessary to speculate about when we will know all that we should about motivation and its relationships to work and to organizations. As long as we continue to change as a nation and as a civilization, all institutions in which people interact will have to adapt. It can only be hoped that accumulating knowledge about why people work will keep abreast of changing human needs. Only in this way can we hope to maximize the quality of organizations and of their accomplishments.

HERBERT H. MEYER

The Effective Supervisor: Some Surprising Findings

General Electric Company

Because of job simplification, which breaks work down into highly repetitive tasks, many factory jobs are simply boring. Employees respond to the tedium with high absenteeism, excessive turnover, work slowdowns, waste, and high accident rates. A corporation can minimize some of these problems by means of sound personnel policies, programs, and procedures. But the actions of the individual supervisor—his ability as a leader, and the way he applies the company's personnel policies—determine, in large part, whether or not those who work for him are as satisfied and as productive as they ought to be.

In order to learn more about how the first-line supervisor achieves or fails to achieve sound employee relations, the General Electric Company's Personnel Research unit undertook a major research program. It sought answers to the following questions:

☐ How does the effective first-line supervisor operate? What method does he use to stimulate cooperation and to develop interest in the work?

☐ How many employees can he supervise and maintain good relations with under different conditions? What kinds of responsibilities should he have?

☐ How does the structure of the total organization affect the worker on the assembly line?

There were also many collateral questions which we felt such a research program should answer, such as:

What are the manager's training needs?
How can he best receive this training?
How should new supervisors be selected?
How should the supervisor's employee-relations skills be evaluated?

Our researchers conducted a series of four studies designed to determine how foreman's jobs were structured. An initial survey of twenty-one plants covered the number of persons supervised by each foreman and the scope of responsibilities assigned to him.

The second study in the series focused on finding the different ways those foremen who were rated "very effective" and those who were rated "relatively ineffective" perceived their jobs. The third study intensively analyzed differences in the ways effective and ineffective foremen actually carried out their jobs. The fourth involved controlled studies of shop organizations that had been experimentally altered in an attempt to improve relationships between supervisors and workers.

In the initial study, care was taken to select a variety of manufacturing operations so that the sampling would be fairly representative of General Electric's total operations. The operations surveyed ranged from the manufacture of large turbines and generators to the assembly of miniaturized electronic components.

At each location researchers gathered information both about the general nature of the operation and about specific characteristics of an individual foreman's job. Data included details of work-group composition, the nature of the work, and the foreman's responsibilities for meeting production schedules, providing technical services, dealing with employee-relations problems, and other such operating functions. This information was obtained for 142 types of foremen working on day-shift jobs involved in direct manufacturing or process operations.

Individual General Electric plants are given a great deal of autonomy. Therefore, practices varied from one plant to another almost as much as they might in a survey of unaffiliated companies. Great variations were found, for example, in the number, or "span," of employees reporting to individual foremen. While the average was about 30, the span ranged from 8 to more than 150. Table 1 offers a summary of the differences between small and large work groups.

We also wanted to find out how achievement and supervisory activities were related to the size of the work groups. We wanted to know, for example, whether the foreman who supervised a small group was more people-oriented and had better relationship with his subordinates than the foreman who headed a larger group.

The single, clear-cut conclusion that emerged from an analysis of the data was that foremen of very small groups tended to behave more like technical specialists, while foremen of large groups behaved more like managers. Foremen who supervised large groups spent more time on personnel and administrative functions than the foremen of small groups.

One of the byproducts of the study was the finding that a foreman's responsibilities are highly ambiguous. In trying to define them, we found, for example, that an expert in methods, or quality control, might say

Table 1. Major factors or job characteristics found to differentiate between large and small work groups.

MAJOR DIFFERENTIATING FACTORS	CHARACTERISTICS OF LARGE GROUPS	CHARACTERISTICS OF SMALL GROUPS
Supervisory assistance provided the foreman	Likely to have leaders, instructors, or related forms of assistance.	Foreman carries out all supervisory responsibilities personally.
Nature of the manufacturing operation	Perform "mass production" operations.	"Job shop" type operations.
	Employees work in gangs or on paced lines.	Employees work individually.
Composition or characteristics of the work group	Homogeneous work groups in relation to kinds of jobs performed.	High percentage of different kinds of jobs performed.
	High percentage of female groups more likely to be above average size.	High percentage of male workers.
	Workers on incentive pay. (Group incentive especially characteristic of large groups.)	Workers on nonincentive jobs.
Characteristics of the product	Small products manufactured.	Large products manufactured.
	Simple products manufactured; jobs require short learning periods.	Complex products manufactured; jobs require long learning periods.
Supervisory method	Foremen spend more time on "personnel" or employee-relations functions.	Foremen spend more time on "production" and related technical and operating functions.

that the foreman had little or no responsibility for functions in his specialty. On the other hand, the foreman himself might claim that he had full responsibility. A foreman and his superior (the General Foreman) often disagree markedly about the foreman's responsibilities. It was decided to study this surprising lack of agreement between foreman and superior more intensively.

It seemed reasonable at the time to expect that the foreman who *disagreed* with his superior over responsibilities might be regarded by his superior as performing less effectively than the foreman who usually *agreed* with his superior. It also seemed reasonable to expect that if such conflicts were resolved, the superior might feel the "disagreeable" foreman's performance was improving.

To test these hypotheses, we constructed a questionnaire listing specific responsibilities or job functions that foremen might perform. Foremen were asked if they performed such tasks as submitting formal periodic production reports, or keeping track of work coming up for their groups. The questionnaire asked if foremen made requisitions for additional employees needed in the work group; whether they interviewed and made the final selection of new employees; whether they explained pay computation to employees; whether they approved piecework rates before they became effective.

It asked whether a particular foreman had "complete," "partial," or "no" responsibility for each job function. If the respondent was not sure about the extent of responsibility, he could indicate that, too.

Foremen were also asked to describe their own jobs, and general foremen were asked to describe the jobs of the foremen reporting to them. Each general foreman was also asked to identify his most effective and his least effective foreman.

We then selected for analysis the questionnaire returns from general foremen who said that the foremen they had nominated as most and least effective had exactly the same jobs. This selection yielded fifty-one sets of forms completed by general foremen along with their most and their least effective subordinates.

Our hypothesis that general foremen would more readily agree with their "most effective" than with their "least effective" foreman was not confirmed. On the average, in fact, disagreements were equal for the two groups. But we come upon something significant. This was a marked difference in the direction of the discrepancies in the responses. In general, those foremen who were rated by their supervisors as "most effective" claimed to have a significantly greater amount of responsibility than did the foremen who had been rated as "least effective."

Perhaps this finding provided the key to "effectiveness." In other words, *the effective foreman assumes that he has full responsibility whereever there is any ambiguity about who is in charge. The ineffective foreman assumes that someone else is responsible.* Those results led us to seek a clearer picture of the differences between effective and ineffective foremen on the job.

An intensive observational study of foreman job activities was carried out in a large factory employing about 120 foremen. The performance ratings of these foremen were obtained through carefully conducted "field review" interviews with their superiors. Each general foreman and superintendent (the next level up) was asked to rate foremen on various aspects of their job responsibilities.

At the same time, an attitude survey was conducted in the same plant. The employees were asked to rate the effectiveness of their foremen. These "reverse ratings" covered not only interpersonal aspects of the foreman's job, but production and administrative responsibilities as well. Interestingly, the composite ratings of foreman by subordinates did not agree very well with composite ratings of the same persons by superiors. Obviously the two groups attached importance to different performance characteristics.

Two groups of twelve men were selected for intensive study. These two groups included 10 percent of the highest-rated foremen and 10 percent of the lowest-rated.

Each of the twenty-four selected foremen was observed on the job for eight 2-hour periods—a total of sixteen hours spread over various times of day and days of the week. This covered a four-month period in order to assure a representative sampling of normal job activities and behavior. Observers followed each foreman closely and made detailed notes on all his activities and the length of time spent on each. Observers were not only highly trained for the study, but each had worked as a foreman at one stage of his career. They could thus establish rapport with their subjects and judge whether the subjects were behaving normally. Sometimes an observer found it necessary to repeat an observation because he felt that his presence had significantly changed the foreman's conduct. For the most part, however, the work pace did not allow foremen to alter their usual activity patterns.

Careful statistical checks were made on the reliability of observations. These revealed that sixteen hours of observation yielded consistent job-activity patterns. In addition, a second observer checked consistency by making comparable two-hour observations of several foremen during matched time periods of the day and week.

Observers placed heavy emphasis on the foreman's role as a communicator in the manufacturing process. Observers noted not only the activity in which the foreman was engaged, such as establishing job priorities, determining work status, or working on production schedules, but also the people whom the foreman contacted and those who contacted him. The reason for the contact was recorded, as well as whether information flowed primarily from the foreman to the person contacted, or vice versa.

It was found that a foreman's day contained a great number and variety of brief activities. It also showed clearly that the least effective foreman engaged in *more* activities than the most effective. Specifically, the least effective foreman engaged in an average of 270 different activities and contacts during the working day. The most effective foreman engaged in only about 200. The better foreman, on the average, shifted his activity every two and a half minutes. The poorer foreman did so every one and three-quarters minutes.

Figure 1. Percent of time spent by foremen on four major areas of foreman responsibility.

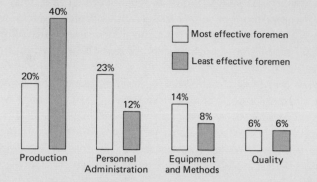

When the time spent on specific activities was examined, even greater differences appeared. As Figure 1 shows, the poorer foremen spent twice as much time on production and related activities, and only about half as much time on personnel activities, as the most effective foremen. Although the two groups spent the same amount of time dealing with quality-control problems, performance rating by superiors had shown that the most effective foremen achieved much better results in that area. Perhaps their success could be attributed to their spending significantly more time dealing with equipment and methods problems than the least effective foremen.

The least effective foremen occupied more of their days seeking immediate solutions to short-range production problems, while the most effective foremen put in more time planning and organizing the longer-range aspects of the job. The low-rated foremen devoted more effort to checking work progress, securing materials, supervising materials movements, and similar activities. The more successful foremen usually delegated these tasks.

Apparently a foreman who spends time with his subordinates does not necessarily improve his relations with them. Figure 2 shows that

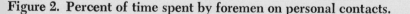

Figure 2. Percent of time spent by foremen on personal contacts.

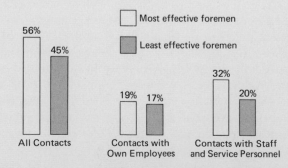

although the better foreman spent more time in contact with others, most of that contact was not with his own employees. Instead, he spent the extra time with staff members who serviced his employees. The difference in the number of contacts with services personnel was attributed to the better foreman's inclination to take advantage of such services. Poorer foremen tended to ignore them and work on a do-it-yourself basis.

When we examined the flow of communications, the better foremen seemed to show superior patterns. "More effective" foremen, on the average, spent more time in each contact with another person. They engaged in more two-way conversations on job-related matters. Also, they spent more time communicating information to their employees and giving *general* work orders. Low-rated foremen gave many more *specific* and *direct* work orders.

Why are some foremen considered "tops" by their managers and regarded so poorly by their subordinates? And, conversely, why are some foremen judged very effective by subordinates and very ineffective by their superiors?

To answer these questions, we developed a "self-report activity questionnaire." Foremen were asked to estimate the frequency with which each job activity normally occurred. The questionnaire included such items as:

> *"An employee asks me for a work assignment."*
> *"An inspector suggests a way for me to correct a reject."*
> *"My general foreman asks my advice on a production problem."*
> *"I am notified about a change in my production schedule."*
> *"An employee tells me of a safety hazard."*
> *"I tell an employee how to do a job."*
> *"I check jobs in my area to see how they are coming along."*
> *"I discuss with a planner a job rate that is too high."*
> *"I discuss an employee's attendance record with him."*
> *"I ask another foreman to expedite a job for me."*

We found that those foremen rated high by their superiors but low by subordinates were the busiest and most production-oriented of all the men studied. In general their activity patterns were similar to those of foremen who had been rated low by both groups. Evidently this activity pattern is not popular with subordinates but fits some superiors' ideas about the ways in which a good foreman should operate.

The foremen rated low by superiors but high by subordinates showed almost the opposite pattern. They were the least busy of all the foremen, spent less time on production and related kinds of activities, and reported relatively few contacts with their own employees. Their supervisory style could best be described as laissez faire. We can only speculate on the reasons for subordinates' high rating of these foremen. Perhaps in the highly simplified jobs that characterize most factory operations, the employees really do not need much supervision and therefore prefer a boss who is not continually looking over their shoulders and giving them orders.

In sum, foremen rated high by both superiors and subordinates were more likely than others to give general supervision. Those rated low by subordinates gave much more detailed supervision, regardless of how they were rated by their superiors.

Foremen have a very frustrating job. Their responsibilities are very broad, but are shared with many other people. In fact, studies show that foremen have *almost no complete responsibility*. The production-control experts decide when a job is to be done; methods engineers decide how and to what standards; quality-control specialists set quality standards and monitor results; other specialists provide maintenance. Even in the personnel area, if a grievance is filed the specialist in union relations usually takes over.

The foreman's lack of complete authority often seemed to undermine his relationship with those in his work group. His decisions were often reversed, and he frequently found it difficult to get things done when they required the cooperation of others. In many instances he had little influence up the line. His role seemed that of a straw boss, and the pressures of the job allowed him to be merely a troubleshooter. The study showed that he was often so harried that when a personnel problem did arise, he mishandled it.

Other problems in running the shop seemed to stem from the long lines of authority in each of the critical functional areas, for example, production control, methods, quality control, maintenance. The centralization of these functions apparently made it more difficult for a foreman to make decisions that would be appropriate to conditions at the moment. Long-range planning and development activities tended to get short shrift.

These characteristics of highly centralized shop systems, combined with findings from the foreman's job studies, provided important clues on how the shop could be better organized—and especially how the first-line supervisor's job could be redesigned to get better results.

The facts suggested that a decentralized form of shop organization would be more effective, making the first-line supervisor's job less frustrating and more manageable.

It seemed best to divide the shop into relatively independent units. Each unit would be completely responsible for its own production objectives. These units would contain two or three times more employees than the average foreman's group. A single manager would then be given full responsibility for the unit. He would receive whatever help he needed to get the job done. Thus, he might have reporting to him one or more specialists in quality control, maintenance, and the like. These specialists would not only carry out the work they normally performed, but would also take over some tasks formerly done by the foreman. They would no longer report to others higher up in their specialty.

In the decentralized shop, each manager can give only general supervision because of the size of his work group. But the hourly employee can also call on technical experts for help within his own work group. Control of operations is achieved by holding the unit manager responsible for results. Since he has complete control of all functions needed to perform the work of the unit, he may be held accountable for costs, quality, and schedules within his unit.

As part of our research, this unit type of organization was established experimentally in two kinds of operations. The first unit was in a plant that fabricated and assembled a *single* product. In this instance, units were organized to carry out subfunctions in the manufacturing sequence. The second unit was set up in a plant that produced a *variety* of products. Here the experimental units were established to manufacture a total product or product line.

After the reorganized units had been operating for several months, an intensive study was made of the activities of the key personnel. The same research approach was used as in the study of effective and ineffective foremen.

The observed data showed that the new unit managers were spending a higher percentage of their total time on longer-range, "planning ahead" activities than were the typical foremen. As Figure 3 shows, they spent

Figure 3. Percent of time spent by unit managers and foremen on short-range and long-range production activities.

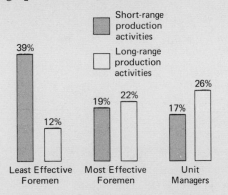

26 percent of their time on longer-range activities, such as working on methods, equipment, time standards, scheduling, and cost reduction. Only 17 percent of their time was spent on such short-range activities as checking the status of jobs, arranging for materials, establishing job

priorities, and such. This was an improvement on the pattern of the "effective" foremen in the previous study. It was in marked contrast to the pattern that characterized the least effective foremen.

It was surprising to find that unit managers were not spending as much time on activities classified as "personnel administration" as the effective foremen were in the previous study. As Figure 4 shows, unit

Figure 4. Percent of time spent on personnel administration activities.

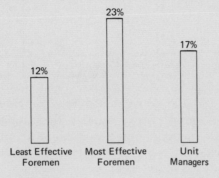

managers spent approximately 17 percent of their time in these activities. The most effective foremen had spent an average of 23 percent, and the least effective foremen had spent only about 12 percent. This discrepancy was surprising, since the number of workers reporting to each unit manager was at least 50 percent greater than in the previous study. Since the managers were able to delegate much of their short-range production work to specialists, we had expected that they would spend more time on personnel or employee-relations activities. We did find that effective leaders spent more time in personal contact than ineffective ones.

Though less time than we expected was spent in activities classified as personnel administration, when total time spent in contact with other people was measured, the unit managers were well ahead of both foremen groups (Fig. 5), but like the foremen, the managers did not spend the extra time with their own employees. They spent it with other managerial and staff personnel.

Observation of the functional specialists showed them spending almost all of their time on short-range problems. Consistent with the theory of the new organization, the major responsibility for technical leadership was delegated to these specialists. They seemed to be carrying out their task very well.

Communication patterns also appeared to be superior under the new system. The unit managers had fewer informal contacts, but they held more regularly scheduled formal meetings with their specialists and line operators. They engaged in a significantly higher percentage of two-way

Figure 5. Percent of time spent by foremen and unit managers in contact with others.

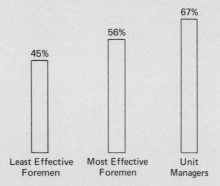

discussions than did the conventional foremen. Moreover, a majority of production-line employees expressed the opinion that, since the change, they were "getting more information about what is going on in the department or plant." In other ways, too, communication patterns for unit managers were found to be more like those of the most effective foremen.

The survey of production-line workers showed that most of them liked the unit form of organization better than the old setup. Some workers, however, expressed confusion about who was the boss in specific situations. Because of the distinction between managerial and technical leadership, they were not always sure where to turn for guidance. Their confusion may have been compounded in many instances because the man who had been their foreman under the old setup was now their group's production specialist.

Many departments of the General Electric Company have adopted the unit type of shop structure. In fact, a majority of General Electric departments now use some adaptation of the structure described here. Where departments have reported difficulties with the new system, often these have stemmed from a lack of understanding by key personnel of the nature and extent of their responsibilities. Problems also have arisen when units grew too large. In such cases, many production-line employees felt that they no longer had a boss to turn to with their problems.

Overall, however, organization of the shop into decentralized units, each with more complete autonomy than is usually assigned to foremen, seemed to provide a solution to a surprising range of the difficulties encountered in traditional shop organizations.

HERBERT H. MEYER

Feedback
That Spurs Performance

General Electric Company

The ways that managers motivate their workers have been studied in a major research program at General Electric. One factor was common to the various techniques surveyed: in some form, all involved a knowledge of results, or feedback. If a person is to do a job effectively, he must know the results of his past performance. With such feedback, he can guide his subsequent work and take any appropriate corrective actions. This may sound like nothing more than common sense. But application of this principle has proved much more complicated than it appears.

Carefully controlled studies have shown that a number of factors must be present in order for feedback to be useful to a worker. The most obvious is that the information fed back must be *precise*. Suppose the worker is merely told that the last ten parts he produced had to be rejected because they did not meet specifications. He would clearly not be able to correct his performance as quickly as if he were told that the parts were rejected because they were approximately one ten-thousandth of an inch too large.

Feedback must also be *timely*. Weekly performance reports are much less useful than those prepared daily, or, better yet, hourly.

Usefulness also varies with *the worker's ability to correct his performance*. A golfer gets immediate and continuous knowledge-of-results feedback. The ball either gets close to the hole or it doesn't. But without the skills to correct his performance, the golfer will show no real improvement. Similarly, a worker may not be able to apply his knowledge of results constructively because he lacks needed skills.

Probably the single most important condition influencing the effect of feedback in an organizational setting is the *source* of the information. Our golfer is likely to have one reaction to an opinion fed back by a professional, and a somewhat different reaction to the identical opinion fed back by his wife. In the case of a worker, feedback from a boss

199

is likely to be colored by the knowledge that he has control over one's career. Any worker must have *incentive* to maintain or improve his performance. Without some such desire or incentive, there can be no improvement.

Reactions also vary according to the worker's judgment of whether the information is *subjective* or *objective*. This is especially true if the feedback includes not only knowledge of past results, but also suggested corrections. Subjective feedback may be seen as ambiguous, biased, or open to challenge. In industry, unfortunately, much of the data fed back to the worker is subjective. This seriously weakens its effectiveness.

We considered all these factors in setting up our research on the motivational impact of feedback. Our program included examination of objective feedback in highly structured factory jobs. Part of the project was intended to demonstrate dollars-and-cents gains to be realized through the application of feedback principles to jobs found in a shop. We also studied indirect means of improving feedback in complex professional positions, where measuring results is difficult and largely subjective.

We focused on operations that were causing management serious problems. One of these involved the machining of a cylinder for a compressor. The machines that performed this operation generated slight variations in bore size; therefore, workers were required to measure and classify each finished cylinder by bore size. They were to stamp a "1" on those within the lower half of the acceptable range, and a "2" on those in the upper half.

This seems a relatively straightforward operation. Yet many of the cylinders delivered for assembly had to be rejected because of misclassification as to bore size. Many that should have been stamped "1" were stamped "2," and vice versa. Since there were several operators involved in this machining and classifying, there was no way to identify who was at fault. Various approaches were tried in an attempt to solve the problem.

The first stage of the study lasted seven weeks and used commonly employed procedures: communication, persuasion, and instruction. The foreman talked to each operator individually, informed him of the problem, showed him examples of misclassified parts. They discussed the need for improvement, and reviewed the work-methods sheet. As Figure 1 illustrates, this traditional approach was a disappointment. It yielded no significant or lasting improvement. Moreover, the operators' reactions were negative. Each disclaimed responsibility; each expressed resentment at the foreman's apparent insinuation that he had not done the job well.

In a second seven-week stage, knowledge-of-results feedback was added. Performance measurement and feedback were accomplished sim-

Figure 1.

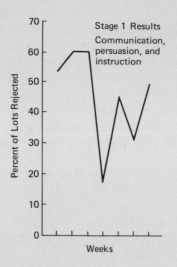

ply by adding a distinguishing mark to the numeral stamp used by each operator to classify the finished parts. Thus, a worker could be notified immediately of parts rejected because of misclassification made by him. The results of this method are illustrated in Figure 2.

For a while, the percentage of lots rejected because of improper classification dropped to about one-fourth the old level. But toward the end of the seven-week period, performance drifted back toward the previous poor levels. At first, each operator was somewhat surprised, embarrassed, and anxious when he got clear evidence that it was he who was misclassifying cylinders. After a few weeks, however, this reaction wore off until all the operators seemed quite unconcerned about poor performance.

Figure 2.

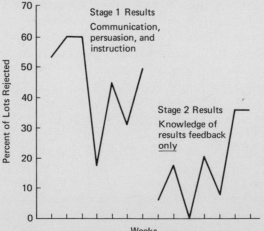

During the final seven weeks of the study the primary intent was to observe the effects of reinforcing the established feedback procedure with *reward for good performance and penalty for poor performance.* Unfortunately the use of positive rewards proved to be so difficult that we settled for negative rewards only. These were penalties in the form of reprimands, written warning notices, and threats of more drastic disciplinary actions.

The results were dramatic. Figure 3 shows them. The number of lots rejected for misclassification of bore size dropped abruptly to zero, where it stayed throughout the last six weeks of the study.

Figure 3.

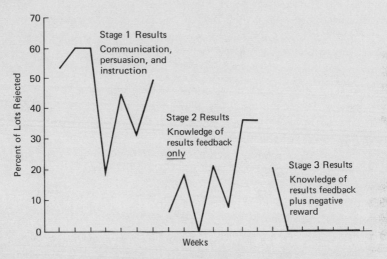

Our ensuing studies also tended to focus on one or two particularly troublesome operations, although one study involved all of the tasks on a complete assembly line. In every instance, significant improvements in quality of output, and in total manufacturing costs, were realized when the following specific conditions were present:

☐ The operator knew what aspect of his performance was not up to par.

☐ He knew precisely what corrective actions on his part were called for to improve his performance.

☐ He had the ability to take the corrective actions called for, or was provided with the necessary instruction or training to improve his operation.

☐ He perceived that it was in his own best interest to undertake the corrective actions demanded; in other words, he had some *incentive* to improve.

This may seem an elaboration of the obvious, but experience indicates that these conditions are often overlooked in the design of factory jobs. After the results of our research in this area were published, we received reports from other managers that confirmed our results by describing the benefits realized by application of these simple principles—especially where quality or quantity of output had been a critical problem.

A man should know where he stands, and toward that end a manager should periodically discuss an employee's performance with him. Yet we frequently got reports of negative results from these exchanges. In fact, managers would almost invariably drop the program if they were not strongly pressed to carry it out. It seemed logical to assume that if the manager had found this a valuable technique, he would have been eager to continue its use on his own initiative.

More evidence on the negative side came from interviews with employees after experience with such appraisals. Very few could cite examples of constructive action they had taken, or of significant improvements they had achieved, on the basis of suggestions made to them in the annual interview with their boss.

Because of this contradictory evidence, an intensive study was clearly in order and several surveys were therefore undertaken.

First came an analysis of the psychology of the appraisal interview process. We began by assuming that our theory of the value of feedback was sound. Innumerable psychological studies seemed to confirm this. In fact, experience since the beginning of time had demonstrated that a man's knowledge of past results could help him improve his future performance. Yet we also knew that appraisal interviews based on this theory were often ineffective. Why? We focused on the different methods of conducting appraisal interviews and on other typical situations in which knowledge-of-results feedback had proved helpful.

The crucial difference seemed to be this: the appraisal interviews usually involved communication of *subjective judgments by a person who had a good deal of control over the listener's fate.* It was therefore easy to suspect that the feedback might be biased, inaccurate, or incomplete.

A person with sound mental health, it had been shown, has an image or concept of himself that he values. He will strive to maintain or enhance this image. If his favorable self-image is threatened, he is very likely to use some form of rationalization to protect, or defend, himself. He may blame his co-workers or his work environment; he may minimize the importance or validity of the criticism. He tries to maintain his sense of self-approval.

The essential point about defensiveness in this context is that it is a rejection of criticism. Thus, in an appraisal interview, the subordinate who reacts defensively to criticism is, in effect, rejecting the validity of the feedback. In such circumstances, no one should be surprised if he fails to take constructive action to improve. A study was designed to test the validity of this expectation.

Almost all General Electric Company units have some sort of formal appraisal program. Each calls for periodic interviews, to be conducted by a professional, with administrative personnel; some also include other salaried or hourly-paid employees. Since the company setup is decentralized, however, the procedure varies considerably from one department to another. To test the effectiveness of performance appraisals fairly, we selected for the study a department judged to have an especially good program.

In this department, appraisals were based on job responsibilities rather than on personal characteristics. Intensive training had been given to managers in the use of the appraisal system and in techniques for conducting the interviews. The program had the strong backing of the department's top manager and it was policed diligently by the personnel staff. As a result, more than 90 percent of the exempt employees were interviewed and appraised annually.

The appraisal program was designed to serve two major purposes. One was primarily administrative: the appraisal was used as a means for justifying recommended salary changes. The second objective was of greater interest to us in our research: it was to provide feedback to each worker. The interview was used as a formal opportunity for the manager to express approval and appreciation of a worker's good performance, or to discuss needed improvements. To this end, the manager was required to draw up for the subordinate a blueprint of plans and goals that would help him improve his performance, as well as to develop general skills to qualify him for promotion in the future.

However, preliminary interviews with managers and subordinates dictated a change in the usual procedure. It became evident that the issue of salary so dominated the appraisal interview that neither party was left in a good mood to discuss plans for improving the subordinate's performance. We decided, therefore, to alter the format. We asked the managers to split their usual appraisal discussion into two parts. In one interview they were to discuss appraisal and salary. A second interview, about two weeks later, was to be devoted entirely to planning for performance improvement.

A cross section of employees at professional and administrative levels participated in the study. Included were engineers, engineering support technicians, foremen, and specialists in manufacturing, customer service, marketing, finance, and purchasing. Ninety-two persons were appraised. We interviewed them, and they completed questionnaires both before and after they were judged by the managers.

Our interviews were designed to serve two purposes: first, to assess changes in the attitudes of the subordinates toward their managers and toward the appraisal system in general after each of the discussions; second, to obtain from them a self-appraisal before they met with the manager, and a report on the manager's assessment after they had met. This was required in order to determine how a discrepancy in appraisals might affect an employee's reactions to the program.

In addition, each of the appraisal and goal-planning discussions was recorded by trained observers—graduate students in the industrial management program of a local university. In the appraisal discussions, for example, the observers recorded the amount of criticism and praise offered by the manager and the employee's reactions to these comments. In the goal-planning sessions, the observers recorded the amount of say the subordinate seemed to have about the goals that were formulated and agreed upon.

As the last step, a follow-up check was made approximately ten to twelve weeks after the goal-planning session. The purpose was to obtain estimates from both the managers and the subordinates of the degree to which goals or improvements discussed in the appraisal had been achieved.

In general, managers participating in the study completed their appraisal forms in a thorough and conscientious manner. Appraisal interviews ranged in length from approximately thirty to ninety minutes. On the average, the manager covered thirty-two specific performance items, offering praise on nineteen items and criticism on thirteen items. Typically, praise was more likely to relate to general performance, whereas criticism was more often focused on specific items.

The average subordinate reacted defensively to seven of the manager's criticisms per interview, or about 50 percent. Constructive responses to a criticism were rarely observed. The average was less than one per interview. The discussion of salary usually took place at the end of the interview, after the appraisal of performance.

Not surprisingly, the more criticism the boss had to offer during the session, the greater the likelihood of defensiveness on the part of the person being appraised. Men who received an above-average number of criticisms showed more than five times as much defensive behavior as those who received a below-average number of criticisms. The ratio of defenses per criticism increased with the number of criticisms. Men who received a below-average number of criticisms reacted defensively only about one out of three times. On the other hand, those who received an above-average number reacted defensively almost two times out of three.

Before the discussion, each subordinate was asked to assess his own performance. This self-appraisal was based on a comparison of his performance with that of others in the department who were working on similar jobs. A percentile scale was used for the comparison. After the session, each man was asked to indicate on the same scale where he thought his manager had put him.

The average preappraisal self-estimate of performance of the men in this study was at the seventy-seventh percentile. Only two out of ninety-two participants estimated their performance below the average point on the scale. This finding is consistent with the results of previous research on self-esteem.

The same men were asked, after the sessions, how they thought their bosses had rated them. The average figure had dropped to the sixty-fifth percentile. The majority (75 out of 92) saw their manager's evaluation as less favorable than their own. To these men, obviously, the discussion with the manager was a deflating experience. It is not surprising that they reacted defensively in the interview.

Ten to twelve weeks after the appraisal, *men who had received an above-average number of criticisms generally showed less improvement* in the areas in which they had been criticized than men who had received less criticism. (See Figure 4.) At first we thought this difference

Figure 4. Achievement of goals set during appraisal process (percent).

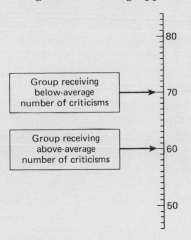

might be accounted for because the men who received more criticism would probably be poorer performers in general. There was little evidence, however, to support this idea. Those men who got an above-average number of criticisms also received, on the average, slightly lower summary ratings of overall performance. They did not suffer lower salary increases, however, even though salary increases were supposed to reflect differences in job performance.

An alternative explanation seemed more plausible: A large number of criticisms undermined self-esteem enough to disrupt subsequent performance. We had assumed that the destructive effects would be greater among those who were already low in self-esteem and that the employee who had greater self-confidence in his ability to do the job would react more constructively to criticism. The study proved this expectation to be correct.

There was still further evidence that criticism had a negative effect on performance. It showed up when we looked at performance in areas given special emphasis by the manager's criticisms. In the interview following the discussion, each man was asked to indicate which aspect of his performance had been most criticized by the manager. A follow-up check revealed that subsequent improvement of these most-criticized aspects was considerably *less* than improvement in other areas.

If criticism has so negative an effect, common sense might lead us to assume that praise would have the opposite result. It seems reasonable to expect, for example, that the man who receives a lot of praise would be less defensive when criticized, have more positive attitudes toward his appraisal discussion, and try hard to "keep up the good work."

Actually, no such effects were observed. We compared the reactions of men who were praised many times with the reactions of those who received little praise. We found that the well-praised were just as likely to be defensive when criticized, that they achieved no higher percentage of goals, and that they showed no differences in their attitudes toward the manager. We found, too, that the number of times a man was praised was related to the number of criticisms he received: The man who was criticized more was also praised more. Evidently, the managers were using the "sandwich" technique; when the manager wanted to mention a shortcoming, he sandwiched it in between two compliments. As a matter of fact, the observers who sat in on these sessions noted that those appraised typically gave no response of any kind to praise. They were sensitive only to criticism. After the manager had used the sandwich technique a few times, the subordinate seemed to become conditioned to expect that any praise would be followed by criticism.

Most of the goals formulated in the goal-planning sessions related to details of performance that had been discussed in the earlier appraisal interviews. Nonetheless, many areas of needed improvement which managers had pointed out in the discussions were not subsequently translated into goals in the goal-planning sessions. In fact, for many who were appraised, that aspect of performance which the manager had emphasized as *most* in need of improvement was never translated into a goal.

When goal achievement was being measured ten to twelve weeks after the goal-planning sessions, a check was made on progress or improved performance of (1) items subsequently translated into goals, and (2) other items that had been mentioned in the appraisal discussion as needing improvement, but which had not been subsequently translated into specific goals.

As Figure 5 shows, the average estimate of accomplishment for those

Figure 5. Goal planning and improvement in performance.

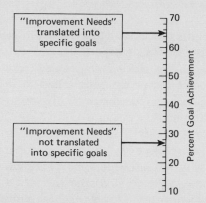

items that were translated into goals was 65 percent. The rate of accomplishment for those items that were *not* translated into goals was about 27 percent. It is obvious that significantly greater progress in improving performance was made on those items for which specific goals were set. Our conclusions were these:

1. Periodic appraisals are of questionable value, and may be frustrating for everyone concerned.
2. Coaching should be a day-to-day activity, not once a year.
3. Knowledge of results is important for improvement.
4. Far superior results are achieved when the manager and his subordinate set specific goals rather than merely discussing needed improvements in performance.

The study did not lead us to the conclusion that all appraisal activities should be abandoned merely because some effects were negative. If the right atmosphere could be created, it still seemed probable that discussion of past results between subordinate and manager could be helpful in guiding future performance. Thus our next experiment was an attempt to *create* a favorable atmosphere for such discussion.

When a manager discusses his appraisal of a subordinate's performance with his employee, he is automatically cast in the role of judge. The subordinate becomes the defendant. If, on the other hand, responsibility for the performance review were placed in the hands of the subordinate, and if he were to bring his appraisal to the manager for discussion, the manager would be cast automatically in the role of counselor. Upon such a restructuring of roles, we would expect the subordinate to be more willing to reveal shortcomings and areas for improvement. The manager would be in a better position to provide coaching without creating the threatening atmosphere often associated with appraisals.

This study was carried out, therefore, to compare results in subordinate-prepared and manager-prepared performance reviews. Some of the specific questions we attempted to answer were:

☐ How do the two parties react to subordinate-prepared appraisals?
☐ Are subordinates likely to be constructive, rather than defensive, if the discussion is based on a self-appraisal?
☐ Under what conditions is one approach superior to the other?
☐ What effect does either approach have on subsequent subordinate-manager relations? On subsequent performance?

This investigation was based on appraisal interviews for eighty-one professional and administrative employees. Thirty-five managers agreed to take part. Each employee had at least two appraisal discussions within a one-month period. Several had three or more appraisals scheduled.

Employees and appraisers were interviewed before and after each discussion to assess reactions. A follow-up check was also made twelve weeks later to find out how much improvement in performance had actually been achieved. Each manager was asked to carry out his first scheduled appraisal in the normal fashion—that is, based on the man-ager-prepared appraisal form. After he had completed the first discussion, he was told the purpose of the study. He was then asked to instruct the next subordinate scheduled for a session to rate his own performance on the standard form, and to bring the completed questionnaire to the interview. The ensuing discussion was based on the subordinate's own appraisal. The manager was told, however, not to accept the subordinate's ratings without protest if he disagreed with any of them. The manager was instructed to insist that self-appraisals he didn't agree with be modified to satisfy him with the final ratings at the conclusion of the discussion.

Forty-one appraisal discussions were based on the usual manager-pre-pared forms; forty others were based on the forms prepared by the subordinate. The two experimental groups did not differ significantly in average age, education, service, or position level. They were also comparable in attitude and other variables as measured on a question-naire, which was administered before the appraisal discussion.

The majority of the managers who participated in this study felt that the employee's self-prepared appraisal was an improvement over the one prepared by the manager. Typical comments were:

"The employee got a better feel of where he stands."
"It helped both of us more than the standard appraisal would have."
"I think we should adopt this approach."

In general, their comments suggested that more information had been exchanged, and that both subordinate and manager saw more clearly into problem areas. Most of the managers also thought that employees appraised their own performance quite accurately. In most of the cases where they felt that the self-appraisal was not accurate, it was because they thought the employee had underrated himself. Managers also reported that when the employee's rating was higher or lower than the manager's, the manager had an unusually good opportunity to find out what the employee's problem was. An inaccurate appraisal was often more useful to the manager in getting at problems than an accurate self-appraisal. Many managers commented that they uncovered new, or more comprehensive, information when this approach was used. They learned something about the way a subordinate perceived both his work and himself. The method created a useful upward flow of information.

As Figure 6 illustrates, those employees preparing their own appraisals

Figure 6. Performance ratings three months after appraisal.

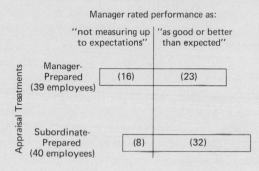

were only half as likely to fall short of their manager's expectations in subsequent performance as those appraised under the manager-prepared approach. At first, some managers were hesitant to use the subordinate-prepared appraisal with employees whose performance was only fair or poor. They felt that an appraisal discussion based on a subordinate-prepared form would make it more difficult to coach the employee on improvements. Not only were their fears unfounded, but the opposite proved to be true. The subordinate-prepared appraisal had much greater impact on employees considered below average than on employees whose performance was above average.

The study showed that low-rated employees who had discussions based on manager-prepared appraisals were often found, three months later, to be performing at a level which did not measure up to the manager's expectations. Low-rated employees in the self-appraisal group, on the other hand, were much more likely to be performing at a level exceeding the manager's expectations.

Feedback, too, was superior under the self-prepared approach, even though the manager's feedback was not as direct as in the traditional interview. For example, employees who were rated low in performance before the appraisal and who used the self-prepared form were more likely to say afterward that they now understood better what their managers expected them to achieve on their jobs. They were also more likely to consider the appraisal discussion an important administrative tool than were the men exposed to the manager-prepared appraisal treatment. Several managers even volunteered the observation that the most fruitful appraisal sessions they'd ever had were those with poorer performing employees in which the discussion was based on a subordinate's self-assessment.

Discussions based on self-review were not, however, equally effective with all employees. There were two situations in which the more traditional approach seemed preferable. The first was with employees who had never had an appraisal discussion with their present manager. The manager-prepared appraisal was preferred in most such cases, since it seemed to be a useful way for the employee to learn something about the manager's standards of performance and his measurement of results.

The second was with managers who had a reputation for being rather authoritarian in their style of leadership. Here, the self-review approach seemed to be regarded by both parties as somewhat inappropriate. The authoritarian boss was unwilling to give much weight to a subordinate's self-assessment, and both sides knew it. Employees with a high need for independence reacted most favorably to the self-review approach. In the questionnaire given before the appraisal interview, several items were designed to measure this "need for independence." Employees whose score was high in this measure gave more favorable responses regarding the benefit they had derived from their appraisal discussions than did those who had scored low.

The study indicated strongly that discussions between an employee and his manager which focus on specific, short-term plans and goals yield much greater returns in improved job performance than do conventional appraisal discussions.

As a result, another study was set up in the same department to test a formalized procedure incorporating work planning and goal setting as methods for achieving superior job performance. The new plan, given the name "Work Planning and Review," called for periodic meetings between the manager and each of his subordinates. In the course of these meetings, new goals were established, progress relating to previously set goals was reviewed, and solutions were found for job-related problems. The purpose was to create a meeting in which the manager and the subordinate could discuss job performance in detail without the subordinate becoming defensive.

This new approach differed from the usual program in that (1) there are more frequent discussions of performance, (2) *there are no summary judgments or ratings*, (3) salary discussions are held separately, and (4) the emphasis is on *mutual* goal planning and problem solving. In the employee-manager discussions, the two parties consider specific work goals. Measures are agreed upon and deadlines set whenever possible. These goals stem, of course, from broader department goals. They are defined in relation to the position or function of the employee.

About half the key managers in the department decided to abandon the comprehensive annual appraisal program in their groups and to adopt the new Work Planning and Review program. The other half were reluctant to make a major change at that time and decided to continue with the performance appraisal program. But they decided to try to make it more effective.

This division provided a natural way for us to compare the effectiveness of the two approaches. We decided to evaluate the new program in the light of the objectives usually stated for the annual comprehensive appraisal, namely, to provide knowledge of results to employees in order to motivate and help them to do a better job.

The design of the study was simple. Before any changes were made, a survey was conducted among the employees who were to be affected by these programs in order to provide baseline data. The Work Planning and Review program was then implemented in the groups whose managers had elected it, while the other groups continued with periodic appraisals. One year later, the same questionnaire was used again to assess the attitudes of those affected by the two programs.

The results were convincing. The group that continued with performance appraisal showed no change in any of the areas measured. The group that participated in the new work-planning program, by contrast, expressed significantly more favorable attitudes in the second survey than in the first on nearly all the questions. Specifically, their attitudes had changed affirmatively with regard to:

☐ The amount of help the manager was giving them toward improving on the job.

☐ The degree to which the manager was receptive to new ideas and approaches.

☐ The ability of the manager to plan.

☐ The degree to which the manager made use of their abilities and experiences.

☐ The degree to which they felt their goals were the proper ones.

☐ The degree to which they received help from the manager in planing their future job development.

☐ The overall value of job-performance discussions with the manager.

Even more dramatically, there was strong evidence that employees exposed to the Work Planning and Review program were much more likely to take specific actions toward improved performance than were those whose managers continued with the earlier appraisal approach.

After our study, the new program was recommended to all managers. A number of departments in the General Electric Company adopted it. Most of them found the approach beneficial. In a few instances, however, managers had less success than they had hoped for. We decided therefore to conduct an intensive study of the manager interviews.

By finding out just how Work Planning and Review discussions were being conducted, we hoped to gain some insight into how these interviews could be made even more effective. A special goal was to learn how variations in the way managers conducted these interviews affected the degree of improvement in job performance. Each employee was interviewed and completed a questionnaire. Then an observer sat in on the discussion between the employee and the manager. Both were interviewed after the discussion to assess reactions, and a follow-up check was made twelve to fourteen weeks later.

Altogether fifty-six discussions were observed. Two general findings stood out.

First, most of the Work Planning and Review discussions were highly *participative* in nature; in other words, the subordinate contributed as much to the discussion as did the manager. This had not previously been true in most performance-appraisal discussions, which were distinctly manager-dominated.

Second, most of the time was spent in finding solutions to problems related to carrying out job assignments and achieving goals. Figure 7

Figure 7. What managers and subordinates discuss in W.P.&R. interviews.

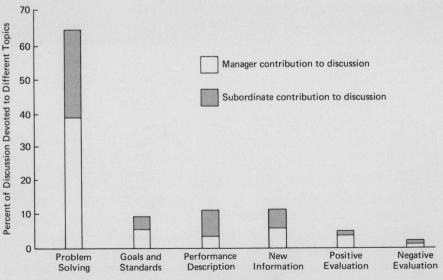

illustrates how time was spent in these discussions, and to what extent each party contributed to various topics. The sessions typically involved very little evaluation of performance; this was usually not touched on by the manager. Somewhat more time was devoted to a straight description of performance—that is, reporting what had happened without rating the results. In this discussion, the subordinate usually played the leading role. The setting of specific goals and standards of performance took a relatively small portion of the time. Goal setting usually resulted from a problem-solving discussion. In some instances, the goal was stated first. Then there was a lengthy discussion of the problems associated with reaching it.

Perhaps the most interesting findings of this study concerned the effects of various approaches used by the managers. A *participative* approach was found to be especially effective for employees whose performance rating was below average before their Work Planning and Review interviews. As Figure 8 shows, below-average employees who

Figure 8. With below average performers, subordinates who improved in subsequent performance contributed more in problem-solving discussions.

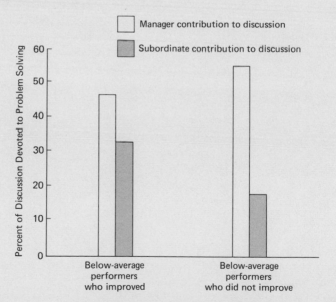

showed subsequent improvement contributed more to the discussions than those who later showed little or no improvement. This finding does not conclusively prove that the greater opportunity to participate was responsible for the improvement. Other explanations could account for it. The manager may have allowed subordinates in whom he had confidence to have more say in the discussions. These employees may also have had more potential for better work. In any event, the employees who participated least in the discussions were the ones who improved least. Thus, it is possible to conclude that domination of the interview by the manager has no positive effect, even though there may be a natural inclination to direct a poorly performing employee.

A second interesting finding crops up in relation to subsequent job performance. The least change for the better was noted among those men whose Work Planning and Review interviews had been conducted as though they were performance-appraisal interviews. The old cycle observed in the performance-appraisal study was repeated: the pattern of criticism by the manager prompts defensiveness on the part of the subordinate, followed by a lack of improvement on the job. This effect was especially noticeable among employees who had been rated below-average before their work-planning discussions. As Figure 9 shows, em-

Figure 9. Below-average performers who improved in subsequent performance received more positive feedback from the manager about past performance.

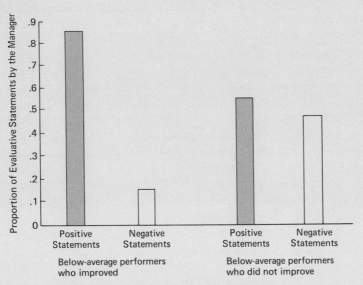

ployees who received the *most* criticism from their managers in the work-planning conferences showed the *least* improvement thereafter.

Our research certainly suggests that feedback of the results and indications of past performance is a necessary condition for improvement of future performance. It is also plain that the manner in which such information is communicated is a vital factor in determining its effects.

It has been shown, for example, that objective information fed back through impersonal channels results in improvements in performance—provided the recipient has the necessary abilities and the incentive to do better. On the other hand, subjective information communicated personally may in many instances have no effect, or even a negative effect. If it is perceived as an ego threat, it provokes a defensive emotional reaction.

These findings present difficulties for the manager. The idea that carefully thought out and documented suggestions for improvement can be self-defeating seems to violate common sense. But, unfortunately, most measures for gauging results or efficiency are largely subjective. This is especially true in the complex jobs found at professional and administrative levels.

Fortunately, there are at least two approaches or techniques the manager can use to motivate improvement. The first entails more systematic planning activities than most managers normally use. Careful planning, setting specific goals, and explicitly defining and agreeing upon expected results can translate what might be ambiguous and subjective feedback into relatively objective terms.

The second technique is to permit each employee to participate, both in appraising the results of his past performance and in planning improvements for future performance. One of the fortunate elements of the Work Planning and Review program is that it accommodates subordinate participation easily. Participation is natural in the processes of planning work, setting goals, and reviewing performance.

By systematic planning the manager can effectively control performance in his organization. Systematic planning helps to insure that each member of his unit has a clear understanding of (1) the objectives of the organization as a whole, (2) the plans and goals of his particular component, (3) the way these plans and goals contribute to overall objectives, and (4) the role he plays in achieving all these goals and objectives.

These conclusions, drawn from an extensive research program, may seem obvious. Experts in administrative practices have long emphasized the importance of planning, and social scientists have extolled the motivational value of participation in decision making. But we believe that our research has added something more. It has contributed a much more thorough understanding of the behavioral dynamics underlying many motivational techniques. We can now translate general recommendations into specifics, and we feel confident that significant, tangible, and practical improvements will be realized.

MELVIN SORCHER

Motivating the Factory Worker

General Electric Company

I started in classification, and I couldn't understand why people sent me devices with bent leads. I moved to the assembly area and understood bent leads, but now I couldn't understand why I got bad pellets. Then I moved to processing, and I saw how the bad ones got out. But I didn't appreciate why we got all the faulty wafers. I moved on to wafer processing, and now I've got the whole picture. I think I can do my job better now that I know what problems I'm giving those other girls.

WORKER'S COMMENT TO HER FOREMAN AFTER A PLANT TOUR MADE AS PART OF A JOB-TRAINING PROGRAM.

Despite advances in technology and changes in our culture, the content of most factory jobs and the style of supervision in the shop are not very different from what they were at the turn of the century. The result, in many cases, is a late twentieth-century American in an early twentieth-century job; and the two are incompatible. The typical approach to factory management takes into consideration neither the personal desires nor the expectations of employees. Jobs are designed for "efficiency." Consequently, assembly line workers report that their tasks have little meaning to them, that they are simply endless and boring.

Job simplification enables management to hire unskilled employees at minimum rates, reduces training costs, and limits the possibility of costly errors. But job simplification has eliminated the interest and challenge that employees need in their jobs. The resulting boredom, indifference, and resentment find expression in poor workmanship, high turnover, absenteeism, grievances, and even in wild-cat strikes. In the long run, it may well be that the negative effects of simplification outweigh the planned savings in cost.

The personnel research staff of the General Electric Company decided to study this problem because of its enormous practical implications. If the causes of poor morale could be isolated and corrective steps undertaken, the company would be better able to keep its employees, improve performance, lower costs, and attract new workers. The research program was designed to answer such questions as these:

Can factory jobs be made more meaningful?

Can the factory employee be motivated to become more involved in his work?

What would be the effect of higher motivation on workmanship, productivity, and job attitudes?

The first step was to identify some of the factors in jobs that influence attitudes and performance. Supervisors in five large plants were asked to identify groups that had consistently shown either very high or very low quality of output. From this number, twenty-five groups judged to be at the high end of the quality-output scale and twenty-five groups at the low end were selected for study. The foreman of each group was interviewed to find out about such aspects of jobs as cycle time, repetitiveness, and training required. In addition, a random sample of employees from each work group was selected to complete a brief questionnaire designed to measure several other job-related attitudes—pride in work, sense of accomplishment, monotony, identification with the product being made, and attitudes toward management. The sum of the scores in this attitude questionnaire constituted the measure of "motivation" for this exploratory study.

Comparison of high-rated and low-rated work groups showed that, in most instances, factors associated with poor performance were also associated with negative job attitudes. The following sections discuss the factors that were found to contribute importantly to the employees' level of performance.

Job Training. In general, positive work-related attitudes were associated with a greater amount of job training. Among the fourteen groups working on very simple jobs for which workers received little technical training, ten were low-performing groups. In other groups that had been given more extensive training, the performance level was significantly higher.

Job Understanding. In forty-one of the fifty work groups studied, employees had no conception of the completed product on which they were working. Many, particularly those doing highly repetitive operations, reported that the work just seemed to go on and on, endlessly. Most of the groups either received feedback only when quality dropped below acceptable standards or got none at all. In these groups, performance was low. Why should anyone care about endlessly inserting screws into parts whose final destiny he or she never knows?

In the few groups in which members received regular feedback, performance was high. Such job understanding can be provided in a number of simple ways. Employees can be informed of the destination and end use of the equipment which they are working on; it might be a TV camera for a football stadium, a sonar for a particular submarine, part of a transformer that will provide power for 800 new homes in California.

Repetitiveness. Performance was lower among groups doing work with very short cycle times, groups in which the number of operations was limited to one or two, and groups where freedom of movement during work was markedly restricted. Thus, it appeared that the oversimplification of jobs actually contributed to higher rather than lower costs.

Added Responsibility. A factor that seemed to improve performance was the assignment of a greater amount of responsibility to each worker. To test the effect of giving employees greater responsibility, a follow-up study was planned. Seven plants at widely scattered locations were involved, and about 700 factory employees served as subjects. They constituted about eighty functionally different work groups, ranging in size from three to forty employees. Measures of attitudes were obtained on a questionnaire completed anonymously and identifiable only by work group. Estimates of quality of workmanship (typically measured by the number of defective units) were obtained from the quality-control and supervisory reports. Measures of the number of units produced were not used in this study, since management established the minimum production rate. Quality, however, was more directly under the control of the employee.

Work groups performing similar operations were classified by the amount of responsibility they had in carrying out their jobs. Comparisons were then made between the groups having greater responsibility and those having less. The results confirmed earlier studies: Performance was higher where responsibility was greater. The employees were less bored, took more pride in their work, and felt a sense of achievement. Attitudes toward the job, the supervisor, and the company were more favorable.

The same results were found when comparing the performance of employees in the day shift with those working at night. In several departments, identical operations were required on the first and second shifts. The second-shift groups generally had less supervision and greater freedom in their work. In this situation, where the workers had more discretionary responsibility, the quality was significantly higher at night.

As an additional check, several first- and second-shift groups that had the same amount of responsibility were compared. The comparisons showed no differences in quality. It seemed evident that greater responsibility offset the negative effects of less popular working hours.

Examination of the effects of an occasional change in work station or task came up with an unexpected result. It was expected that higher performance would be associated with regular rotation, and lower performance with no rotation at all. But no rotation at all turned out to be better than occasional rotation. Why this is so merits further study.

Job Orientation and Role-Training. Seemingly endless routine is often marked by a decline in motivation. But if a worker can somehow be provided with successive goals which are meaningful and logical to him, he may well regard his arrival at each such landmark as an accomplishment. Once he experiences this sense of achievement, he may be on his way to higher performance. Each goal must be worked out in its own unique setting. There can be logical units of production within which it is possible to reach objectives. An imaginative use of goals, adapted to particular work situations, can go far in combating the feelings of futility arising from seemingly endless and unaccented routine.

At the same time that we were considering the use of goals, we obtained evidence that the majority of the workers in every plant were not aware of the importance of their personal role in the manufacturing process. In general, they were even unaware of other operational procedures in the plant.

It was against this background that role-training was carried out on an experimental basis. The employees in this study held jobs either on assembly lines with conveyor belts or at individual work stations where they operated a machine.

Role-training attempts to give the employee an understanding of how his job fits into the entire operation. It embraces a good many activities: plant tours to see how one group's work affects others; talks by managers and specialists; vestibule training to increase proficiency in a given operation; and formal, in-plant training programs. In short, role-training lets the employee see his own job in its total context. All this is a departure from the conventional practice of putting a new employee to work as soon as he has mastered the basics of a simplified job. It adds an extra expense to the training overhead, but it pays off handsomely.

One department provided an opportunity to study effects of role-training in two contrasting types of jobs. A was a high-responsibility area containing eight work groups in which employees had an unusually high amount of responsibility, discretion, variety, and physical movement in their jobs. Here they used different kinds of electronic testing equipment and moved about the floor as they worked. B was a low-responsibility area containing six work groups in which the jobs were more typical of assembly work; employees had very little responsibility, discretion, or variety. They stood or sat at one station and worked with a single tool. The research aim was to introduce role-training in both A and B areas, and to measure and compare the changes in the performance that occurred.

Discussion meetings with foremen were held separately for each work group, and the meetings focused on the part each employee played in manufacturing the product turned out by his department. The groups also learned how their work affected that of work stations down the line. They were taken on a tour to establish a more personal relationship between their own work and that of others. Some of the workers visited a local firm where the departments' products were used. Each group was also asked to set quality goals for itself and to discuss ways of meeting them.

The effects of role-training on quality of performance were rather striking. In Area A (high responsibility), which has a very long job cycle time, the manufacturing engineers anticipated that no measurable improvement would be possible until at least three months after the beginning of the program. Yet well before that time there was substantial improvement in two of the three small work groups, and a modest improvement for the third. In Area B (low responsibility) the results were even more favorable.

For the eight weeks preceding the program, the average proportion of output rated acceptable at two control points was 57.9 percent and 66 percent. At the third control point, machine downtime averaged 3.3 percent. For the nine weeks *following* the program, acceptance percentages rose to 69.2 and 92.1. At the third control point, machine downtime was reduced by 50 percent. Foremen in Area B reported a productivity improvement of about 20 percent.

An engineer who participated in the role-training activities for Area A, but who was not part of the research staff, wrote a report to his own manager. He pointed out that operators had set as one of their own goals a reduction in losses from 26 percent to 15 percent by the end of the month. They proceeded to better this goal. He also listed seventy-two good, directly applicable suggestions contributed by employees during group meetings. On the subjective side, he stated that employees in both areas had expressed great satisfaction in having the chance to see how their work fitted into the total operation—so much so that a number of them had remained after work on their own time to ask questions about the manufacturing process. New employees had subsequently come around to ask when the program would be repeated so that they, too, might participate.

In the third step, management encouraged the operators to assume more responsibility by scheduling some of their own activities and setting their own quality goals. Each operator was informed of the total output required of the area. He was then asked to use this information to determine the order in which he would work on each of several units and to decide how he would approach the diagnosis and repair of these units. In effect, the operators were told to do their own work planning. They were given the necessary information, rather than receiving these assignments from the foreman. For the first time, all those in the group were aware of the output expected from them. Each day, a graph depicting group-performance-to-schedule was posted prominently in the work area. This provided performance-results feedback.

Defects per operator were reduced substantially. Productivity, based on dollar output results, also improved markedly. In addition, records of performance-to-schedule showed that although perfect performance was achieved in only four of the fourteen weeks before the "employees-involvement" programs were introduced, it was achieved in nine of the fourteen weeks following the introduction of the plan.

Job Enlargement. The assembly line was originally set up as a series of sequential processes. Each worker on the line performed a particular operation, then passed the product on to the next operator until the job was complete. The shop manager decided to change this procedure. Instead of having each worker perform one small and discrete operation, he had each employee assemble the entire product.

The program resulted in significant increases in productivity. An average of about forty units per month was turned out in the nine months before the change in assembly methods. In the first month after the change, production increased to fifty-two units, and it continued to rise thereafter, reaching sixty units in the second month and seventy-one in the third.

In another department, the time allowance for the completion of the product had been set at five weeks. Instead, it was taking ten. The manager designed an action program that included role-training to give employees a better understanding of the total operation and its importance, and increased responsibility for daily and weekly schedule planning.

To measure the results of this program, the changes were introduced in only one work group. A second group performing similar operations was considered the control and no changes were made in their customary way of working.

The experimental group showed a striking improvement. Their cycle time was reduced from ten to five weeks—the goal set in the past but never achieved. The control group remained unchanged at ten weeks.

Unless all manufacturing operations become completely automated, which is unlikely, the most efficient functioning of the factory will depend largely upon the efforts of highly motivated employees. The studies we have reported indicate that adding meaning and importance to jobs, and giving increased responsibilities to employees, can result in significant improvements in performance, which can be measured by a decrease in errors and by increase in productivity.

WILLIAM MCGEHEE

Better Training
on the Production Floor

Fieldcrest Mills

Psychologists have been studying the learning process for over a century, yet until recently their research has had minimal influence on the training of factory workers. But this situation is rapidly changing. Training directors and behavioral scientists are now collaborating in a search for scientific answers to problems that have been troubling industry for years.

Industry has turned hopefully to the behavioral sciences for help in reducing training costs while getting better results. And increasingly, as industry faces the challenge of absorbing large numbers of disadvantaged workers, behavioral scientists are being asked for methods to modify the behavior of those who for generations were considered untrainable, or trainable only for menial jobs. Traditional methods have proved to be inadequate to the task of changing the chronically unemployed, or underemployed, into desirable workers.

The failure of learning theorists to test their concepts outside the laboratory too often becomes apparent when their principles collide with the harsh reality of the factory. There are always dangers in applying generalizations from one source of data to another, different situation. The plant or warehouse floor is not the psychologist's laboratory, and vice versa.

At Fieldcrest Mills, Inc., near Danville, Virginia, efforts to develop training programs at all levels have depended consistently on data from scientific research on the process of learning and motivation. Supervisors, instructors, and others concerned with teaching workers have been exposed formally and informally to these data. To be sure, production requirements have often taken precedence over sound educational principles, but this is, perhaps, as it must be. In an industrial organization, training should always be a means to an end and not an end itself.

There has been no careful experimental testing of either single learning principles or total training procedures in the design of our programs at Fieldcrest. Occasionally, however, we have been able to isolate certain

223

variables which seem to account for heightened efficiency. In one job, for example, the introduction of pacing—a process in which an apprentice paces his work against that of an experienced operator—seemed to have been the major factor in reducing time. But there was no controlled experiment to verify this.

There is no need to apologize for failure to conduct carefully controlled experiments to determine the efficacy of various learning principles in our training programs. We are confronted with the practical problem of working in an industrial organization whose major purpose is to produce textile products at a profit through the effective use of its 17,000 people, almost all of whom it has to train at its own expense.

At Fieldcrest, instructional programs have been designed for jobs ranging from unskilled to highly skilled. The majority of jobs for which training procedures have been devised are semiskilled. Yet even in these jobs certain tasks require high degrees of perceptual skill and complicated eye-hand responses.

We focus on the employee first, and only secondly on training procedures. These must be flexible enough to accommodate the different capacities and aptitudes of each learner. We must take the beginner where we find him, in terms of his knowledge and skills, and move from there. This has led in some instances to designing training procedures that are essentially tutorial in nature.

We have searched for a suitable model of behavior modification, but no one model existing today covers adequately all the aspects of learning which are expected of an industrial employee. Accordingly, we have used principles based on research generated by various learning models. Of all those current, we have borrowed most heavily from what is called "operant conditioning." In following it, we have consistently utilized these practices:

Careful definition of the behavior to be acquired.

Organization of learning units in small steps.

Provision for active response by the trainee.

Use in initial phases of immediate feedback, and of reinforcement schedules in later phases.

Developing, utilizing, and gradually fading out external cues to signal-required response.

Provisions for low error rate in desired responses for the individual trainee.

We also looked for outside factors which could help or inhibit the learner. This led us naturally to a key figure: the instructor. As a result, we have carried out an intensive program for "instructors" to familiarize them with teaching techniques, as well as with what happens to beginners as they acquire new complex skills.

The starting point in designing an effective training program is a specific job analysis. It is now widely recognized that difficulties in analyzing jobs for training purposes often arise from a failure to use clear, meaningful concepts that are convenient to learners. This problem is compounded when the training specialist must use terms that convey precise meanings to supervisors and instructors who may have somewhat limited capacities for thinking in conceptual terms. Consequently, we abandoned technical terminology. This led us to collect job information from the persons who knew these jobs best: production workers and supervisors.

Each job to be taught is first analyzed into tasks. A task is defined as a part of a job with a definite starting point and a definite ending point. Some tasks are discrete—there is no flow from a previous task or to a later task.

A second technique helps the learner acquire the ability to rely on senses other than his vision for cues and feedbacks. It is a process of moving the trainee from reliance on vision alone to reliance on "feel" to get the signals for appropriate task behavior.

The trainee is also told how quickly he is performing his tasks. Pacing is used to increase speed. If the task is performed by pairs of workers, an experienced employee or the instructor can serve as a pacer. Where the task does not involve partners, signals are devised to pace the learner.

Certain jobs, particularly those involving the use of more than one machine, require that the learner develop not only the psychomotor skills, but also skill in organizing his duties. The learner must acquire the knowledge of how to establish task priorities and manage his time. In many jobs, once psychomotor skills have been gained, teaching job organization requires scheduling the learner gradually from part- to full-job assignment on a battery of machines or on other multitask jobs.

People who want to learn direct their energies more effectively toward changing their behavior than those who are basically indifferent. We attempt to provide these aids to motivation:

Prepare the trainee for learning by familiarizing him with the training environment, that is, his department, shift, supervisors, instructors, and other employees.

Provide individualized attention, particularly at crucial stages in the learning.

Set goals or targets for learning and achievement.

Keep the trainee informed of his progress.

Keeping the trainee informed of his progress requires the development and use of reliable and relevant measures of performance. For example, it is not enough to indicate that a trainee's speed at a task falls below the standard. The trainee must be assisted in analyzing *why* his speed is low, and how to improve it. We also devise means of diagnosing his mistakes in an effort to help overcome them.

Both instructors and supervisors play important roles in our training effort. To ensure that they are qualified, we run courses for both, based on a guide to job instruction. These courses provide information on the learning process and its proper management. They also furnish practice at applying the general principles to instruction for specific jobs.

At Fieldcrest, acceptance and use of this training approach for production employees has varied from mill to mill and from department to department. To force it on a superintendent or a supervisor does not work. Thus, we have tried to demonstrate the value of the approach by contrasting it with existing teaching procedures. We have involved the supervisors in the development of training plans for their departments. We have persuaded some managers to use behavioral science data instead of depending solely on past experience. But it is a slow process.

Turnover, growth, expansion of the workforce, changes in job tasks, and new products all create a constant need for training new people. But the suggestion by an operating executive that a training program should be created to solve a troublesome problem is sometimes misguided. Very often elaborate instructional programs are developed without ascertaining whether the problem at hand really arises from lack of training.

Several years ago, for example, we were asked to plan and carry out a program to improve the effectiveness of first-line supervisors in communicating with their subordinates. After considerable study, it was found that the problem was not primarily one of poor communication skills—it was lack of clarity about what a supervisor's job entailed. The supervisors and their manager seemed to have very different perceptions of their jobs. After discussion with supervisors it was agreed that the structure of the supervisor's job would be surveyed.

The results indicated clearly that the central problem was clarification of job structure, objectives, and priorities. Both the supervisors and their bosses perceived that the supervisors' main responsibility was to "get the work out." To do this, most of their time was spent troubleshooting, looking for materials, and maintaining machinery. This left a minimum of time for contact with subordinates. The supervisors were too busy to stop and talk. Even if they were skilled communicators, they would still be unable to find time to discuss difficulties and problems. If training had succeeded in improving their communication skills, it probably would also have increased their frustration. They would have possessed a new ability they could not use.

In another instance, it was discovered that a task required of inspectors was impossible to perform in the time allowed. Training cannot improve the performance of an impossible task. And in one mill, an attitude survey indicated that a program of economic education not only would fail to improve the employees' attitude toward the company and the mill, but would make it less sympathetic. Training is an investment of corporate resources, and these resources should not be used helter-skelter.

A current companywide problem for which Fieldcrest is seeking a science-based solution is the growing incidence of turnover among production employees.

Numerous discussions of this perplexing problem—and some actions to meet it—have taken place over the past several years among managers, but turnover has continued to go up. It has become obvious that explanations for the higher quit rate have been mostly guesswork. No dependable data have been assembled as a guide for directing efforts toward reduction of turnover. A decision was made to investigate the possible causes in two ways, first, by a statistical analysis of existing records to determine when, where, and among whom turnover is occurring, and second, by the use of a consultant as a participant-observer.

Though this study is still in process, significant modification of current employment and training procedures has already been accomplished in our experimental unit. On the basis of further results, a decision will be made as to subsequent attacks on the problem. But we already know enough to be sure that new strategies are needed to solve this costly problem, and we are clear that it is better to get reliable data than to depend on untested nostrums or simply to attribute turnover to the current social malaise.

part four

Two Basic Techniques

DAVID N. BEACH / WALTER R. MAHLER

Management by Objectives

The technique of management by objectives has been popular for almost a decade. MBO, as it has inevitably come to be called, is one of the most frequently offered subjects at management conferences in the United States, in Europe, and in South America. If asked, most companies will say they use the method. The basic idea of management by objectives is to set measurable goals and try to meet them. It is such a reasonable idea that it may seem almost self-evident. Yet almost all firms that have tried to implement it in systematic programs report they have had a difficult time. And some, after their initial efforts, have given the technique up. Indeed, there have been more clear failures than successes.

Companies getting started with the method encounter unexpected complexities and a good deal of human resistance. There is often confrontation with long-established organizational practices and delicate interpersonal relationships. Use of the technique may lead to management changes that were not anticipated. But management by objectives can be achieved, and the many success stories already reported are tantalizing. They prove the rewards can be great.

The trouble is that while management by objectives sounds simple in theory, it is far from simple in practice. In truth, even the theory is not as simple as it sounds. The concept of management by objectives had its origin in "performance appraisal," an idea that also seemed simple at first. An employee's motivation and performance, it was thought, would be improved if, at year-end, his superior appaised his performance while reviewing his salary. The procedure would let people know where they stood and how they were doing.

The idea was adopted by many firms, including General Electric. Superiors met with their subordinates once a year, appraised their work, and told them whether or not they would be getting a raise. In the mid-1960s, General Electric evaluated the process and published results. The findings were surprising. As it was being conducted, performance appraisal *did not work*. Employee motivation and performance had not been improved, and may even have been harmed. The General Electric study found very negative attitudes toward the process on both sides. The employee discounted praise as sugarcoating for the criticism to come. The criticism by superiors led to considerable defensiveness by employees and a worsening of relationships.

The study recommended a number of changes, including frequent reviews throughout the year, more day-to-day coaching, and, significantly, separation of salary discussion from performance appraisal.

One of the main weaknesses of the appraisal procedure, the research team reported, was the lack of agreement by the manager and the subordinate on specific goals. Much better results could be expected if goal setting became a joint venture. These findings supported an important theory about the relation of goal setting to motivation first expressed by Kurt Lewin in 1928.

He stated that when an individual decides to reach a specific goal, the intention itself builds up a system of psychological tension, and that the need to release this tension serves to sustain goal-directed activity until the goal is reached. Lewin postulated that as long as the goal is not fulfilled, the tension continues and makes its influence felt in a push for action.

Lewin's theory about the role of tension in goal achievement has since provoked a number of probing questions about goal setting. What factors, for instance, go into the decision to try for the difficult goal rather than an easily achieved one? What reactions are produced by failure to reach the goal? Or by success? These questions are just now being explored.

With both Lewin's theory and the findings of General Electric in mind, we like to define management by objectives as a process, a means of setting goals, that is particularly designed to foster self-management. The aim is as much to increase motivation and satisfaction on the job as to increase profits and improve the organization.

Most successful management-by-objectives programs today have several elements in common: the objectives are specific; they are jointly set by those involved in reaching them; there is concrete and periodic feedback; and the higher echelons participate, particularly in giving support at the beginning. Again, it sounds simpler than it is. Each of these elements offers pitfalls to the unwary.

First of all, it is never easy to define objectives. Generalized objectives, such as "lower production costs" or "make more profit," mean no more than "let's get together sometime," which people say only when they have little intention of meeting again. To be meaningful, an objective must be specific, or quantitative, and also time-bound. You must project something like "Reduce production costs of Model A 7 percent by December 31," or "Average a 28 percent share of the national market for product B during 1973." These are measured objectives. You can know if you attain them.

Objectives at the lowest managerial level can be set for three months or a year; at the top corporate level, they are set for five years and ten years ahead. Long-term objectives, of course, involve considerable uncertainty. What is the average growth of trade or industry likely to be in the next five years? What market trends can be expected? What technological advances? Long-term machinery capability? Profit levels? Competitive positions? Political and social influences?

In general, companies aim to maximize profits (usually measured by return on investment) and to grow and survive. Still, a company needs to determine the share of the market it wants and can reasonably expect to get. It needs to determine its real return on its total investment, including the investment of its shareholders, and what that should be in comparison with others in the same business.

Despite the problems involved, companies, one after another, have been able to set specific long-range objectives. For example:

☐ The Ford Motor Company: *"Double net worth per share every ten years."*

☐ IBM: *"Increase sales and profits 100 percent at least every five years."*

☐ Socony Mobil Oil Company: *"Earn at least 7.5 percent return on all investments."*

☐ The Lodge & Shipley Company: *"Obtain for stockholders a minimum of 10 percent return on net worth, as an average over any three-year period." "Conduct our business so that sales will grow at a rate of not less than 7 percent per year on the average." "Assuming no major product or company acquisitions . . . be a commercially oriented company with at least 70 percent of our sales volume generated by private industry." "No single customer shall be responsible for such a large percentage of our business as to cause the loss of independence in our customer relations."*

Specific objectives such as these obviously require a great deal of thought. Even for the short range, however, specifics can be tricky. "We shape our buildings," Churchill said. "Thereafter they shape us." It's the same with objectives. Once set, they tend to take over; if they are inappropriate, they can lead a company astray.

For example, a certain firm known for giving good service wanted to make its objective of "improving customer service" more specific. Yet the only measurable items it arrived at concerned the amount of time spent per customer and the number of customer calls, things that really had little to do with the kind of quality service the firm was noted for. Nonetheless, these were used as a guide, and imperceptibly the objective shifted from *improving* customer service to *reducing the cost* of customer service. The less time spent per customer and the fewer the calls, the more costs were cut and short-term profits increased. It worked for a while, but in the long run it ruined the firm.

Some specific goals simply reflect narrowness of vision. One company's billing department, for example, established the objective of reducing the time spent in preparing invoices by 10 percent. The objective was clear enough; but it overlooked the fact that if the sales department achieved *its* objective of increasing sales volume, new accounts would be opened and more billing time would be required. The 10 percent reduction would be impossible to attain if the sales department exceeded its goal. The appropriate measure, as hindsight made clear, would have been to reduce the average time spent *per statement*.

Finding the right objectives, and making objectives interlock both horizontally, among departments, and vertically, from the bottom to the top of the organization, is obviously time consuming. It often requires negotiation talents of a high order. The goal-setting process most often goes astray when attention is focused merely on the activities involved (answer letters within two days, have all reports in on time) instead of on the results those activities were designed to support.

There are still other errors to which those who set objectives are subject. They can set objectives too high—or too low, with no "reach" in them. The objectives can cost too much to be worth meeting. They can be too complex to keep clearly in mind. Or too numerous. The time span can be too long, or too short. Objectives can create an unbalanced emphasis by focusing on only part of a company's operations.

Even when the objectives set are good ones, however, the process is far from over. Next, plans or strategies must be designed to meet them. The strategies have to be feasible within the level of competence of those who must carry them out. They must mesh with the overall corporate strategy. Responsibilities must be assigned and priorities set. All this involves hard, time-consuming work.

"Over twenty years of industrial experience in many countries has shown me time and time again," a Belgian industrialist has written, "that the human problem in corporate life is the only really serious one." The greatest obstacle confronting any organization seeking to set goals systematically is the human resistance to change. Management by objectives implies change.

For a management-by-objectives program to succeed, the organization must be "unfrozen." Readiness for change must be stimulated; openness, candor, and trust must be increased. This is a tall order, but is the very one that the technique of management by objectives is expressly designed to meet. It sets as its first priority, remember, the goal of allowing the people responsible for carrying out objectives to have a role in setting them. Change is more acceptable to those who have had a hand in calling for it. Management by objectives also demands decentralization to some degree. It means surrendering authority, too, by those who may not want to give it up. It calls for behavior change.

The key to making it work is *participation*. As one consultant put it, "Participation tends to increase commitment, commitment tends to heighten motivation, motivation tends to make management work harder and more productively, and harder and more productive work tends to enhance the company's prosperity. Therefore, participation is good."

The reverse is also true. The lack of participation can "demotivate." Thus management by objectives emphasizes participation, from the very beginning, by all those to whom the objectives and strategies apply. It means that the boss and his subordinate work jointly, not only in setting objectives but in reviewing and revising them.

In some programs, lower-level managers are allowed to redesign their jobs, change salary differentials within their departments, and propose modifications of their superior's responsibilities. Often the man one step down has the very suggestion the man one step above needs if he is to set attainable objectives.

In many effective programs, it is the man who must meet the goals who does all the planning, once the objectives are agreed to. The plan has become his, not his superior's. The joint setting of objectives enables the superior to become more of a coach than a judge. "How can I help you meet your objectives? What do you need from me?" The focus is on the job, not on personalities.

Of course, performance has to be measured against the goal. Feedback must come fast. Consistently high performance should be rewarded without undue delay. Incompetence must also be dealt with regularly and frequently.

Salary discussion must be kept separate from performance appraisal. A recent survey by the Conference Board found that "Satisfaction occurred when management by objectives had become a regular way of managing and when it was carried out as a series of periodic reviews. . . . Dissatisfaction occurred when the program was used primarily for performance appraisal or compensation adjustments such as salary increase, bonus, etc."

When management by objectives is confined to performance appraisal and linked to compensation, the program is stymied by being placed on too narrow a basis. Rather paradoxically, we have learned that the more limited the program, the less satisfactory the results.

Experience has shown that goal setting does produce results. Costs have been cut and new products have appeared on schedule. More useful management information has been furnished and reports have been made more timely and pointed. Planning has been better and contingencies have been allowed for. Development needs and profit potential have been identified more correctly.

To use a dollar-and-cents example provided by the Conference Board, one division of a nationally known company undertook to estimate the cost and contribution of each one of the hundred objectives set by the division's management for the following year. It couldn't believe its own figures. A half-million dollars more profit than expected would probably accrue. It didn't seem possible that such a potential profit had gone unnoticed. Yet, a year later, the profit was $400,000 more than previously anticipated.

With management by objectives, control is tightened. Even better, the control tends to be self-control, which reduces the need for close supervision. This sometimes introduces a problem for managers who are reluctant to surrender their authority, but it usually results in increased trust between subordinates and superiors and better relationships all around. Benefits accrue in part because subordinates have a better idea of what is expected of them. Sound measures of performance have been laid down; authority has been clarified.

There is an important principle at work here. Psychologists repeatedly have shown that performance improves when measurement data on it are made available. Anyone is helped by knowing what the standards are and whether he is performing successfully or not. Quite apart from money, most find intrinsic satisfaction in work well done.

In a way, it's like a game. What makes a game fun is that it's clearly structured, the rules are well defined, and the score (or feedback) is instantaneous. In an organization, the simple existence of authority or standards is not what causes dissatisfaction. Fuzzy standards and confused lines of authority cause the trouble. Management by objectives can help clear things up. In doing so, it can make work more enjoyable.

By setting clear performance measures, management by objectives replaces weak appraisal methods, which constitute one of the biggest blocks between subordinates and bosses. The relationship is strengthened when it emphasizes objective measurements and the job at hand, when it moves toward coaching and away from judging. More cooperation flows both ways.

Management by objectives has now been fully tested. It's beyond the trial period. It has passed the test of profit improvement. It has been applied successfully to profit-making organizations of all types, to public-service organizations, educational organizations, universities, hospitals, consulting firms, administrative organizations, governmental organizations, and the military, at all levels.

Why, then, have so many *other* organizations searched in vain for the benefits of an MBO program? The answer, we feel, is that they have been unaware that a successful introduction generally requires several years of intensive work before it produces real benefits. The preparatory time is necessary because of the basic problem—the traditional resistance to change by the staff. People generally find a variety of reasons to avoid committing themselves to a procedure that links them to specific and measurable goals.

Our experience with programs that have succeeded, and with some that have failed, leads us to conclude that success depends on three basic conditions:

☐ Top management must understand what the program is all about. They must see it as demanding rigorous planning and follow-up by all members of the organization, including themselves.

☐ The process of setting the goals must be practical and simple.

☐ Managers must be trained to help their subordinates set realistic objectives. They should know how to conduct progress reviews and lead problem-solving discussions. Though these skills are rarely self-taught, few firms really make adequate allowance for the kind of training, both formal and informal, that objective setting requires.

The two examples that follow, one drawn from a large organization, one from a small, illustrate the kind of training that can be provided.

The Glass Division of Pittsburgh Plate Glass Industries has nearly two dozen manufacturing plants scattered across the country. It supplies automobile manufacturers, home builders, and commercial contractors. When it decided about two years ago to install a management-by-objectives program, the division brought in an outside consultant group to help. The program was designed to begin with the top manufacturing management and go down, one level at a time. One plant manager was chosen to head the program. His job was to show the other plant managers how to conduct the necessary in-plant training. He was also to serve as monitor of the written objectives that were submitted and to recommend changes as needed. Formal training began with the plant manager who was to head the program. The other plant managers were later given a week's intensive training. Surveys of current management practices in planning and control were then conducted.

Significant improvements have already been reported. Overlapping responsibilities have been identified and the lesser responsibilities pushed downward in the organization. The need for measures of performance has been revealed at various levels. Communications and integration across organizational lines have been facilitated by written progress reports—now commonplace—and by regularly scheduled monthly or quarterly individual and group reviews.

In contrast to PPG's enormous Glass Division, the various plants of the U.S. Envelope Company are small. One of these operated sixteen machines, each producing tens of thousands of envelopes an hour. Before setting out on a management-by-objectives program, the plant's manager participated in several seminars. He then chose a three-step approach: First, the "areas of responsibility" were determined (for example, quality, quantity, timing, inventory, scrap, safety); then, indicators to serve as performance measures in each area were chosen; finally, short-term objectives were set.

After the plant manager had trained his management team in the approach, written objectives were obtained for every supervisory position in the plant. The supervisors, in turn, worked with each of their subordinates in developing similar documents.

Several problems immediately became apparent. As at PPG, several areas of responsibilities were found to be overlapping. Also, many objectives had been stated in terms of work activities rather than results. In addition, a number of performance measures were found to be subjective.

With the help of an outside consulting firm, the plant manager and his staff worked out the solutions to the problems before proceeding further. Agreement was reached on who would make the subjective judgments and what "evidence" they would look at in arriving at their decisions. In addition, performance measures were improved for each level of management.

In the four years since the plant's program was set up, performance has gradually improved, not spectacularly, but enough to make goal setting and regular progress review a standard operating procedure. However, surprising gains were made almost immediately in one area: cutting down waste. Before the program began, the only measure for paper waste was a weekly one—waste as a percentage of the total paper used each week. The new measure required a comparison of the actual number of envelopes made from each foot of paper entering the machines with the standard expected per foot. The workers operating the machines made the comparisons and adjusted their presses accordingly, assuming responsibility for daily waste. If they needed assistance in meeting the standard, they called on their supervisor, who otherwise received only daily reports. The supervisor sent weekly reports to the plant superintendent, and the superintendent sent monthly reports to the plant manager. Waste was cut by fully 25 percent in the first half year of the program, and since then has dropped an additional 10 percent.

Management by objectives can be tailored to suit any company's needs. At Honeywell, Inc., the chairman begins by writing a memorandum each spring, setting forth some general goals for the corporation over the following three years. He indicates roughly what various divisions might contribute. On the basis of this memorandum, the division managers prepare their own detailed plans, with specific goals in terms of profits, sales, volume, return on assets, and new products. These are entered as the first chapter in their fall planning book. The remaining chapters list the goals for each of the major units within divisions, with cross references. Thus, while the top of the corporation provides the direction, the lower levels supply the specifics.

It's not always necessary to start at the top. A divisional manager, for example, can set objectives for his own organization even though no formal effort may have been made to set companywide objectives. Similarly, a plant manager might set objectives for his own plant even though objectives have not been set for the overall manufacturing organization. It's not the sequence, but the opportunity for interaction that is important.

Experience suggests that goals can be set at all levels of an organization. It is quite possible to have goals used by every supervisor and every professional and technical employee. If one thinks of a small number of rather specific goals, it is also possible to have goals prepared by nonsupervisory personnel. However, as one moves to lower levels, two changes take place. The time period for which goals are set shortens considerably, and the number of goals needs to be limited.

Management by objectives not only tends to decentralize authority, it sometimes calls for realignment of unsound organizational structures and administrative practices. This can prove embarrassing. For example, three highly regarded vice presidents of a large manufacturing firm, whose jobs were to provide coordination among various divisions, found nothing uniquely attributable to their efforts when they tried to set objectives for their work. Reluctantly, the firm agreed their jobs were superfluous, and finally the positions were eliminated.

The vice president of a Canadian firm found himself in a similar position. His job was to supervise four managers of profit centers. But in trying to determine his specific responsibilities, he found he had none. He wasn't specifically responsible for profits, the managers were. He agreed, at a team meeting with the managers, that his job should be dissolved. Fortunately, in both cases, the men displaced were assigned to new positions of equal status that included real duties.

Cases like these underscore the crucial importance of relating the *personal* objectives of executives to the objectives of the organization. Objectives handed down from on high will not create significant incentives if they are forced on employees regardless of their private aspirations and dreams. It's not always easy, of course, to identify subjective needs, but specificity is not as important as making it safe to explore such feelings. If there are discrepancies between a man's personal goals and the organization's, the matter can be explored to see whether the discrepancy is significant and alternatives are available. If personal goals are ignored, management by objectives can backfire. It can create hostility instead of trust, dissatisfaction instead of incentives. It can be interpreted as mere manipulation.

The manager of the U.S. Envelope Company plant elected to include personal objectives in his program. His comments, written several years after the program began, emphasize their value:

> In our program the personal growth of each individual and his self-improvement objectives are related to company and plant objectives. These objectives are reviewed and reset each progress review. I feel these discussions have been one of the most useful outcomes of our entire program.

To many companies the harnessing of personal goals has, in fact, become part of the definition of management by objectives. Humble Oil puts it this way:

> Management by objectives is a dynamic system which integrates the company's need to achieve its goals for profit and growth with the manager's need to contribute and develop himself . . . . It is a demanding and rewarding style of managing a business.

LELAND P. BRADFORD

How Sensitivity Training Works

Imagine, if you will, your participation in a week-long Presidents' Conference.

The session opens on a Sunday afternoon with twenty to twenty-five top executives present, fifteen of them accompanied by their wives. The afternoon is a get-acquainted time, but with a difference. In twos, threes, and fours, people come to know each other not just in terms of name, rank, and serial number, but in terms of what they hope to get from the week, what human problems—at work or at home—are most trying for them.

On Sunday evening each T (for Training) group of about eight people has its first meeting. The staff member in the group starts by saying that each member faces the task of learning about his own and others' behavior from his experience in the group. He adds, among other things, that he will not be the leader, but will try to find ways of helping the learning as time goes on.

A long silence follows.

If not he, who will lead the group? Is a leader absolutely necessary? As a chief executive, accustomed to command and action, each group member faces an unusual situation. Inevitably various individuals try, in differing ways, to lead, move, push, prod the group. None of the efforts is successful for long. The group seems to sway first in one direction and then another. The behavior of some irritates others. At intervals the professional staff member asks what they think is blocking group progress. He may share his feelings about the difficulty in the hope they will indicate theirs. Or he may comment on someone's behavior and suggest possible consequences of it. The first evening seemingly leads nowhere, but a great deal of data is accumulated about frustration, behavior of various members, and feelings. Members have built, destroyed, and rebuilt stereotypes about each other. Subgroups have formed as individuals have sensed others reacting as they did.

The T-group meeting the next morning is intense, frustrating, full of action in many directions. Although nothing is solved, the participants have a growing feeling that they have their teeth into something, no matter how amorphous. The four morning hours pass more swiftly than seemed possible. The session ends with the total group meeting in a general session to discuss theories about individual and group behavior that will hopefully shed some light on the morning's experience.

The evening program offers an exercise in intergroup competition. Members of each group find themselves loyally identified with their group, and are somewhat chagrined at the end of the evening when they examine their behavior and the intensity of their feelings about the other groups. Husbands and wives, having been in different groups, have much to talk about when they go to their rooms.

So the week goes. Toward the middle of it, an exercise is introduced in which one group "acquires" the remaining two, and all the dynamic forces in business acquisitions and mergers come into being and are discussed. As trust grows, participants test each other. They are now getting feedback from time to time about their behavior and how others feel about it. Each feels freer to seek the kind of help he wanted but feared getting before. By the end of the program everyone has a lot to mull over—some of it painful. But there is the realization that every member is more likely to understand others and himself better now. Each has a new awareness of how a group can become more than a collection of individuals, how a work team can be developed, and how much more productive a mature group is than isolated individuals.

Finally, those executives who had urged their wives to attend now have a deeper understanding and sense of communication within the family as well.

That, in briefest outline, is the story of a truly new method of education—the T-group, perhaps the most significant educational innovation of the twentieth century. It is a dramatic development known by a number of names: sensitivity training, laboratory training, encounter group, group dynamics, confrontation group. None of these fully describes its character. It is an innovation in the manner or process of learning, and it has been adopted by many management leaders, in government, education, and civil rights. But most of all it is being effectively used by men in business and industry.

The first T-group training center, established in 1947 at Bethel, Maine, by the National Training Laboratories, continues to be the principal laboratory training center in the United States. Currently, training labs are in use at more than 100 educational institutions in the United States, including Columbia, Harvard, M.I.T., the University of Michigan, the University of Chicago, the University of California, Yale. By now, more than a million people, it is estimated, have shared the training laboratory experience.

The T-group provides learning values difficult to secure elsewhere. To begin with, the training differs from that usually provided in the classroom, the seminar, or the workshop. The subject matter is not a body of knowledge, but a group of people. You do not simply gain knowledge of people; you *experience* their behavior and your own as well in a way that is useful to you in life. Further, the emphasis is on changing individual conduct rather than on imparting scientific knowledge.

The learning may be focused on the process of social organization, or the dynamics of group behavior, or personal relationships, or individual perceptions and motivations, or individual and group values. The raw data for learning is what goes on among members of the T-group. The data come from the participants' own behavior in the group as they struggle to create a productive and viable organization—what amounts to a miniature society—and as they work to stimulate and support one another's learning within that society. In a sense, members write their own textbook as they read it.

The T-group is relatively unstructured. Most of what the trainees learn in the T-group meetings they learn from one another rather than from the lab staff. The interaction of the participants is the distinctive element of the daily sessions.

The emphasis in the training lab is not on lectures, though there are some. It is not on reading material, though this is part of the course. Rather, the emphasis is on the group itself. We understand its history: what happens to it from the first time the members come together. We understand its composition: the people who make it up, how they act individually, and how they behave together. From the very first session, the participants are put on their own. The agenda, if it can be called that, is provided by the dilemmas that develop in the process of building a group. This happens to them without their being told what to do, who is in charge, what to talk about, or who should say it.

Group interaction is the essential condition for learning, but it's not the only part. The T-group is set in the larger context of a carefully designed development program. A variety of other learning activities, such as lectures on management and behavioral theory, skill-practice exercises, and simulated cases, are provided as integral parts of a design for learning about oneself, about small-group teamwork, and about broader organizational behavior.

The training is designed to help good managers become better managers. The participants are successful people seeking more effective ways of using and improving their management skills. Effort is also devoted to planning for the application of these lessons after the conference to achieve individual growth and organizational improvement.

The first thing the participant in a typical one-week lab does, after he arrives at the conference center, is to attend an orientation session which brings together the entire group of fifty or sixty trainees. Here the men are given their schedule: T-group sessions morning, afternoon, and evening, interspersed with skill-practice sessions and occasional theory sessions. Before they leave the assembly room, they are divided into T-groups, the basic unit of eight to ten people.

Generally, no two members of the same company or of directly competitive companies are assigned to the same T-group. At some training centers, however, groups of managers from a single company have come together for training in "family" groups. These may be further divided into groups on the same management level.

Each T-group has its own professional leader, usually a trained psychologist. But the leader does not exert control. Instead, he serves as a catalyst and guide to channel the group into the most productive learning situations. The professional leader faces the task of encouraging and occasionally helping the group members do the kinds of things that will produce relevant data about themselves, each other, and the group as a whole. With the data, the participants can experiment with new ways of behaving, but the professional generally stays out of the way. The T-group is an unstructured, self-directed group with no predetermined agenda to cover. There are no fixed rules; the group makes its own rules in a highly permissive atmosphere.

This method is often referred to, for good reason, as "laboratory training." The laboratory is the special environment in which the participants learn new things about themselves. Each one is encouraged to examine his own behavior and to experiment with new ways of relating to others. The important point is that he can experiment in a setting where experimentation is safe. In addition, the information concerning how effective one's own actions are can be obtained from others and subjected to examination. Since the immediate behavior of participants is the basic subject matter, the participant is in the unique position of being at the same time the experimenter and the subject of the experiment. Here the trainees analyze each other's attitudes, react to each other's behavior, compare the way they see themselves with the way others see them.

Each trainee learns about his own motives, feelings, and strategies in dealing with other persons. He learns also of the reactions he produces in others as he interacts with them.

He learns a good deal, too, about groups, since he is helping to build one. Participants have the experience, guided by a skilled trainer, of creating a productive work group out of an unstructured situation. In the process of creating direction, order, and leadership from their own resources—and in the process of making decisions, dealing with conflict, and working on tasks—participants gain, often for the first time, a clearer view of the strong and weak points of their own characteristic methods of working with people.

In a unique way, these groups provide each participant with a microcosm for studying the same kinds of human problems he faces daily in his own organization. As the participant learns to deal more effectively with problems arising in the T-group, he learns to work more effectively in his managerial position.

He may develop new skills in group membership, skills in giving and receiving help, and skills for changing and improving his social environment as well as himself. From this laboratory approach to learning, each person can review the effectiveness of his own behavior as he comes to master the very difficult skill of learning with the help of others. It is this new understanding of himself, combined with new skills in dealing with others and new insights into company organization, that helps the trainee to tap the inner resources and powers which he may not have been using and may not, in fact, have known he had.

A first purpose of the T-group is to help individuals *learn how to learn from their everyday experience* in the areas of self-awareness and sensitivity to different kinds of interpersonal behavior. There also is an effort to impart an understanding of the consequences of behavior. Learning in these areas requires a willingness to explore openly one's own motivations and feelings. Participants learn to utilize the reactions of others as feedback about the consequences of their own behavior. And they experiment with new ways of behaving.

Since each of these steps requires emotional support, the T-group faces the dual task of creating a supportive climate and of developing situations in which members can learn through examining their own experience. As they analyze the interpersonal difficulties they encounter in doing this, they learn important truths about themselves and their relations with others.

The T-group rarely delves into the genetic causes of behavior. It deals mainly with present, here-and-now behavior and its consequences, and with conscious and preconscious motivation rather than with unconscious motivation. The T-group makes the important assumption that persons participating are well rather than ill.

Most people adjust only partially to the conditions of their lives. Their understanding of themselves in inadequate. Fearful of upsetting the precarious balance of their relationships, they find little opportunity to become more aware of themselves and thereby to find greater meaning in living. The intense personal nature of involvement in T-groups, however, provides the energy—the motivation—for learning of considerable depth.

The experience is frequently a deeply moving one. It often means a reevaluation of a lifetime of values and beliefs. Anyone who has participated in a T-group has experienced an extraordinary amount of emotional involvement and energy expenditure. After each session, people feel emotionally drained, but still eager to continue. Extra sessions often last long past midnight. Small clusters of T-group members continue to talk during meals and recreation periods. Various members sit through long evening hours, playing back the tape recording of the previous session to squeeze out further meaning. This degree of involvement continues throughout the life of the T-group.

One cause of emotional involvement, particularly in the initial sessions of the T-group, lies in the ambiguous situation created by the unstructured beginning. This ambiguity seems to produce stresses related to individual identity and group survival. The question as to whether one wants to be a member of the group, the uncertainty as to how to proceed, the very unpredictability of the situation, cause people to forget much of their learning purposes and become deeply concerned, first about their own identity and position in the group and then about the survival of the group itself.

The session opens with the members feeling conflicted and uncertain about power and leadership, about goals, about norms to guide behavior, about which efforts will secure a place in the group, about rewards and punishments, and about what will happen to each individual. This situation provokes individual defense systems to operate until greater predictability is secured.

Each individual is not only uncertain about how he should behave, but he is also unable to find, in the beginning, any obvious pattern of membership that will suggest what is expected of him. The group has not yet established ways to evaluate or utilize contributions. It has developed no way to confer membership. It has not even determined what constitutes membership. Increased anxiety causes each person to listen more to his "internal noises" than to what others are actually feeling and saying.

The uncertainty with which individuals enter any new situation is thus compounded in the T-group. Individuals react in a variety of ways. Some deny that there is an uncomfortable and unpredictable situation. Members will say, with hands clenched, that they are relaxed and comfortable. Some seek to handle the situation by withdrawing into the role of observers. They are here, they say, to learn by watching others behave. Others attempt to work out their own survival by trying to force one group to become a traditional and predictable group. Still others try to coerce the trainer into saving them; when this fails, they may punish him.

An early and basic problem facing the T-group, therefore, is how to handle anxiety. The early hours of a T-group are spent in trying to "place" other people in relation to self; in discovering their motives, their power or superiority, and their ability to hurt. There is a search for comfortable and familiar situations; to find out whether one is liked; to try to win power or approval. Some of the dependent, and independent, reactions to the trainer grow out of the desire to have him, as the one known power figure, reduce the discomfort. Since members differ in their perceptions of what is desirable and what is uncomfortable, early efforts to lead the group around the shoals of discomfort generally result in a clash over leadership.

In the first day or two of a new T-group, members are concerned almost exclusively, but not consciously, about their individual situations. Can I survive? What will happen to me? What will be demanded of me? Can I accept feedback from others? Dare I give it?

Each individual faces, in heightened form, his own personal problems of membership in the group. As in any other group, he is asking: What gain—at what pain—may I expect? How close do I want to be to these people? How much of myself am I willing to invest in this? He is concerned, too, about whether he can measure up to expectations. He is uncertain about what to contribute or how to measure his effectiveness. His defenses against correction are high. Yet discussion usually wanders in apparent aimlessness from descriptions of events back home to discussions of abstract or harmless topics and thence to suggestions for immediate group actions without adequate diagnosis. Discussion, interestingly, centers on group procedures or on events not overtly related to individual concerns and anxieties.

However, trainees are constantly urged to look back and see what their behavior has revealed. Feedback is important. For instance, in the beginning some may have been overly anxious or impatient to get started. Some may have played it safe, said nothing, and thus contributed nothing. Some may have shown a need to dominate the meeting and organize the group. "We can't just sit here," a member may say. "Now, I'll tell you what we'll do. . . ." And what he has said is on the record, to be studied. In subsequent sessions the men analyze their own experiences in the struggle to create a working group. They examine the way one member tried to control the group; the three-man clique that railroaded a decision on how to fill the time; the chairman they elected who couldn't cope with some of the members. Although in the early hours there is desire to communicate with other people about oneself, it has to be done in "safe" ways and it must not reveal too much. Members tend to discuss themselves in terms of their organizations or events back home. Only much later does it come out how little of this early effort to communicate is really heard.

This is the paradox in the history of the T-group. When individuals are feeling their own anxieties and fears most keenly, they seem to conspire to keep the discussion centered on group action or on events unrelated to the present anxiety. Later, when some predictability has developed, some norms for sharing feelings and perceptions have been constructed, and greater understanding of one another has been established, there is much more discussion of individual feelings, perceptions, and needs. Indeed, group problems are resolved through open discussion of individual reactions.

But the stress over problems of individual identity is never relieved because new events present new threats. Gradually, however, individuals learn that they need to alert their defenses less frequently. They see that openness in sharing feelings and motives and willingness to give and receive feedback are not only less dangerous than imagined, but can be extremely helpful if one's goal is to improve interpersonal behavior and to discover more fully one's own identity.

A characteristic of the T-group is the candor and the sense of intimacy generated. At first participants are strangers. All they know about each other is that they are there to help not only themselves but everyone else. Eventually, they tell each other how they feel and what they think—frankly, freely, and fully. They learn to communicate their feelings accurately.

The essence of this learning experience lies in the "transactions" that occur as each group member attempts to influence or control the stream of events and to satisfy his personal needs. Individuals learn by exposing their needs, values, and behavior patterns so that perceptions and reactions can be exchanged with others. Thus, behavior is the currency for transaction. The amount each invests helps to determine the return.

Through this negotiating, the individual can validate or correct his assumptions. He can learn to recognize and use feelings, and he can evaluate his behavior and learn to make it more consistent with his intentions. As individual members grow in these directions, the group itself grows in its capacity to encourage still further individual learning. The group learns that the barriers to learning—defensiveness, withdrawal, fear, distrust—can be reduced so that problems of relationships can be dealt with on deeper and more realistic levels.

Investment of self requires considerable awareness of one's own motivations and personal defenses. It also requires awareness of personal identity and sufficient ego strength to relate to others interdependently rather than dependently or aggressively. Yet to invest himself constructively, the individual has to be able to diagnose what is happening in the group.

The transactional nature of the learning process is illustrated by the fact that individuals can more effectively use feedback about their own behavior when they help others do the same.

Resistance to learning may be more clearly seen in others than in onself. The individual does not feel so *alone* if others are involved with him in learning. Collaboration lessens the possibility that an offer of help will be interpreted as an attack. As these discoveries are made, individuals learn that giving help and receiving help are extremely difficult, but that they can assist one another more than they had thought possible.

Thus the T-group provides opportunity for developing, at successively deeper levels, insights and skills that are necessary for carrying out membership responsibilities. Participants learn through experience that apathetic, irresponsible, or ineffective membership reduces the effectiveness of the group; that silent or withdrawn members withhold from the group the resources needed for individual and group growth; that irresponsible members distort the group to serve their own purposes. Participants learn that full membership necessitates continuing questioning of assumptions and values underlying behavior, and continuing validation of perceptions and diagnoses.

A T-group, then, is a group formed for individual learning purposes—

☐ Where the data are created and analyzed by the work of the group and not fed in from outside and interpreted by a teacher.

☐ Where learning is a group task entered into jointly.

☐ Where the professional does not deny the group members the experience of creating and maintaining their own group identity, even though this experience will be difficult and may produce anxiety.

☐ Where the motivation for learning comes from the high degree of emotional involvement of the members.

Today there are many kinds of T-groups, many different approaches, different purposes, different expectations. New methods are constantly being tried. One of the most recent exciting innovations has been the establishment of T-groups for top executives. These were first set up at the National Training Laboratory in 1965. Since then more than 300 chief corporate executives have participated in the Presidents' Conferences on Human Behavior.

More than anyone else perhaps, today's top executives need new and specialized skills in human relations if they are to diagnose and solve the human problems of organizations. The role of the chief executive is becoming increasingly uncertain, complex, and demanding. He is faced with an explosion of technical knowledge and with technical breakthroughs that become obsolete before they are fully implemented. He is faced with organizations which are expanding in size and complexity. He is faced with rapid and far-reaching social and cultural changes that affect his organization and the people who make it up. Traditional patterns of management no longer seem adequate. Creativity, the ability to adapt to sudden changes in conditions, and the ability to motivate people to do their best, rather than the ability to give and carry out orders, are desperately needed executive qualities.

Perhaps the greatest problem—and the greatest challenge—confronting executives today lies in working with people. This is particularly true for top management. If the chief executive and his organization are to grow and meet new challenges, he must find the answers to a number of perplexing questions. For example:

☐ How can a collection of managers be turned into a real management team in which individual abilities and interests are raised to their maximum potential without becoming destructive of each other?

☐ How can new and more effective ways of working be evolved so as to receive wholehearted acceptance?

☐ How can the chief executive convert *knowledge* of human behavior and organization development into *practice?*

☐ How can the chief executive improve his own skills in working with human problems of organization?

☐ How can he get more fun and fulfillment out of his work?

These questions are fully explored at the Presidents' Conferences. A primary value of the conferences, of course, is the opportunity to share ideas, experiences, and dilemmas with other senior executives. But emphasis is placed on helping the top executive attain the skill and understanding required for working more effectively with others.

Understandably, when the question is posed of whose behavior in the organization is to be changed, the average top executive's answer is: "My subordinates.'" He doesn't think of changing himself. But recent research suggests that change in the top executives should come first. If these men are to give genuine leadership, they need to know a lot more about their motives, their values, their emotional maturity, and the impact they make on the men they work with. Self-knowledge is a business necessity if the manager is to develop the cooperative relationships that will turn his subordinates into a working team with good morale and high motivation.

A first step, therefore, is for the man who manages others to take a good close look at himself: He must examine his attitudes, recognize his inadequacies and failings, and then reshape them into new insights and skills. The dynamics of the T-group, then, are almost tailor-made to meet the chief executive's needs.

"I discovered," one chief executive said after participating in a presidents' conference, "that a number of mannerisms, some quite unconscious, resulted in the personality I was projecting being neither my true one, nor even the one I was trying to project. The false projection must have been a starting point for false relationships. It therefore formed a barrier to the creation of new and fruitful relationships."

"I think the most important aspect has been my personal growth as an individual," said another top executive. "It is clear this has benefited my company greatly. I have found my subordinates less tense and more open with me. We have been able to take some major steps forward as a management team."

In learning about group behavior, the chief executive may become more aware of how complex the behavior of groups is, and of the unspoken feelings of group members. He may come to recognize the importance to group productivity of team building and team maintenance.

One president reported: "Three of the presidents of subsidiaries reporting to me decided to attend a presidents' T-group program. There is no question in my mind that the common experience we all had produced a much more effective and productive working team."

Executive T-groups have a special relevance to company-based organizational development programs. As time goes on, executive T-groups are more and more closely tied in with organizational development, for the chief executive plays a crucial role in the success of any organizational improvement plan. In fact, it was with the express purpose of helping chief executives initiate and support programs of organization development that the Presidents' Conferences were established.

As a consequence, the conferences are specifically designed to help a chief executive test his openness to change. The reason is compelling. Unless the chief executive is seen by others as open to change himself, both in his own behavior and in his relations with others, others will see no reason for change themselves. Instead they will view change as unnecessarily risky. They will doubt the consistency and endurance of the program and fear that "going alone" might leave them in left field if the boss shifted to another approach.

The chief executive must be vitally committed and personally involved in any program of development. Otherwise the program will not be taken seriously by others in the organization. Change is usually threatening, and inertia is powerful. A sustained development program aimed at improving the working relations in a company has many implicit threats for individuals and groups who have built strong walls around their operations. Mandates from the top are not always clearly understood; some are not agreed with. A typical approach is to "wait out" the efforts to change.

If there is any evidence that the development program does not have strong commitment from the chief executive, or that he only partially understands its ramifications and the long-range efforts needed, individuals and groups will cautiously stay uninvolved. Thus the problem of creating credibility in a development program rests in large measure with the chief. His behavior, as well as his words, will be studied as evidence of credibility.

In one very large organization, massive and expensive efforts were made to bring about improvement through training and team building. The managers close to the top were fully committed to the program, but the top management was not. The chief executive was informed, and although he acquiesced, he was committed only in part. Significant progress was made until a temporary budget retrenchment was necessary. Then a small pocket of resisters formed to convince the chief executive that the training program could be eliminated. Because he was not committed to it fully, the program was killed.

Another company with a development program behaved differently in a period of retrenchment. Here the chief executive, who had been involved in learning about his own and the organization's behavior, was deeply committed to the development program. Although the program's expansion was temporarily halted, he made it very clear that it was by no means dead and the company would continue to support efforts toward improvement in working relations.

The Presidents' Conference focuses on other aspects of organizational development as well. The top executive can examine, with the help of an expert consultant, the careful steps he can take to begin a program of organization development in his company. He can learn about some of the mistakes and traps he might fall into. He can find out from chief executives of other companies the problems they have faced. The T-group can give him needed insights into why change is often so difficult.

The chief executive needs to become more aware of the slowness of change. Otherwise his expectations may be too high. "I guess I was really holding things up in my company," one chief executive confessed. "I expected things to happen as soon as I decided they should. I know now how much uncertainty, anxiety, and discord I created. My group taught me how difficult and slow is change in human behavior, and how much continued support is necessary if any change is to occur."

Just as the chief executive has more than others to gain from an improved organization, he risks more than others in the process of organization development. By virtue of his role and power, he may be the target of blame for the problems of the organization. He may be a focus of competition, covert or overt, from subordinates. He undoubtedly causes fear in others. He may believe that, as a model for others, he must show himself to be above mistakes or human weaknesses.

The chief executive is in a lonely position. There are areas where he cannot share his anxieties and uncertainties without creating greater anxieties in others. He may feel that to share uncertainties with even immediate subordinates might weaken his power and authority. He probably doesn't find in subordinates the ability to feel sympathy for his problem, since they are looking to him for stability and security for themselves. Their envy or desire for his position may preclude understanding and empathy.

One of the advantages of a training laboratory for the top executive is that it takes him away from the home company and puts him, for a change, in a society of peers. He is no longer top boss; but by putting aside status he opens up new avenues of learning for himself.

In group situations with other chief executives, reactions to any one top executive's behavior are not likely to be as guarded as those of subordinates. When the executive's defensiveness signals resistance to change, he will more readily be made aware of it. He can learn the need for openness, and can practice ways of encouraging it.

Because the chief executive signals through his behavior so much more than through his words, he needs a chance to test his reactive and defensive behavior in a "safe" environment. Accepting and absorbing information critical of one's behavior is always painful. People need time and experience to cope with their defensive reactions. They need to develop trust in the motivations of those supplying the information, and they need practice and skill in inviting reactions to their behavior. Certainly, the top executive needs to be able to accept feedback from his subordinates with minimal defensiveness if he is to secure meaningful help from them.

Often company problems are so close to the chief executive that he can't see the forest for the trees. He, himself, may be so much a part of the problems that he cannot recognize them or interpret them accurately. Distance lends perspective. T-group simulation of organizational problems permits the chief executive to play a role different from that in his company, and usually as a result back-home problems fall into place and solutions come to hand more readily.

As one president, whose group had run through a merger exercise, said: "Our experience that morning was truly amazing to me. I saw my company flash before me, and the confusing problems I had been struggling with became amazingly clear. I saw now why some acquisitions we had made turned out unsuccessfully. I went back home with greater confidence and with plans for action. While it would be too much to say that they all worked out, I can say that the program started us on a productive path."

Another president reported: "Through becoming more aware of others' problems, I found that my problems were not unique. As a result, I achieved more inner peace and ability to face some of the problems of our team."

Many chief executives have gone on to initiate organizational development programs in their home companies after their participation in a presidents' conference. The following example illustrates the steps involved.

One company president who had participated in a conference asked afterward about the next step he might take in developing a team-building program in his company. The long-term nature of such an undertaking was stressed, as were the dangers of starting too rapidly and with too many people. I asked if his vice presidents would understand what he wanted to do, or would be as aware of the human problems as he now was. He didn't think so. There had been a number of recent changes in his top staff and he wasn't certain how much tension existed.

It was suggested that it might be best for some of his top vice presidents to attend the conference. Within a year four had. The president had also returned for another program. I then agreed, as the next step, to come to his company and talk to the top eight people, and to report to the entire group what I had learned. My conversations pinpointed the following major problems.

□ Although the president was close to retirement age, the others were young, energetic, highly competent, and restless. There was need for the group to gain a sense of responsibility for the management of the company as a whole as opposed to responsibility for their own divisions.

□ There was need to help the president gradually share some power and authority with his associates.

□ The intense competition between several of the vice presidents had to be reduced and a number of other long-standing interpersonal problems solved before any cohesiveness could occur.

□ One of the vice presidents would have to be selected to assume a chief role under the president.

□ There was need for the president to receive direct feedback from the others on the impact of his behavior.

After the report was received, I agreed to meet with them for two 3-day sessions over the next few months to help them work on the problems. At the same time, the vice presidents who had not yet attended a key executive conference made arrangements to do so.

The three-day meetings with me, plus a number of other meetings among the executives, resulted in several significant actions:

1. After much sharing of competitive feelings and hostilities, an executive vice president was selected whom all could accept and work with.

2. The president relinquished some power after expectations and role boundaries between himself and the new executive vice president were talked through.

3. The group coalesced into a team after painfully working through personal differences and boundary feelings between major divisions.

While a total organization development plan for the company as a whole was not achieved, the attitude and morale of the top group had significantly improved. Future team-building work was to continue as a regular part of company growth.

The chief executive is frequently out of communication with his wife in crucial areas of his life. The complexities of his role, the responsibilities he faces, the demands of the organization upon him, the pressure of time, all gradually reduce important areas of communication at home. Each reduction tends to close off further areas of communication, as if, with Avenues A and B gone, Avenue C cannot be reached. And so a potential source of support, understanding, and help may be absent. As a consequence the executive carries the burden of *unshared* problems in addition to the problems themselves.

The wives of chief executives say they face a different problem: a problem of identity. They feel they are viewed by their husbands as a collection of functions—hostess, children's chauffeur, mother, house-keeper, community leader, mistress—but not as persons.

Actually both husband and wife, busily fulfilling the roles demanded of them, see each other as the doers of specific tasks. The more they become concerned with their own roles, the more diminished becomes their understanding of each other's problems. Communication becomes superficial. Mutual support withers away.

Inclusion of wives in the presidents' conferences is a recent development. How does it help?

"I gained a deeper understanding of the tremendous stress and strain my husband is constantly under," one wife said. "What is more important, we both learned ways in which I could help him with this strain. I had not understood his problems before and tended to blame him for poor communication. Now we both realize our joint responsibility for communication, and more importantly, how we can go about it."

Both husband and wife are, almost in a literal sense, captives of the organization. Their behavior and the image they project to the public world must be carefully controlled. The demands of the company greatly determine their family life, the clubs they join, the schools their children attend, even their dress and social behavior. For the prestige and power the chief executive possesses, a family price is paid. The price frequently creates conflict between husband and wife, and revolt by children. Learning to face this problem as a family team was one purpose of the Presidents' Conference.

One chief executive's wife said: "The insights both of us gained regarding our love-hate relationship with that important creature that gives us so much and demands so much from us—the company—were thunderous. I am not certain that I have quite resolved the bitterness that built up within me over the years when it seemed that all critical issues in our lives were subordinated to the non-negotiable, ever-present priorities of the company. But it did help my husband to arrive at a stand that set some boundaries on the claims the company had on our lives."

The Presidents' Conferences have aimed to help the chief executive and his wife not only to gain greater insights into their relations to each other, but to become a working team that could improve both family and company. Many chief executives have found the benefits surprisingly direct.

"The conference made a vast difference in our family relations," one president said. "As a result, I was freer from stress and more effective in the company. And improving communications in our family taught me how to improve communications in the office. I no longer ducked human relations problems because I was afraid I would make them worse. Now I was better able to open them up."

Said another: "By learning to communicate better with my wife, I gained in ability to work more openly and effectively with my team of subordinates."

And a third: "Home was a less risky place to try out some of the things I had learned about myself. I was afraid that I would look awkward and phony if I suddenly tried to be different in the company. My wife helped me in testing greater openness with others."

And yet another: "I remember we discussed how far the effect of the conference was likely to operate in the individual's private life and how much in his business life. I now feel this discussion to have been unreal. A good training group operates at a depth of penetration where there is no distinction between one type of human contact and another. *It operates where a man's personality is.* I also believe, from the evidence I saw, that if a man volunteers to take part in the conference, the company should actually press him to take his wife along. As an experience shared, if it should have any effect upon his married life it is likely to be a beneficial one. But as a disturbing experience not shared and difficult to communicate, because the wife did not attend, it could conceivably have a divisive effect."

Not everyone, to be sure, benefits from sensitivity training. Its value varies from individual to individual and company to company. But most people do benefit, and the majority of participants have learned and grown.

part five

Organization Development

New Strategies of Organization Development

Heads of organizations have discovered that, no matter how logical their mechanical arrangements, how modern the technology, or how clearly responsibilities are assigned, work flow is anything but smooth. The difficulties grow out of poor relationships, faulty distribution of responsibility, bureaucratic practices, work overload, day-to-day pressures, and the like.

Most organizations operate substantially below their capacity. Their staffs don't set realistic goals, they plan poorly, they make decisions too slowly, too quickly, or without enough information, and they somehow never really solve their problems in a way that keeps them solved. It is, therefore, to the human side of industry—the capacity of people to give and receive help, to develop interpersonal skills, to respond constructively to questions of authority, influence, and power—that new strategies of organization development (OD) are addressed.

OD is far different from the "efficiency systems" introduced to speed up production in the past. OD in its current form is a collaborative effort by the members of an organization to develop their capabilities so that the organization can attain optimum levels of performance. The members of the organization are involved in planning, problem solving, and decision making with the question always in mind: "What can we do to improve the effectiveness of our organization?" An essential strategy of OD is to work on the total system, not on a part.

An OD program involves all the staff in a common effort to improve the way information is shared, decisions are arrived at, and teamwork developed. The involvement of top managers is essential, because it is often the failure of top managers to build trust and to be open with each other and with their subordinates that causes the indifferent performance of the people in the organization.

OD programs introduce techniques that promote openness and candor and establish a collaborative problem-solving climate. These can lead

259

to greater acceptance at all levels of solutions arrived at or changes made. Through the encouragement of greater self-management and self-direction, all members of the organization may find greater satisfaction in their work and feel greater commitment to setting and meeting high performance standards.

To get an OD process started a company will initially need the assistance of a behavioral science practitioner who can help the supervisors and managers assess the strengths and weaknesses of the organization and offer solutions for improving it. His objective is to help the members help themselves and to transfer his skills and values to the staff as rapidly as he can.

By helping the members of the organization to gain insights into what is going on around them—the consequences of the human interactions that accompany the normal flow of work, the significance of the attitudes expressed at meetings or informal encounters—he helps them learn to identify and confront the trouble spots on their own and gradually to learn to solve their problems without him.

Among the most widely used OD methods—though there are many others—are data feedback, sensitivity training, confrontation sessions, team building, process analysis, and third-party intervention.

The interdependencies among people in an organization make conflict inevitable. A moderate level of competition is healthy. It increases motivation and stimulates a variety of viewpoints. But excessive disagreement can be debilitating. Organization development accepts a manageable amount of conflict and focuses on building the capacity to deal with it, or at least to minimize antagonisms that can't be resolved under prevailing conditions.

A confrontation session can make some staff members apprehensive. But when the purpose is to clarify and improve relationships, to recognize what triggers conflicts, and to find ways to de-escalate them, the risks are minimized.

One way of lessening the risks of direct confrontation is to have the behavioral science practitioner present when the individuals involved in a dispute meet with each other. As a neutral third party, he can improve the relationship by helping the principals find ways of resolving the conflict. As an outside third party, he can prevent polarization of the differences and contribute to the likelihood of a constructive solution. He acts in some ways like the referee or umpire in a sporting event, or the mediator or counselor in a labor or marital conflict.

Openness, trust, and candor are not truly understood or appreciated until they are experienced. That is why top management must understand what an OD effort really means. For unless top management is totally involved, the effort is unlikely to prove successful.

In the next decade organizations will need optimum utilization of their human resources if they are to meet the pyramiding demands of employees, stockholders, and customers. The striking success that some companies have already had in improving their operations brightens the prospects that the OD strategies will be used much more widely in the years ahead. The chapters that follow describe the successful application of OD techniques in a variety of organizations.

A.J.M.

SHELDON A. DAVIS

Building an Organization for the Future

TRW Systems Group

The typical complex industrial organization contains many problems that are difficult to deal with even after they are identified. People compete with one another instead of working together in a common effort to get the job done. They harbor hidden resentments and resist having them brought out into the open. They go home and tell their wives or husbands what is really bothering them on the job instead of discussing their problems with the colleagues with whom such problems must be solved. Managers are constantly being surprised by the sudden emergence of long-brewing problems. The reason is that no one under their supervision is able to communicate openly with them.

It has long been the clear policy of the TRW Systems Group to be concerned with the attitudes and satisfactions of its people. Top executives of the group are aware that so diversified and technologically advanced an enterprise depends on cooperation among a lot of highly educated people, trained in a wide variety of disciplines. Fully 20 percent of the group's salaried employees have advanced degrees, including nearly 350 Ph.D.s.

Each employee's goals receive the most serious consideration. Company policies, although explicitly stated, are nevertheless administered whenever possible in a manner flexible enough to take into account individual situations and personal needs. This is feasible because the company's work is spread over a variety of projects, avoiding concentration of all resources in only one or two major contract areas. Major dislocations in people's plans, which could occur in the event of the cancellation of a very large project, can often be prevented.

The Space Technology Laboratories of Thomson Ramo Wooldridge came into being in 1953. When the name of the parent corporation was shortened to TRW Inc. in 1965, the unit was renamed TRW Systems Group. At present this group of scientists, engineers, and manufacturing workers is turning out many exciting products of advanced technology—

planetary probes, antisubmarine warfare systems, Apollo lunar module descent rocket engines, urban traffic control systems, and a host of others. The Systems Group employs 10,000 people in twenty-five locations throughout the world.

The group achieved a high degree of diversification by the time it was about ten years old. It changed from being essentially a one-customer contractor (to the U.S. Air Force as systems engineering and technical direction contractor for the ballistic missile programs) into a fully competitive "aerospace industry" contractor. Organizational expansion and broadening of capabilities qualified it for participation in a diversity of technical markets. This expansion, together with rapid growth, inevitably brought on many of the traditional problems of corporate bigness, increasingly entrenched functional interests, internal politics, personality conflicts, organizational parochialism, obsolescence of spirit on the part of long-time members of the professional staff, and a general lack of insight about possibilities for further professional growth and career development. It was generally agreed by the early 1960s that many of the organizational characteristics of the TRW Systems Group needed to be improved.

Employees and outsiders considered the Systems Group "a good place to work." But it was clear that a more explicit and formal approach to career and organization development was desirable. As a first step, a statement outlining the group's management philosophy was drafted by the industrial relations staff and circulated to top executives for comment (although not necessarily for official endorsement). A number of changes and revisions were made, and the outline was then tested with a larger group of managers. What finally emerged was the following statement of philosophy:

□ The individual employee is the company's most important resource, and major focus is placed on providing him with the things he needs to work at his best.

□ Work should be challenging, interesting, and personally rewarding. Assignments are made and responsibility and authority are delegated with this aim in mind.

□ A great deal of trust is placed in each person; there is a minimum of controls, constraints, and external forces telling him how to do his job.

□ The management systems created within the group (formal policies, procedures, and standards) are intended as a platform from which each person can operate rather than as a set of inflexible rules confining him.

□ A "technical democracy" exists in which there is a society or group of peers rather than a rigid hierarchy; there is a relative lack of social distance between the employees and their supervisors at every echelon of management.

□ Great emphasis is placed on quality, on technical excellence. The management philosophy is to attract the best people, provide an excellent work environment, give challenging assignments, and compensate adequately for good performance.

□ Long-term career opportunities and personal growth potential are available to a high percentage of key employees. Emphasis is placed on internal upward mobility and on offering individuals diversified job assignments.

□ In assigning responsibility, bias is toward giving "too much too soon" and toward stretching each person beyond his apparent capabilities, rather than toward pigeonholing him in an assignment where he has already proved himself.

□ There is a minimum of office politics. On issues of conflict the solution comes from direct confrontation of the people involved, rather than from passing the buck to higher levels for an arbitrary decision.

□ Stress is placed on delegation of authority and on spreading responsibility downward through the organization; a relatively large number of employees have personal responsibility for important tasks.

□ The management approach toward new ideas and concepts is experimental, rather than cautiously traditional.

□ Persons who will be directly affected by management decisions are given a greater-than-average opportunity to participate in the decision-making process.

TRW Systems Group has long regarded itself as an organization operating under D. M. McGregor's Theory Y assumptions, namely, that employees are trustworthy and capable of exercising personal initiative. Organizationally, the group is structured as a "matrix." In accomplishing a given task or project—such as the design of a spacecraft—resources and functional capabilities in many different parts of the group are asked to contribute according to specialties.

For example, the sponsor of a large spacecraft development project, the Orbiting Geophysical Observatory, is the OGO Project Office in the Space Vehicles Division. However, a lot of the technical work is done by specialists in various functional disciplines—electrical power systems design, flight trajectory design, propulsion system development, and others. These men are assigned to divisions of the Systems Group like the Electronic Systems Division and the Science and Technology Division. The matrix organization requires that there be open access and cooperation between various persons and units within the company regardless of established boundaries or lines of operational direction and reporting. Moreover, communications between all employees, at all levels in Systems Group, should be trustworthy, and employees should identify and resolve conflicts in the normal course of doing business.

Communication blocks among different parts of the organization, however, frequently caused problems. People in one area didn't trust or didn't understand what people in another area were saying. By bringing the two groups together in an informal, away-from-the-office environment, and encouraging them to discuss their differences freely, it was often possible to bring hidden problems into the open. Planned confrontations provided ways to get conflicts on the table early and to resolve them before they became serious impediments.

When the Systems Group management seriously began to consider establishing a formal program of organization development, the primary objective was not to improve morale, or "make people happier," although these were recognized as desirable side effects. The primary purpose was to improve the company in ways that would enlarge profits. It was stipulated from the start that changes made should be tailored to work projects on hand and aimed at their support.

In 1961, Herbert Shepard, a psychologist then on the faculty of Case Institute of Technology, spent part of the summer at TRW. He and a number of key executives examined the possibility of such a program. He returned for a month the following year to explore it further.

Just prior to Shepard's second visit, TRW's director of industrial relations and his associate had attended a "leadership development laboratory" (also called sensitivity training) conducted by the University of California. This experience strengthened their belief that sensitivity training could play a useful role in bettering the division's operations.

A white paper was prepared on the subject, stating the following aims: (1) to increase the leadership skills of managers, (2) to develop interpersonal and group membership skills, and (3) to create an environment in the company more conducive to individual and group effectiveness. It was recognized that the Systems Group would continue to grow only if the people in it were able to deal directly with the interpersonal problems constantly arising.

The first step was a decision to experiment with a "team building" meeting for the key members of a new project, to introduce them to sensitivity training. The project director and a dozen or so of his associates met in an off-site location for a couple of days. They explored the best means of carrying out the new project. The atmosphere was informal. The personal relationships existing within the group were frankly discussed; barriers and constraints that hindered them were examined.

This first team-building meeting was viewed as a preliminary test. If those present could feel free to look objectively at their own and one another's behavior on the job, to question some of their own premises, to examine some of the assumptions of others in the group, then they could work out their own approaches to better collaboration. Group members told the director of industrial relations and the president of the company that the group had found the team-building experiment very helpful.

The response of top management was to explore the process further. The idea was: "Let's try things. If they work, continue them. If they don't, modify them, improve them, or drop them." Out of the first successful team-building experience came a company-sponsored leadership development laboratory, held in the fall of 1963. It was attended by forty-eight employees. Again results were very encouraging, and those who attended urged that more such laboratories should be held.

Outside consultants were employed as co-trainers for the laboratories, along with a member of the TRW staff. The aim was to combine outside expertise and objectivity with inside familiarity and understanding of company problems and needs. Over the years, a number of outside consultants who are members of the National Training Laboratories network have assisted in the program. In addition, TRW retained a practicing psychiatrist, Dr. Gordon Goodhart, as a permanent consultant. Both in laboratory training activities and in on-the-job consulting, outside experts are always paired with a company staff member.

These outside experts have become closely involved with the organization through extended assignments to operating divisions and major functional sections of the company. They have become familiar with our problems. We have encouraged them to experiment with a wide variety of training techniques, including various forms of sensitivity training. The sensitivity training experiences proved to be very helpful to most participants. Attendance at a leadership development laboratory is generally viewed as the first step in a much broader program that has evolved since 1963. These days much emphasis is placed on simulating real-life intergroup problems. For example, a group working on a spacecraft project office may feel that it is not being adequately supported by an electrical power subsystem design unit. By bringing the two groups together in an informal, off-site atmosphere, with a consultant present, it has often been possible to reach much greater mutual understanding of such matters as how each organization manages its budget, what kinds of personality differences there may be, what other unrecognized forces may have engendered distrust between the units. Such team building across organizational lines has frequently been started during a project's proposal-preparation stage and carried forward through the life of the project. The intergroup sessions produce written suggestions for action.

At present, team-building labs represent perhaps 10 to 15 percent of the total organization development program. The balance of the effort is in on-the-job situations, working out real problems with the people who are involved. This has led to some very important changes in the decision-making and problem-solving processes at TRW.

It has also made considerable difference in the coaching of subordinates by supervisors. The program covers such areas as the evaluation of the subordinate's work performance, reasons behind decisions regarding pay raises or promotions, and other aspects of the boss–worker relationship that frequently cause friction or anxiety. By creating an atmosphere for the open exchange of ideas and feelings, a far better relationship between the supervisor and his team is established.

A great many of the Systems Group leadership development labs have been held in off-site locations such as Ojai, California. Ojai is a small town about eighty miles from Los Angeles, offering typical resort facilities of the sort frequently used for business conferences or seminars. The atmosphere is attractive, relaxed, and away from ringing telephones and other office distractions. The early labs lasted an entire week. Recently a number of successful labs have been held in only two or three days. In each lab there is generally a mixture of employees drawn from similar levels throughout the company, but from a number of different staff and operational units. They may or may not be personally acquainted with one another. In other words, they are usually organizational "cousins." This tends to preclude preoccupation with a particular job problem, and helps prevent discussions from deteriorating into gripe sessions.

Since the first experimental leadership development laboratory was started in 1962, more than 1,100 employees have taken part in formal leadership labs, and more than 6,500 have participated in team-building and intergroup meetings.

With the increasing maturity of the program, the relative proportion of leadership laboratories to application laboratories and team-building and intergroup meetings has decreased. A good deal of sophistication has been acquired about how to conduct application labs and team-building activities that help to develop skills around specific company problems and that provide training in organization development techniques.

Attendance at the leadership development laboratories has always been voluntary. Procedures ensure that those present remain fully aware that they have a choice about participating. The selection of candidates to attend a leadership laboratory is based on the following criteria:

Voluntarily expressed interest in the program.

Apparent readiness to profit from the experience.

Likelihood of making practical use of the experience.

Relevance to team-building or intergroup training activities in which the candidate may participate later.

Some supervisors seem to want employees in their unit to attend "for their own good" or so that "all my people will be on the team." There have been instances in which a manager acted in accordance with what he perceived to be company policy, even though there is no policy—written or unwritten—for mandatory participation in the leadership training portion of the program. Whenever such interpretations are discovered, actions are taken to check them, since they could threaten the usefulness of the leadership laboratory concept and are counter to the values of the program, which emphasize self-determination.

The following are some of the procedures currently used in the TRW Systems Group organization development program to deal with difficult human problems. The procedures are continually changing and the ones in use now may endure, or they may not. It is what works that counts at TRW, and thus far these procedures have proved themselves.

Behavioral Science Consultants. An outside consultant skilled in human behavior, sometimes called a "third party interventionist," comes into the organization to assess behavioral problems and suggest remedies. Organizations tend to become locked into their own particular way of operating. They have difficulty in obtaining fresh perspectives. Outside consultants can be very useful as diagnosticians.

Diagnostic Techniques. There are several effective diagnostic techniques. One found very helpful at TRW Systems Group is referred to as "sensing." This involves the simple process of having an executive or supervisor—at any level in the organization—sit down with a group (typically a random or representative sample) several levels removed from him in the chain of command and attempt to "get his finger on the pulse." He encourages everyone to speak freely. "Sensing" can take various forms, from relatively formal and structured discussions to quite informal gripe sessions. The goal is to get a sense of how people feel about the work situation, what is bothering them, what they feel about the organization or their type of work. It may also be more action-oriented. The sensor may say: "I'd like to listen to any of your ideas or suggestions and make specific recommendations for changes."

An example of a specific use of "sensing" is in the preparation of material for the annual report to employees from the head of the Systems Group. The report consists typically of two parts: the first is the report of top management to the employees, and the second is the employee's report to top management as brought out in sensing sessions. To find out staff attitudes, the head of the Systems Group has a series of meetings with groups of about a dozen employees, drawn from different parts of the Systems Group. The meetings are explained as opportunities to talk to the boss, tell him what is bothering them, and ask questions. Of course the meetings not only give the employee a chance to talk to the boss, but also give the boss a valuable opportunity to find out what people are thinking.

Organization Mirror. This refers to various techniques by which a particular unit collects data from other units with which it works. The procedure is intended to provide feedback about how well the unit is performing its job, particularly with respect to its interaction with other units.

If a unit (or an individual employee in the unit) is having difficulty in dealing with others, one reason may be that they are not hearing each other. Each group is thinking, "Why can't you understand my side of this? How come you don't see that I am doing it the way the customer, system, or boss requires me to do the job?"

The mirror technique, in which members of one unit examine the problems raised by members of other units, usually with the impartial assistance of a consultant or trainer, will often convert such attitudes into more constructive ones. It might be summed up in this manner: "Look, obviously something about our group and its method of operation is bothering you. What are we doing that is getting in the way?" Once this attitude is established, then cooperative progress, which can lead to identification and solution of the trouble, is frequently possible.

A typical example of the use of the mirror technique resulted, a few years ago, from some operating problems that had developed between the "product assurance" staff and certain engineering units. Friction was evidenced by an increase in complaints from engineers. They said the inspectors were "going by the book," that they were more interested in exposing problems than in solving them, as well as other related complaints. When the two groups were brought together with a consultant, it was disclosed that each group felt the other was unaware of its operating difficulties: "You guys don't appreciate how I have to do my job." Candid discussions led to great improvement.

Intergroup Building. Closely related in many ways to the mirror technique is intergroup building. In the TRW Systems Group, this can be done across line and staff, or across functional areas such as electronic design and mechanical integration. Frequently it is discovered that groups, which should be working cooperatively, are really acting in a highly competitive and destructive manner.

One approach to intergroup building is to simulate a merger. Two groups are combined into a single operating unit; a competing or complementary company or two technical functions are joined; or there may be a new arrangement of staff functions. In practice, an intergroup building session involves a "committee" from each organization. Each side first draws up a list describing how it feels about working with the other. Then, with the assistance of a trainer to assure that the emphasis is on "hearing," each group listens without comment to the other's list. This opens the way to a cooperative approach. A desirable end result is a combined list of proposals for action.

Leadership Development Laboratories. Leadership development techniques, such as grid labs, sensitivity training, and other types of laboratory training, constitute a means to an end rather than ends in themselves. As a result of experience and evolution over the years, the approach has been to stress personal values rather than the more impersonal phenomena of group dynamics. An individual's interest is aroused much more by matters that concern him directly than by impersonal, theoretical issues. Most of the laboratory time is spent in groups of not more than ten to twelve persons, with two co-trainers. One may be an outside consultant, the other a Systems Group employee.

Several experimental laboratories have examined the employee's career goals, taking into account the needs and desires of his family. The object is to help him develop keener insight into what he really wants to do with his life and, where possible, to help instill optimism, a feeling that he can actually realize his (perhaps unperceived) true objectives. For certain employees, this special form of laboratory has been particularly rewarding, perhaps even more valuable than the traditional leadership development lab approach.

Whether it is the special life-career planning format or the more conventional, personally oriented, leadership development laboratory, most of the employees who have participated over the past several years have agreed strongly that the experience is stimulating and rewarding. In many instances, moreover, leadership laboratory training serves merely as the first step, or initial point of entry, into the process of organization development. The employee goes from this initial experience into other group-oriented activities, such as team-building and intergroup-building labs, which aim more directly at changing the basic climate of the organization.

Team Building. Team building involves a special application of organization development. A trainer, preferably an outside consultant, works with a supervisor and the people he directs. The objective is to improve—in a modified laboratory environment, usually at an off-site location, in a somewhat informal atmosphere that is a brief respite from the daily grind—the personal relationships among the team in the context of their organization and projects. Team building has been used quite effectively both with established groups working on a long-term project and with new groups that are being assembled to undertake a new enterprise.

Although there are many variations in the team-building technique, the presence of an outside third party is essential. He can be someone from the internal staff, such as a member of the personnel department who is skilled in organization development methodology, or a consulting psychologist brought in from the outside. The head of the company group sets the basic agenda in a first brief meeting. He begins by asking:

"How can we increase our effectiveness in doing our job? We will be working together as a group for the forseeable future. We are highly interdependent. I can't accomplish my job without your help, and vice versa. Let's spend a little time looking at our procedures, our methods of reaching decisions, how I relate to you, how you relate to me, and how we cope with other parts of the company."

Another frequent practice is for the outside consultant to interview each member of the group to develop a more detailed agenda. Then at the start of the meeting, the consultant reviews the data he has collected and the group begins to sort out the really significant agenda items.

The meeting then moves into the "general phase." Improvements in the way the group works are suggested. These bring out personal likes and dislikes, as well as attitudes toward operating procedures. Discussion frequently clears the air, and the group becomes receptive to a more constructive approach. Later, the meeting enters a new phase: the group examines how it relates to other groups and teams within the company. During this phase, the team often develops new insights that help its members to see that they themselves may be causing some of the problems. A common follow-up activity is to have one or more meetings with the other group.

Organization Development Workshops. A series of workshops have been conducted to expose more executives, mostly at the middle-management level, to the tenets of the organization development program.

Intern Program. In recent years, a program has been developed through which personnel managers and others who want to participate in the organization development program can receive specialized training. The faculty includes outside consultants and company staff.

Research Effort. TRW currently supports, through the industrial relations staff, a number of research activities associated with organization development. These activities are aimed at fostering acceptance of a broad range of desirable values and actions. Among them:

☐ Recognition that an employee is involved in a growth process rather than fixed in a permanent position.

☐ Acceptance and utilization of individual differences instead of resistance to individuality.

☐ A view of workers as whole persons rather than primarily in terms of their job description.

☐ Encouragement of appropriate expression and effective use of feelings rather than a walling off of emotions.

☐ Encouragement of authentic behavior instead of maskmanship and game playing.

☐ Use of status for organizationally relevant purposes instead of for personal prestige and maintaining power.

☐ Encouragement of appropriate confrontation rather than avoidance of facing others with relevant data.

☐ Willingness to accept necessary risks.

☐ Emphasis on collaboration rather than competition.

Many people would agree with these values, and in fact might claim that they use them in running their own companies. However, there is often a large gap between expressing belief in these values and actually practicing them. A number of organizations have adopted a management-by-objectives program which may include many of the above values. But, too often, the process can become mechanical.

How has our organization development program worked out?

Experience shows that the kinds of evaluation data that interest academicians do not necessarily satisfy industrial executives. Some measure of the impact of a particular strategy has been obtained with questionnaires. In one case, a questionnaire was administered "before and after" to a relatively large cross section of employees who participated in a team-building meeting at one of the company's major systems project offices. These questionnaires attempted to determine changes in attitude to various quantifiable aspects of their jobs—number of internal misunderstandings, frequency of rejection of work output by superiors, frequency of complaints regarding personal or group performance.

The results were not of nearly as much interest to top management as were qualitative answers to questions about the relations of employees with customer representatives, the relationship between the project office and supporting functional laboratories, and similar matters.

An effort was made to check on the effectiveness of one of the early team-building sessions by interviewing the project manager six months afterward. Although he could not translate the result into dollars, he was certain that his group's effectiveness had significantly improved after the team-building meeting. He had observed marked changes in the attitude of key staff members, and estimated that the two-day team-building meeting had made possible an acceleration of the project schedule.

Management generally agrees that there are many direct and indirect benefits. In some instances, team-building work has been closely correlated with a reduction of conflict between two groups. Perhaps even more obvious has been the improvement in working relationships between key people whose jobs require them to work cooperatively. The procedure used to improve a relationship between key individuals is similar to that in intergroup meetings, except that two men, rather than two organizational units, meet with a consultant or internal trainer and explore contentious issues. Although this approach to organization development is used only in very special cases, it has provided several opportunities to observe an explicit change in relationships.

The organization mirror technique has also offered clear evidence of improved performance and better interaction between the unit in question and other parts of the company. This has been measured, again in qualitative terms, by interviews with employees, by the observations of the industrial relations staff, and by the assessment to top executives made before and after the sessions.

The top management of the Systems Group has steadily supported the program. It has also resisted overenthusiastic claims of those partisans who suggest it will solve everything.

In recent years we have seen some signs of what may be termed "obsolescence of spirit" on the part of employees and supervisors. This has shown itself in decreased interest in such resources as organization development and a growing feeling of satisfaction with the status quo. For example, there have been some problems applying organization development activities to the assimilation of new employees. The problems generally arise because the TRW Systems Group has managerial practices different from those of other organizations.

Some newcomers occasionally have difficulty in sorting out what they see as permissiveness. To the new employee, the unusual freedom characteristic of TRW often presents a picture of organized chaos. It is difficult for him to perceive the underlying management discipline which, although actually present, is exercised only on exceptional occasions. (Similar confusion sometimes results after an employee has attended his first training laboratory and then returns to the "real world" of business as usual in the peer-group society of his office. However, this happens less today than six or seven years ago. The office environment has changed to the point where values are now more supportive to the employee's laboratory learning.)

Although the formal organization development program is now about seven years old, there are still many gaps in the way it is implemented in the company as a whole. Cooperative working relationships have been built at the top three echelons of management. Below this level, however, there are still many strained relationships. As the base of the pyramid widens, conflicts increase. Many of these could be helped by an organization development program, but obviously the costs of extending organization development to all parts of the Systems Group would be high in time and money.

The broad assessment, up to the present, has been that the program warrants increased financial investment. The results of the sensitivity training program have shown that unfavorable side effects are insignificant. In the five-year period through 1968, nearly 7,500 employees participated in laboratories of one sort or another. Out of this large number, there have been only three cases in which emotional difficulty of some kind was reported to have occurred after the experience. Of the three, two reported later that the laboratory experience was of real benefit even though it temporarily triggered anxiety. In the third instance, the information obtained was not sufficient to make any determination.

Despite the small number of such incidents, several precautions are taken in assembling participants for a laboratory. A consultant psychiatrist is employed. One of the most significant factors in limiting the frequency of difficulties is strict adherence to the policy of *completely voluntary* participation in the leadership development laboratories. Other routine precautions include prelaboratory orientation, individual interviews with the laboratory staff personnel, distribution of descriptive literature and questionnaires, and review of each person's history of mental health. These steps have been highly effective in identifying those who may have a tendency to react adversely, and a number of candidates have either voluntarily withdrawn their application or arranged to defer their participation at the suggestion of the laboratory staff.

Within the Systems Group, we anticipate a steady growth of the program, including the use of new techniques. The possibility of adapting other kinds of laboratory experience continues to be explored. There is a need to experiment, to innovate, in order to maintain the vitality and excitement of the organization development effort.

WILLIAM J. CROCKETT / ROBERT E. GAERTNER
SAM FARRY

Humanistic Management in a Fast-Growing Company

Saga Administrative Corporation

While profitably managing their college dining room during the 1940s, three college students converted the routine style of institutional feeding into an "as much as you want" family atmosphere. After graduation they went on to start their own company, Saga Administrative Corporation, and to offer similar service at other universities. During the 1960s the company grew explosively—revenues increased nearly thirteen times to a 1970 figure of $147 million, and earnings per share increased elevenfold. Today, Saga provides food service to over 450 universities and other institutions and is beginning to diversify into related fields.

The company's operations are widely dispersed geographically. The food service manager at each client institution exercises substantial autonomy in his own operation. Managers are supervised by district managers, who travel extensively. Most of the district managers are young—the average age is twenty-eight—and many came to Saga after working as students in Saga-managed college dining rooms. As a result of the company's rapid growth they have come to expect frequent promotions.

In 1968, members of top management, seeking to clarify their management concepts and practices in the field of human relations, initiated an organization development program at Saga. Although management found the concepts hard to verbalize, especially at first, they involved two central notions. First, that there should be an informal working relationship between bosses and subordinates; the company's philosophy is that each person—regardless of status, authority, or responsibilities—is to be regarded as an important human being with a worthwhile contribution to make. The second notion was that the organization should encourage an entreprenurial spirit that will result in personal feelings of power, excitement, fun, and a sense of fulfillment throughout the organization. As the chairman of the board of directors phrased it:

Humanistic management, as I prefer to call our effort, must ultimately be the total way of corporate life. . . . It becomes the most essential and basic standard of our interpersonal relationships and takes its place alongside our moral and ethical code in being one of our most important and fundamental business beliefs. . . . It becomes the measuring stick of our corporate congruence between what we are and what we say and what we hope to become.

The organization development program began as the direct result of a meeting of the top company executives held in February 1968. The meeting was conducted by two senior consultants from the faculty of UCLA. Top executives had become concerned that, as Saga grew, important human qualities were gradually disappearing. They felt that middle and lower-level managers were becoming increasingly dependent on their supervisors for decisions and initiation of action. It seemed as if everyone wanted headquarters to provide far more direction and support than was realistic. These concerns were heightened by the results of two companywide management attitude surveys conducted by the Industrial Relations Center of the University of Chicago, one in 1964 and another in 1967. These surveys turned up a lot of disgruntlement. Common complaints included:

The "Big Daddy" attitude of headquarters: *"Headquarters knows best!"*
Management by decree: *"We have no knowledge of how operating decisions are reached."*
"Decisions are bucked up the line at all levels for fear of having no topside support."
"Why do we preach policies that we can't fulfill?"
"As the company gets larger and larger, there are more and more layers and we have less and less impact upon decisions."
"There is more emphasis on criticism—the bad, no matter how small— than in praising the good, no matter how large."
"There is no atmosphere or climate for working closely with the boss. So the boss doesn't get the information he really needs in order to perform his job."

At the 1968 meeting, the executives spoke of their reasons for wanting an OD program. They hoped it would help managers at all levels develop a management style and philosophy that would preserve and rebuild as necessary the human values key executives believed to be important. They hoped an OD program would support a climate in the company that would permit people to actively influence company decisions on matters that affected them. Though it would initially start at the top, the OD program should eventually include everyone in the organization. All managers should participate in its formulation. Its major thrust, at the outset, would be to address the issues raised by the attitude study.

Precisely what was meant by organization development, or what it would come to mean, was not equally clear to everyone. Neither was it certain that the hoped-for results could be achieved. We all simply knew that there was a pressing need for a more effective organization, and we wanted to move in that direction.

At that first meeting, the skills of the UCLA consultants helped create a climate of trust. There was relatively personal and open communication among the participants about their job relationships. The critical question was: "How can we work together more effectively?" In this context, feelings, attitudes, opinions, perceptions, observations, and assumptions were all considered.

Direct and even abrasive communication was encouraged in order to clear up old misunderstandings. The agenda consisted of issues important to all executives at the meeting. Information or data regarding these issues was collected beforehand. The participants focused major attention on resolving issues in which they were personally involved, taking care to respond to the needs of the organization as well as to those of the individuals involved. The meeting concluded with decisions about concrete steps that were to follow. Some of these related to individual changes of behavior, some to organizational issues, and some to the correction of operational problems.

The tenor of the meeting can be illustrated by the directness with which one knotty issue was resolved. Several vice presidents believed that the president was spending too much time on pursuits which, though important to the corporation, were nevertheless of an outside nature and not directly related to providing the internal operating leadership they needed. They told the president this at the meeting. That discussion ultimately led him to agree to become chairman of the board and to turn over operating responsibility to the man who was then executive vice president. The outcome was beneficial to all involved. The chairman of the board was able to spend more energy on significant outside pursuits; meanwhile, necessary internal leadership became available. This event dramatized for everyone who had been present the potential of the confrontation process in solving group problems and group needs. But even more important, it also set an example of how able leaders can listen to and learn from subordinates and associates. Indeed, this meeting at the top validated the program for Saga managers at all levels.

One of the company's executives was appointed to direct the program full time, and in April 1968 he was ready to go to work. His first task was diagnostic. He had to understand more concretely events and behavior underlying the attitudes expressed in the management survey.

In May a series of seminars, attended by people from all levels of management, were held in various parts of the country to review the survey results. Managers discussed the meanings they attached to the attitudes expressed in the survey. They cited situations which they believed had contributed to these attitudes, and made recommendations for action.

These managers were extremely open in their discussions of problems that needed attention. They nailed their increased feeling of isolation and irrelevance to the company's sudden bigness. They felt that the actions of the top executives and the headquarters staff were inconsistent with what they believed was "the Saga way." Forms and procedures were not pretested in the field; they didn't fit, or were missing columns, and so on. Centrally developed menus didn't offer enough flexibility to meet local needs. Benefit programs were out of date—it now cost more to relocate, maternity benefits were inadequate, and so on. They resented the detailed procedures spelled out to reduce costs, and charged that apparently no one at headquarters understood or cared about the changing demands of activist students and apprehensive administrations.

At each level, managers believed they could no longer shape their own jobs or their own careers, or influence the company's policies. Bosses often handed down decisions without knowing what the subordinates knew or wanted—or, for that matter, without seeming to care. Many at the lowest levels believed themselves to be stuck alone on their respective campuses holding a fistful of resolvable problems.

The issues identified were complex, and there was an undercurrent of resentment and frustration. But there was also an optimistic conviction among the executives that the company leadership did care, and could and would make the necessary changes. The fact that the meetings were held seemed to reinforce good feelings about the company's motives and ethics.

A strategy was needed. Certainly the specific problems of benefits, procedures, systems, and the like could be addressed directly. That work was begun. But something more was needed, for these issues were obviously only the tip of a large iceberg. The most serious problem was the belief of many individuals that they could no longer influence corporate decisions that were important to them. The company and the system had grown beyond them, and they were being excluded.

Many discussions and planning sessions followed, involving the man guiding the program, key executives, managers, and several outside consultants. No one was willing to give up the principles of "the Saga way" and its view of man. Still, it wasn't working the way they hoped it would. It had worked best when the company was still small, when everyone knew everyone else, when they could meet face to face and wrestle things out.

Finally, however, the concept of an organization of interlocking teams emerged. This made sense. It was absurd for the food service manager in Burlington, Vermont, to expect that the executive vice president for food service in Menlo Park, California, could be of much real help to him with his day-to-day operating problems, even though he had handled a similar job only a few years before. What did make sense was for the food service manager to believe that he was part of a team in his own geographical area where he could get real support. He had to count on a district manager who honestly cared about him and his problems, and who in turn felt confident as a member of a larger regional team, and on up the line. Through the vehicle of a functioning team, an individual could make his voice heard in company decision-making processes.

Emphasis also needed to be placed on restoring relatively uncensored communications. If such freedom of communication could be recaptured, it would permit many flexible and innovative modes of contact among diverse parts of the organization when need demanded. For example, headquarters staff could collect information and test ideas in the field. Food service managers could press top executives for needed policy changes. This would help them to keep in direct touch with what was really going on.

It was decided that the building of effective teams throughout the company must become the primary objective of the program. In order for these teams to develop, individuals would have to break through the barriers of assumptions, unrealistic expectations, and fears by which they had gradually isolated themselves. This would not be easy; in particular, it would be hard for subordinates to confront their bosses. However, there was reason to hope that a series of two-day meetings bringing together bosses and subordinates might make it possible for them to identify the behavior patterns that militated against such confrontation. This might help bring about new patterns that would permit the expression of what needed to be said about work situations and personal relationships.

The decision was made to start the team-building program at the top. The executive vice president for food service operations, who had attended the previous diagnostic meeting, and his team of four area vice presidents would have the first two-day meeting in June. If this meeting were successful, then it was believed that the area vice presidents would continue the process with their own teams, and the program would be launched and under way. Potentially, the process could cascade to finally encompass the entire organization. It could be criticized and developed along the way. In addition, at each step in the process managers could assess the value of the effort to themselves, their subordinates, and their operations.

The June meeting was similar to the top management diagnostic meeting. Issues, however, differed, and attention was focused on immediately pressing problems. Results were more than had been hoped for. The vice presidents believed that they had gained significant insight into the complexities of human interaction in an organization. What's more, several of them identified aspects of their own behavior—such as not listening carefully, not supporting one another as a team, avoiding expressing their own concerns to their boss—which they believed were inhibiting their effectiveness as managers. It was becoming clearer to them what the organization development program was all about and how it might be useful to them. They emerged with a renewed sense of team spirit and an eagerness to proceed. In the fall of the year similar meetings were held involving the next two levels of management, with similar results.

Not everyone, however, was equally enthusiastic. At the end of 1968, one executive cornered the vice president of human relations and said: "Bill, this thing isn't working. We're having more fights than we ever had before and it's supposed to bring harmony." The complaint turned out to be useful. After they talked about it for a while, the two men decided the program was not necessarily intended to bring harmony. Hopefully, it would establish enough emotional security within the organization that disagreement could be tolerated.

In another situation, an executive vice president who was having trouble devising a compensation plan for his salesmen decided to let them develop one for themselves. After all, who knew more about the ins and outs of bonuses, leads, and negotiated contracts in their area than they did? He provided them with some rough guidelines and told them to go off for a couple of days and work out a plan. This approach was unorthodox. However, when the project was completed the vice president agreed that the plan was better than any he could have devised himself. What's more, the salesmen liked it because it was theirs.

In January 1969 the executive vice president of food service asked his area vice presidents and regional directors to evaluate the program to date. Despite some specific changes they wanted incorporated in the next phase of the program, two of the directors summarized their reactions this way: "I see considerable change for the better in the attitudes and behavior of people, and there is more openness, trust, and freedom," said one. Added the other: "I was frankly skeptical about the whole process and concept in the beginning. It must be pretty good for you to get a guy like me to admit he was wrong."

This favorable reaction launched the program into what came to be known as Team Building Phase Two, designed to involve district managers and food service directors from colleges and hospitals across the country. The program staff tried to respond to the recommendations by the vice presidents and regional directors. Plans were adopted to:

□ Give managers more decision in the content of team meetings and to have the meetings principally conducted by internal staff mem-

bers in order to reduce the heavy dependence upon outside professional consultants. The staff believed that internal consultants
would be better understood by the company managers and that they
would conduct a less theoretical program, and a less costly one.

☐ Give the meetings more formal structure.

☐ Conduct at least one refresher OD meeting for each team each
year. The staff believed that applications of organizational development would have to become an annual custom if the long-term
objectives were to be achieved.

These recommendations for the Phase Two meetings reflected the
fact that the teams that would attend these meetings were more autonomous than the groups of executives that met first. Each food service
director served an institution which made unique demands on him. He
did, however, share with his peers problems summed up in such questions as, "How did you handle this kind of situation?" or "Have you
had trouble with such and so?" He had a boss in common with them,
too. It might be feasible for these teams to meet three or four times
a year to keep in touch and to discuss new company directions and
problems.

With these things in mind, the staff initiated a three-month process
of trial and error in an effort to develop material which would be useful
to managers participating in Phase Two and to test a presentation style
which would be interesting and credible. As before, all Phase Two meetings included a leader from a different part of the organization. In
each meeting the role of this leader was to establish a climate of trust
and inquiry. All meetings involved five to ten people, lasted two days,
and were held at a location away from the press of telephones, crises,
and temptations to check on things.

By the end of June 1970, most of the management teams had held
team-building meetings. Though each of the meetings was unique in
many respects, and the outcomes varied widely, it was clear that a
pattern of more open communication and a revitalized sense of individual power was beginning to form throughout the company.

The consequences of these initial team-building meetings (Phases One
and Two) upon individuals and upon the organization are difficult to
assess. The following quotations capture some of the reactions of managers to the effort, reflect their diversity, and give some indication of
the possible impact.

*I think OD is probably one of the best tools we've used to help
management people develop. It helps us to put real value upon openness. We no longer feel the need to hold on to the false sense of security that not being open gives us. I think the best explanation of OD is
that it causes people to relate to others—not out of charity or anger,*

but because there is a definite need. That is the whole crux of the matter—the ability to talk and to listen, all based upon a mutual need to communicate.

I believe that we have gained in maturity. By this I mean that we can bring problems and disagreements to the surface and discuss them and give each other feedback about what seems to be inappropriate behavior without fear of hurting feelings or being seen as punishing. I believe we can make more logical, objective decisions now than was the case before.

The initial team-building meetings spawned a range of innovative managerial practices and concepts. Some were initiated by the program staff, others by managers. Teams have reiterated their need to hold additional team renewal meetings. They want them in order to learn more about how people can best work together in organizations.

Groups of managers have met in "life planning" sessions to gain perspective on their own lives and careers. As a result of these meetings, some managers have reinforced their own inclination to leave Saga, and have even been helped to find opportunities outside the company. In efforts at job enrichment they have explored ways to create a better match between what an individual most wants to do now and what his organizational responsibilities are.

Top managers have devised "organizational feedback" sessions where they periodically discuss problems informally with a sample of managers at a given organizational level from across the country.

Several meetings including wives have been held. These explore the relationship between organization life and family life, the demands one places on the other, and ways in which they can become more mutually supportive.

Also, managers have tended more actively and routinely to solicit employee opinions on major issues, and to delegate responsibility more effectively.

"Task teams" are now frequently organized to tackle problems involving a number of people. In a recent headquarters reorganization, the principals of the departments most affected made up the membership of the task team.

On the basis of the experiences of the program staff with the organization development effort, several observations can be made. At Saga, the OD program aims to develop and maintain an emotional climate which will support the expression of differences as well as similarities. The hope is that such a climate can extend beyond the organization to other aspects of life, such as family relations and outside community groups.

In the long-term framework of this effort, many limited and restricted individual perceptions emerge. For instance, some managers tend to see OD as an "it" rather than a process. They identify it solely with their initial team-building experience. Some see it as a quick solution to pressing problems, or as a means of helping a person who is failing to become a successful operator. Others suspect it is another headquarters program to "tell us what to do."

In response to these tendencies, and others equally simplistic, the staff has taken pain to emphasize the program's long-term nature. The staff warns that results can only come in response to the actions people take in their work situation. It is stressed that changes in behavior in an organization tend to come slowly. In addition, they place high value on the "field ownership" of the effort. A team-building meeting is held only if that team and its manager express a desire to have such a meeting.

Despite an emphasis on the necessity of a high level of trust and a caring attitude, there are cases where people were deliberately hurt during meetings. Some managers have bloated expectations that cannot be fulfilled. Unfulfilled expectations lead to doubts about the effort, such as, "Is the company *really* committed?" "Am I the only one practicing OD?" "Do people really want to get feedback on this behavior?" Some of these doubts are well founded, and the recognition of their validity is important. For example, the maintenance of the fine balance between organizational needs and adequate support for an individual's sense of privacy requires constant attention by everyone.

The individuals and teams that appear to experience the most payoff from the effort are those that have continued to explore the implications of their initial meeting on the job, in other team meetings, and by forming problem-centered task groups.

In a recent series of meetings held by the program staff with a number of district managers, some of the 1968 issues were still on the list. In the word of one district manager, "What's changed is not that problems go away, but that we can now find out about them for ourselves, we can discuss them openly, and we don't have to conduct an attitude survey to know how we feel."

Currently, much of the effort of the program staff is directed toward developing concepts, methods, and techniques that managers can use on the job. For instance, one situation which occurs frequently is the starting up of food service operations at a new institution. In order to assist managers cope more effectively with the complexities of an opening, the "start-up meeting" was developed. It is now used extensively.

We are currently looking for ways to involve nonmanagement food service employees in the OD program. Once the staff is satisfied with techniques developed for this purpose, they will train operating managers to apply the techniques themselves.

Much has changed in the company since 1968. In addition to the organization development program, the company has gone public. Diversification has been initiated. Competition has become stiffer. There has been a major reorganization, and many managers have come and gone. Some of the major issues of 1968 have been resolved, some partially resolved. Others clearly remain. However, in general, managers express a greater confidence in their bosses; they believe that they can talk to them about their needs and feelings and do, in fact, get more positive support from them. They likewise believe that they have greater flexibility in running their own operations, that they are more effective at handling the complexities of their own job, and that they can and do influence the system.

SOME OBSERVATIONS BY ABRAHAM MASLOW

In November of 1969 Dr. Abraham Maslow, one of the most original and lucid thinkers in psychology and a past president of the American Psychological Association, sat in on one of Saga's two-day organization development conferences. He made some extemporaneous remarks at the close of the session. A brief excerpt of his comments is transcribed here in edited form.

First of all, it may sound corny and square but the kind of thing that's happened here in the past two days couldn't happen anyplace else in the world except the United States. It's absolutely American. Working together with good will and good faith, doing a good job because you want to, and thinking of your superiors as colleagues and not enemies or rivals—is really a new thing. You can regard what you are doing here as a kind of test-tube experiment for the rest of the world. There is hardly any society on the face of the earth that is affluent enough to afford to take its employees away from their jobs for several days to talk about their work. It just isn't done anywhere else.

Of all the organizations I have seen, this company is the best in terms of openness and the opportunity to candidly discuss solutions to its problems. It is expensive, but the company is willing to pay the bill to get feedback from you. It must make you feel good to know you can influence decisions instead of being helpless pawns in a highly impersonal institution.

These last couple of days are marvelous examples of Theory Y in action. The fact that you're trusted on your own shows in your concern, involvement, and identification with Saga. It is a lucky thing for a person to like his work and to be able to identify with his outfit.

In the two days I have spent here I observed that you were open and courageous in speaking to your bosses. There was a certain amount of caginess, but it was very much less than I've seen elsewhere. There wasn't anyone who avoided a confrontation or who camouflaged his feelings as would happen in most situations.

A healthy means of handling aggression is to be unafraid of it. Aggression is very powerful and we should learn how to use it. This means being able to criticize, to say what you like or don't like or what should or should not be done.

A problem in our society, especially for males, is the ability to express affection. The handling of love, affection, friendship, physical closeness is done much better by other societies. I think we should aim to express more warmth and more affection without considering it self-serving. If you like a guy then show him that you do.

We seem to be afraid of getting sentimental or of looking soft. From my experience as a psychologist, I have found that some of the strongest people in our society are often the softest in the sense of being the most idealistic and altruistic. Part of our difficulty with expressing sentiment and affection is mixed up with our effort to look tough, strong, and invulnerable.

The definition of adult masculinity includes the ability to be sentimental and affectionate. The adolescent male finds it difficult to show affection because it looks like softness to him. But a fully grown, mature adult should be able to openly express these feelings. It is generally the men who are worried about their maleness who have to be tough and overdo the tough things.

One observation that I would like to pass on to you is that your judgments about people could be more varied—deeper and fuller. They were very superficial. People are really very complicated. I also got the impression there was occasionally some restraint in expressing interpersonal judgments. But on the whole, when you had something to say you said it. That's a mature, psychologically healthy attitude.

I appreciate your invitation to observe your conference. This, too, is a sign of maturity. There are many groups who would be tense and ill at ease if a psychologist sat with them. But you have made me feel very welcome.

CARL H. ALBERS

Strengthening the Links in a Hotel Chain

Sonesta (Hotel Corporation of America)

When Sonesta (formerly Hotel Corporation of America) was formed in 1956, it had six hotels. Today it has twenty-six, with approximately 6,500 employees. The policy of the corporation has always been one of decentralized management. Sonesta hotels, resorts, and motor lodges vary widely in size, type, and locale. Each has its own unique character, problems, and chances for growth.

A hotel is a complex economic entity, sheltering a number of different businesses under its roof. It is in the rooms business, the restaurant business, the cocktail-lounge business, the laundry and valet businesses, the garbage business, the newsstand business. There may be as many as seventy job specialities. Employees for all these services have a wide range of cultural, economic, ethnic, and national backgrounds. Yet the nature of hotel work requires a great deal of personal interaction among employees. Moreover, the customers themselves become transient members of the hotel's social system, since there is much interaction between guest and staff. It is a "people business" in every sense of the phrase, and consequently a fascinating organism from a behavioral science point of view.

Sonesta Hotels' first efforts to apply behavioral science concepts in dealing with its problems began as early as 1958. The president, although he wanted to maintain a high degree of decentralization, recognized that the organization could benefit from cooperative efforts in such areas as purchasing, marketing, and personnel. A more integrated management strategy had to be developed. It was clearly desirable to identify and to obtain commitment to a common set of objectives. But how?

There was a marked lack of mutual trust and openness between those on central staff, in charge of different specialities, and the general managers of the separate hotels. The hotel managers were seasoned executives and virtually autonomous in their decision making. Each maintained his own individual management style. Periodically the president held meetings with the central staff and the managers to improve communication, hoping the participants would work together in problem solving and planning.

But too often the meetings merely provided a forum for complaints. Central staff complained that the general managers dragged their feet or rejected new ideas and improvements. The managers, in turn, complained that the suggestions from central staff were unworkable and only caused confusion. They contended that the central staff lacked understanding of day-to-day operations.

The president discovered a similar situation in the hotels. There the general managers operated as autocrats. This is a traditional hotel practice, going back to the days of innkeepers and made famous by César Ritz. In Sonesta's case, the gap between the general managers and their staff members was extreme.

The president felt he should learn more about interaction processes and group dynamics. In the spring of 1958, he decided to attend a sensitivity training workshop under the auspices of the National Training Laboratory. He made an interesting discovery. "I'd been trying to work with our managers as a cohesive group, when a group did not even exist," he recalls. "I had been trying to get them to communicate honestly, openly, and objectively, and this was probably perceived as manipulative."

As a result of his experience, he retained a member of the NTL staff to help the people in the organization to develop into a more cohesive and effective group.

The problems were found to be both organizational and interpersonal. The consultant conducted separate in-depth interviews with members of four groups: the hotel general managers, their subordinates, the central department heads, and their subordinates. Those interviewed remained anonymous, but their replies were coded to indicate from which group they had come. Examples of the kind of data that came out of the interviews are as follows:

The president expects us to introduce changes and maintain and upgrade quality, but we can't get into the hotels to do it.

CENTRAL OFFICE SPECIALIST

Mr. X from the staff comes into the restaurant and tells the head-waiter that the service needs to be changed. This undermines the whole organization within the hotel and creates great confusion.

FIELD UNIT MANAGERS

We can't change anything in this organization unless the general manager can be convinced.

GENERAL MANAGERS' SUBORDINATES

The advertising policy of the company is ridiculous. We talk decentralization, and yet we have no voice in setting our advertising policy.

GENERAL MANAGERS

As a first step toward building a team where none had ever existed, a three-day off-site meeting was convened, attended by the hotel general managers and the central department heads, along with the president and the consultant.

As problems came up for discussion, it was discovered that many stemmed from the attitudes and practices of both central staff members and hotel managers, as well as from the structure of the organization and the nature of the business. The conferees began to realize that solutions could be effected only through joint efforts. At the end of the three days, the participants felt they had finally begun to function as a team. They were eager to continue the discussions.

A second meeting was attended by subordinates of the hotel managers—the directors of such departments as food and beverage, front office, sales, and accounting—to follow up concerns they had expressed in the interviews. Communications again headed the list: second-level managers claimed they had little knowledge of the corporation's future direction and were unaware of what opportunities existed for their personal advancement. They needed more communication with their technical counterparts in other hotels and in the central office.

A series of conferences was set up to bring together the second-level managers with central staff specialists, along with the president and others in top management. Participants explored the current needs of the corporation, its long-range goals, and how these might apply to the present and future jobs of each manager present. The managers were pleased; top management listened and acted on their recommendations.

Encouraged by the success of the companywide meetings, some of the hotel general managers decided to hold similar diagnostic and problem-solving programs *within* their individual hotels. The first began in the fall of 1959. Consultants interviewed all department heads and sub-department heads in one hotel to gather their ideas for improving the operation. Those separately interviewed then met as a group and worked through an agenda of the items raised. At the final session, the general manager received the group's recommendations and took steps to put them into effect.

Good results were readily apparent. New methods and procedures were installed. Communications were better. Misconceptions about the functions of the various departments were cleared up. Most significantly, a start was made toward forging an interdependent team in place of the traditional hotel organization, which is a loose federation of semi-autonomous operations—kitchen, dining room, laundry, office. Sonesta hotels now hold such conferences once or twice a year, with every super-visor helping to collect information, report back, and systematically plan improvement.

By 1964, the company's growing confidence in behavioral science was clear. Not only the president but a number of central staff specialists and hotel managers had attended NTL sensitivity training laboratories. They were committed to moving the organization toward more partici-pative management.

In that year the president called a top management meeting to develop even broader programs. It was agreed at the 1964 meeting to institute a process for setting goals systematically, a necessity for any "manage-ment by objectives" program. In addition, some difficulties that still existed between field management and certain central departments needed attention. Periodic meetings between them would be set up.

Team training was considered essential, especially for staff members responsible for opening and operating new hotels. In addition, reorgan-ization and expansion plans required accelerating the development of managerial talent. More effective collaboration was needed between cen-tral staff specialists responsible for launching hotels and those who would later operate them.

One of the first steps taken was to involve top and middle management in a series of Managerial Grid® laboratories based on original work by R. R. Blake and J. S. Mouton. More than a hundred hotel and central staff managers participated. Most of them had already attended a sensi-tivity lab. They were drawn from throughout the chain, and their selec-tion depended on rank, influence, and apparent potential for growth. All the sessions were held at various properties within the company.

The Grid® programs maintained strong links with "back home" reali-ties. Participants increasingly recognized the relevance of what they had learned to their actual roles and responsibilities on the job. They began to understand how functions and people were interdependent. They saw how open and candid communication in a work setting could lead to more effective collaboration and improved performance.

After the Managerial Grid® program, the company was ready to em-bark on more specific programs to set goals, strengthen cooperation among groups within the organization, and continue with team development.

Not all programs were equally successful. A great deal of time, for example, was devoted to making individual goal setting effective.

This process was aimed at involving each employee and his immediate superior in an effort to optimize guest satisfaction, employee utilization and development—and profit. Targets included faster and friendlier check-in of guests at the front desk; improved breakfast service in the coffee shop; improved menus in the dining room; specified reductions in food costs and number of employees; improved food in the employee cafeteria; establishment of a maids' training program; a specified reduction in turnover among busboys; increased productivity by warewashers.

Individual target-setting activities were begun at both the corporate and hotel levels. The first step was to obtain agreement between superior and subordinate on the subordinate's responsibilities. Following this, the subordinates drew up a specific set of goals, usually for a six-month period, with priorities and target dates for each goal. Here again, agreement between superior and subordinate was necessary. At the agreed-upon appraisal time, the subordinate would review his progress with his boss. The process was an adaptation of elements of Peter Drucker's theory of management by objectives and of the writings of Douglas McGregor and others on goal setting.

Managers at all levels experienced great difficulty with this task. Although problems were encountered during each of the phases of the planning and review process, they occurred most frequently at the appraisal session. The subordinate had concerns about being evaluated fairly. The boss often had similar fears about judging the subordinate's performance. An oppressive atmosphere of rewards and punishments was common.

Often goals were regarded as either too high or not high enough. Valid measures or standards for evaluation were lacking. Factors and forces beyond an individual's control frequently influenced his progress.

In spite of a superior's desire to encourage more self-direction and self-control, and to be "helpful," the dynamics of the individual-oriented planning and review sessions all too frequently created conditions which ran counter to this intention. More often than not, both the superior and the subordinate thought the sessions were frustrating, uncomfortable, and not very motivating.

Our experience with *individual* goal setting had not been successful. Why? No doubt there are many reasons. However, one simple hypothesis has emerged, namely, that a one-to-one goal-setting and evaluation process may be unnatural. The relationships among functions within the company create interdependencies; therefore, planning and evaluation ought to be conducted on a team basis.

Although our experience with individual goal setting was disappointing, what we learned has been helpful in designing our present approach to *group* goal setting. The planning process in our hotels now begins with a diagnosis by work-team members of the hotel's major problems, needs, and opportunities. Priorities are established. Goals are set within three main clusters: financial, guest satisfaction, and use and development of human resources. Responsibilities are defined. Performance measures and target dates are agreed upon. Evaluations are made and corrective action taken. Then new goals are set and new plans made.

During the summer of 1966, a seminar on organization development was conducted as part of our annual management meeting. It was intended primarily as an educational workshop, and the design gave the participants (the top 75 corporate executives) an opportunity to air their views on the major needs of the company. The seminar provided data with which to refine the company's organization development program. It also identified the need for a more equitable and motivating executive compensation program. An international management consulting firm was retained to work with executives on a plan that would be consistent with the company's basic philosophy and goals. The process of developing and implementing the new plan, which is currently in effect, drew on various behavioral science concepts. However, the plan was not developed by outside experts and then imposed on the group. Long and frequently heated discussions took place. The complexities of each executive position had to be talked through to complete agreement, so that it could be related equitably to every other position.

Another major program was initiated to provide team training for executives who are responsible for opening new hotels. The complexities and pressures of opening a new hotel require real collaborative effort. The top managers of each new hotel now get together for a number of days well in advance of the opening. They consider how they are going to work together; they discuss and agree upon goals, review roles and responsibilities, and develop or refine programs to ensure that the opening will be effective. The "new team" training sessions have proved extremely helpful. A follow-up session is usually held a few months after the opening of the hotel.

A dramatic example of a technique known as the "confrontation meeting" occurred in a hotel which Sonesta had acquired in a rundown condition with poor management. Although a new general manager quickly developed an energetic, effective management team and the hotel improved greatly within a year, serious dissatisfaction still existed among certain departments and front-line supervisors. They felt that top management took all the bows while their work, performed well under pressure, went unappreciated and unrewarded. They felt that although they had proved their mettle, their judgment was not properly respected. They resented having to clear decisions with top management, particularly since the higher executives were often unavailable for consultation.

A day-long confrontation meeting was held at the hotel. Information collected at the meeting was quickly fed back to the participants, the general manager, and the top staff. Six months later, the entire climate of the hotel had changed. The practices causing most of the complaints had been corrected, and the group felt great strides had been made in creating team spirit.

There was a general broadening of involvement of the hotel's staff in making decisions and planning activities. Along with this involvement came better implementation of the decisions and plans, which led to improvement of guest services and the quality of the food, as well as to reduction in costs and expenses and a generally improved attitude at all levels of the hotel's staff.

In 1968, Sonesta shifted the focus of certain elements of the organization development program. An Advanced Management Program, covering a broader spectrum of managerial training than had been attempted in the past, was developed for a group of young, high-potential executives who were rapidly moving up. The first phase made use of an elaborate management game simulating a hotel operation. The results and observations were fed back to the group to help them plan and develop the rest of the management training program.

In this, as in many of our previous applications of behavioral science at Sonesta, it is sometimes hard to measure results quantitatively. But there is a strong conviction throughout the company that our efforts have paid off and that we continue to learn from both our successes and our failures.

EDWIN R. HENRY / C. PAUL SPARKS

Fueling Organizational Change at Jersey Standard

Standard Oil Co. (New Jersey)*
and Humble Oil

Standard Oil of New Jersey employs about 200,000 people. It is the largest company in its field. It operates through some 350 affiliated (subsidiary) companies throughout the free world, with about 65 percent of its business outside the United States. Although the oil business is considered capital-intensive rather than labor-intensive, the policy of Standard Oil of New Jersey has been heavily oriented toward the well-being of its employees. The company has tried to provide an open, problem-solving climate and to place problem-solving responsibility as close to the primary sources of information as possible.

From employment testing to retirement planning, the company has continuously aimed at the development of its people. For this purpose it has employed the services of many of the leading psychologists in the nation. From the many behavioral science applications that have been made and are currently in progress, we have selected a few highlights for this report.

The reader should understand that decentralization has been a long-standing corporate policy at Jersey Standard. All operating companies have been given considerable control over their own operations. Thus when we describe an application of a behavioral science practice or method in some part of the parent company, it is entirely possible that in some other parts of the organization the generalization does not hold true.

The role of the behavioral scientists at Jersey Standard has been as varied as the conditions and settings of the operating organizations by whom they are employed. The parent company had early decided not to develop a large central behavioral science staff. Instead, it elected to maintain a small staff in the parent company and to retain professional consultants when needed. It was intended that the behavioral science

* Exxon Corporation after January 1973.

staff of the parent organization would be available as needed to help any operating unit develop research plans, find professional help, or evaluate outcomes of studies. In no way was the central behavioral science staff put in the position of "selling" headquarters' ideas to operating units.

Over the years more than 100 behavioral scientists have worked in the company, either as consultants or on the staff. A wealth of data has emerged. Much of this has already been applied in day-to-day operations, but much also remains to be applied.

Oil is often struck in the least convenient spots, far from any city that could provide a literate or skilled workforce. In the more remote drilling and refining locations, a staff of ten or more behavioral scientists is frequently brought from the United States. After a few years, as the immediate problems are eased or solved, their number usually dwindles to one or two, and the work is carried on by local staff trained in company procedures.

Formal behavioral science programs at Jersey Standard date back to the years just after World War II. Veterans returning to the company reported that in the military they had learned to use psychological tests and measurements for the selection and placement of personnel, that they had been supplied with professional counseling and consulting services to help solve manpower adjustment problems, and that officers had been helped in managing their organizations by periodic reports on the morale and attitudes of unit personnel. Why, they asked, should similar techniques not be applied in the Jersey organization?

These questions led to the formation of a study team to survey and evaluate the uses of behavioral science in other organizations for possible applicability to Jersey. A few affiliates had already felt the need for improved personnel management tools and had added industrial psychologists to their staffs. Several others had retained consultants to help them develop new programs.

One of the earliest problems assigned to Jersey's behavioral scientists was how to improve the effectiveness of the long-established Jersey policy of offering all employees career employment and continuous opportunities for advancement *within the organization.* Company policy has always been to employ people at entry-level jobs and then provide opportunities for their personal growth and development, so that higher-level positions could be filled by promotion from lower-level jobs.

Thus in all our companies, vacancies in supervisory positions are filled by promotion from lower-level nonsupervisory personnel. In a refinery, first-line foremen are selected and promoted from the ranks; office supervisors from the clerical force; sales and marketing supervisors from the sales department; engineering supervisors from the technical staff. Higher-level supervisors are selected from lower-level supervisory groups. In every instance, an attempt is made to promote individuals

who will be successful on the higher-level job and who have the potential
for promotion to still higher levels of responsibility. But many managers
were troubled by doubts as to whether they were always selecting the
best man for the company and not bypassing another who would be
an even better choice. They hoped that their selections were made on
factors relevant to job performance and capacity for growth and not
merely on seniority and social acceptability, but they really didn't know.

A coordinated effort was made to develop new strategies and techniques for measuring performance and capacity for growth. The question
was how to do this with the greatest fairness to employees, and with
the best possible results for the company.

We recognized that the appraisal system would have to answer such
questions as: Is the new employee getting a good start, giving promise
that he or she will be of value to the company? Is the present employee
holding up his share of the load? Has he strong points which suggest
better ways of using his talents? Are there weak spots which must be
corrected so that undue strain will not be placed upon them? On which
employees should we concentrate advanced training or promotion?

Performance and Potential

Too often performance rather than potential has been the basis for evaluating an employee's worth to the company. Current performance must
be evaluated, of course, but it is our belief that the major purpose
of appraisal is to determine whether an employee holds promise of
further progress in the organization. The short-range view often pre-
dominates when candidates are selected for promotion. There is a
tendency to give promotions based simply on a man's ability to manage
the very next step ahead rather than on his long-range promise.

If a man can cope with the next step ahead, it may reasonably be
asked, why shouldn't he have the job? If his performance has been
satisfactory, why shouldn't he get the rewards and salary recognition
to which he is entitled? These are logical questions, but there are dangers
as men move ahead one little step at a time. Each small increase in
responsibility doesn't seem like much, yet, by repeating the process often
enough, the organization may be promoting too many men beyond their
capabilities. This only encourages mediocrity. It can be avoided, however, by comparing candidates and asking not "Can he do the next
job?" but, "Which of these men can go farthest and therefore most
merits this opportunity?"

The senior executives of most large organizations are seeking more
dependable ways of identifying the young people on their staffs who
in twenty years are most likely to succeed them. If they could predict
with accuracy, they could give tomorrow's top executives personalized
and accelerated training and development. The loyalty of these young
men could be sustained by early recognition, and the paths to executive

advancement would not be clogged by men of mediocre promise. One major problem is that technical excellence and executive potential are not highly correlated. And since the first few years of a typical employee's career are usually spent in a technical specialty, there may be little opportunity to observe his leadership skills.

After considerable research aimed at developing methods to assess executive potential, we found the following procedures, when used together, to be especially dependable.

"Alternation" Ranking Report of Present Performance. The names of a group of employees known to several supervisors are listed on a form. Each supervisor studies the names and selects the one whose present performance he considers *highest* and the one he considers *lowest,* then *next highest, next lowest,* and so on. He selects alternately until all names listed have been ranked. No specific guide of factors to consider is available to the ranker. He makes his own definition of what will put one man higher or lower than others on the list.

Performance Description. The supervisor rates how well each of sixty descriptive statements fits the man being rated. Different patterns of marking give different scores, each statement having a weight that has been determined on the basis of companywide statistical analysis. A group of persons holding relatively comparable jobs can be ranked according to their *total score.*

Analysis of Functions. A list of thirty-three functions, duties, and responsibilities characteristic of various supervisory positions is prepared. The rater indicates on a five-step scale how he feels about the way the person being rated performs each function. Simple average scores may be obtained, but the form is primarily designed to provide a profile of the working abilities of the man.

Performance Appraisal. This is basically a "free answer" form. On it the rater records his opinions and reasoning about the man's contributions, his limitations, the help he needs, and the extent to which he may develop in the future.

Our experience with these rating methods over a period of years can be summarized as follows: Formal appraisal methods do help the supervisor to be more analytical in his judgment. A combination of methods fills our needs more effectively than any single one. The use of short (one-page) forms is most acceptable to the majority of raters. The accumulation of ratings drawn from different appraisal methods offers the best perspective.

The rating methods have the advantage of distinguishing among the present capabilities of various employees, but they do not indicate the levels employees may be expected to reach. After much research, we came up with the best approach we had yet developed, which we called the Personnel Development Series (PDS).

This program was based initially upon various assessments we had made of men who had already proved successful in our company. We discovered that with experienced employees a rating of their present performance would be a reliable indicator of their potential competence at higher-level jobs. But with the young employees who most concerned us we did not have long-term performance to appraise. After years of experimentation we arrived at a biographical data questionnaire that has proved to be a reliable predictor. Each question and every possible response of the young employee has been quantified by comparing it with the records of long-term managers whose accomplishments are known.

The basic use of the PDS test data is to give management an estimate of potential in terms of how far the person is expected to rise, and a measure of the value placed on his present contributions in the performance of his job.

The biographical data questionnaire is designed to record early behavior in life—what a candidate accomplished, and how he utilized his opportunities, during his school years and his early business career. Early behavior patterns are identified by means of 292 biographical questions. Similar histories drawn from the personal lives of successful company managers are obtained through the same questionnaire. These are then used for comparison. An extremely significant finding of twenty years of research is that *reliable predictions can be made on the basis of early data, because patterns of activity, interests, and attitudes tend to carry over into adulthood.* The program was adopted for use throughout the organization after preliminary testing of about 4,000 employees over a four-year period.

At the time these studies were started, our behavioral scientists believed that the empirical approach would have very different outcomes in different cultures or countries, even in dissimilar areas of the United States.

Surprisingly, the results of projects in such diverse locations as Argentina, Venezuela, Aruba, Australia, Norway, Denmark, Germany, Saudi Arabia, Libya, Texas, Louisiana, and New Jersey were strikingly similar; in many instances, they were almost identical. It would seem that basic personal characteristics, capacity for growth, style of behavior, and job performance of supervisors are much the same around the world.

By means of the PDS program, we are now better able to uncover promising men earlier, give them early tryouts as supervisors, and take steps to weed out unpromising men.

The questions that are asked most frequently by employees about the Personnel Development Series, and our answers, provide a better understanding of this significant program for identifying managerial talent.

Q *What do the tests measure?*
A The PDS program looks at achievements during the scholastic years. It studies aspects of a person's maturity, interpersonal relations, breadth of interests, and reasoning abilities. The PDS program consists of a four-to-six-hour series of tests and questionnaires designed to record what an individual has done and how he has utilized the opportunities he had during high school, college, and his early business career.

Q *Why does it take four to six hours?*
A The questionnaires are long in order to cover a wide variety of possible experiences. The individual needs a chance to show what he was able to do with the opportunities he had, no matter what they were.

Q *Did you say older managers are used for comparison?*
A Yes. Over 450 high-level managers participated in the original research for the PDS program. With this group as our reference point, we studied what distinguished those managers who had the greatest success, and we use this as our basis of comparison.

Q *In using a previous generation of managers, isn't there danger that we may be measuring qualities that become obsolete because of changing times?*
A We protect against this by regularly checking our program against today's standards of success. So far, some modifications have been made in the questions, but there has been no need to alter the basic system. This is probably because the really successful managers proved highly adaptable. They are more likely to produce change and adapt to it than to let change pass them by.

Q *Are young employees the only ones who get the PDS tests?*
A Not at all. Of course, the majority take the tests during their first two years in the company. But of the 4,000 who have been tested, many had ten years or more of service. Some field units continue to double-check the tests by including people of longer service who have been adequately appraised already.

Q *How is testing handled?*
A The Personnel Development Section at headquarters administers the tests at different field locations about once a year. Employees are invited for testing by their local manager. The individual has the right to decline to participate, but only a very few have done so, and some of those participated later when they had the opportunity.

Q *How are the test results used?*
A The results are made available on a restricted basis to those charged with management development in the region, division, refinery, plant,

or department to which the employee is assigned. The test results can be considered along with what is learned from performance appraisals made by the direct supervisor. One of the company's prime objectives is to locate promising people early enough in their careers so that they won't be overlooked when there are new opportunities. No matter where the person is located, a lot of effort is put into making sure he doesn't get lost. The PDS program helps in this connection.

Q *Does the employee ever see his score?*
A No. The score is only a portion of what the company has learned about the employee's potential. It is much more meaningful for a manager to hold a review with the employee about his job performance and the progress he is making. Then he can provide advice and guidance based on the total picture and not on just the part of it represented by test scores.

Q *Is this program used by other companies?*
A No. PDS is considered an asset in which the company has made a considerable investment. It is not made available to other companies. The program has, however, been extended to affiliates both here and abroad.

There is a very evident need to educate managers on the rationale of the PDS type of testing before it can be accepted and put to use. In the case of one subsidiary company, this has necessitated seventy meetings in the past three years with groups of key managers who were interested in getting enough background to understand the procedure and to evaluate its usefulness.

Even if an organization has considerable sophistication in the use of selection procedures for employment, there are many reasons why management groups are cautious about using tests to determine potential. One concern is with possible misuse of such data. Another is over the appropriateness of the methods of evaluation, and the extent of their accuracy.

With regard to the basic concern about accuracy of test methods, it should be recognized that even the most logical explanations will not normally be enough. The local management does not have much confidence in test procedures until they get trial runs made on some of their own people. In many cases, this has meant getting small validation groups of more senior people in our field organization. We have found that this is both useful and acceptable as a procedure. Our experience has been that a small trial group of twenty or so senior managers from an installation of several thousand people forms a good cross check. It gives the local management a feeling of confidence in interpreting the results of the test program.

Each time we have had trial groups that were heavily oriented toward our basic functions, such as production, exploration, manufacturing, marketing, pipeline, or accounting, the data have strengthened our conviction that the test program is measuring a common denominator called managerial potential.

We now anticipate utilizing the PDS procedure on a recurring basis on all those units of the company that ask for it. The number of these units continues to increase as managers find to their own satisfaction that the data proves helpful and is capable of being used intelligently and not abused.

Employee Attitude Surveys

The use of employee surveys in our company has increased substantially in recent years. We have found that certain principles must be complied with if a survey is to be successful.

Managers using survey data should be prepared to accept that responses represent the perceptions of employees and are the bases for actions and attitudes, even though the managers may believe that the respondents are wrong.

We do not use a standard questionnaire. When a division feels it has a problem of morale, communications, employee-management relations, or the like, an appropriate survey is designed. In addition to reports of the findings to management, the results of these surveys are fed back to the participants for discussion, proposed action, and, frequently, major changes in management practices.

The surveys have helped diagnose employees' feelings on such crucial matters as barriers to communication, degrees of trust, and feelings toward management. The surveys are kept short and uncomplicated, and the items are phrased for ease of response, analysis, and interpretation. All are precoded for computer processing. As a result, a complete survey—from approval of items to be included in the questionnaire to presentation of a report with appropriate visual aids—can now be accomplished in less than a month. Reports to the supervisory staff include illustrations and are in simple, nontechnical terms so that local management can interpret the results easily and disseminate them further. The research staff making the report concentrates on the findings, not on recommendations for action. Implications of the results call for comment only when needed to assist in interpretation.

All data obtained from a survey, it should be noted, belong to the division which sponsored it. One unit is not pitted against another, nor can higher levels of management second-guess the sponsoring group or use the results punitively.

As a tool for organizational improvement, employee surveys aim at understanding how the employee sees himself in relation to his job, his supervisors, his expectations, and the policies and practices under which he works. A simplified answering process enables the employee to express his own opinions.

The feedback from the survey does not include a "Conclusions and Recommendations" section. Instead, the people most involved in using the results are trained to evaluate them. From there, planning and subsequent action work their way upward, downward, across—wherever the needs are. The exact situation depends in part on the. type of survey and the organizational level surveyed. Each survey, developed for a specific purpose, furnishes data that can be used to make comparisons across organizational lines.

Sensitivity Training

Our company was among the first to introduce the technique of sensitivity training into our programs. Several members of the company attended the National Training Laboratories (NTL) at Bethel, Maine, as early as 1948. (It was established in 1947.) Our first in-company lab was held in the mid-fifties. The leaders of these labs at Jersey Standard have been drawn from NTL-qualified trainers, and the emphasis has been on problems of organizational behavior rather than on personal growth.

Generally, our sensitivity training courses have been built around such needs as improving communication among all levels of the division, enhancing participation in decision making, developing openness in personal relations, increasing cooperation among individuals and work groups, and encouraging an innovative spirit. In some instances, the entire staff—from the first-line supervisors up through refinery managers—has attended the same laboratories. Representatives of all levels of management, including some members of the board of directors, have attended sensitivity training workshops.

The programs usually take place in a setting removed from the place of work and generally consist of a number of daily sessions held over the course of several days or several weeks. Unlike most training experiences, participants in sensitivity training strive to diagnose their own "course work" and to join in crucial decisions about course content. These experiences usually increase the trainee's sense of confidence and responsibility for his own actions and encourage him to experiment more frequently.

We have found it valuable to offer the laboratory experience to the top executives of an operating unit first. After participating in sensitivity training, they are better equipped to plan and conduct similar experiences for their subordinates.

In addition to laboratories dealing with work-related problems, many Jersey affiliates have held laboratories focusing on problems of personal growth and group relationships. In these, each group is subdivided into small Development, or D, groups. The D-groups, the core of the program, meet to study and experiment with their own behavior as individuals and as members of a group. Training usually focuses on such specific concerns as the distribution of power and influence in personal and intergroup relationships, causes of hostility and conflict and how to manage them, openness in dealing with others, and the like. An important aspect of the laboratory's approach is the emphasis on continuous data collection and rapid feedback of the data to the participants for their own learning.

Our organization experimented with sensitivity training as a way of finding answers to such questions as these: How does one go about rebuilding morale, initiative, trust, and cooperation in an organization that is weak in these qualities? How does one gauge the state of organizational effectiveness—and then improve it? If a key manager sees his organization as more rigid, authoritarian, dependent, and noncreative than he wishes it to be, how can he change the organization?

More than 5,000 Jersey managers and supervisors have been involved in laboratory training designed to meet challenges such as these. Dozens of social science consultants have brought modern organizational theory to these conferences. Systematic data gathering has been integrated into the laboratory and the plant. Supervisors from all levels have spent many hours in workshops or in groups examining the question, "How can we make ours a more effective organization?"

This work is still in its early stages, yet the evidence accumulated so far suggests that a new and effective route to organizational development is emerging.

The laboratory approach is a training experience. Unlike most training experiences, it strives to maximize the degree to which the "students" participate in diagnosing their own needs, assessing their own capacities, developing their own course work, and participating in decisions about course content. These experiences tend to make the participants feel more responsible for their learning, and encourage them to experiment more frequently and to experience a real sense of confidence, success, and self-esteem.

Some basic assumptions of the laboratory method are these:

□ The training program ought to emphasize the participant's responsibility for his own self-development. It makes little sense to teach participative management in a situation where the teacher directs and the learners remain passive and do not actively participate in the process.

□ Education in human relations is re-education. No one begins from scratch. The problem is to help the learner become aware of his attitudes and behavior, and then unfreeze them, before he makes the decision as to whether or not he will change them.

□ This process of re-education is basically the same as the one by which the individual received his original education. Learning takes place in interpersonal, small-group, and intergroup relationships. The laboratory attempts to make maximum use of all three relationships to create conditions in which human beings will learn from one another.

☐ Human re-education is not simply a matter of intellectual understanding. Re-education requires that emotional learning also take place. One of the crucial problems in human relations is that even after people "know" what effective human relationships are, few are able to behave accordingly. Even more tragically, fewer yet are aware of this discrepancy in themselves.

☐ The most effective development in an individual (or an organization) occurs as he becomes more aware of himself and then more accepting of himself. One can best change if he first develops a deep understanding and acceptance of himself. True self-acceptance will not tend to lead to stagnation or complacency. A complacent person does not respect or accept himself. A person with self-esteem realizes that complacency is akin to psychological stagnation.

☐ As a person's sense of responsibility, self-esteem, and self-acceptance increase, he tends to be more understanding of others and to show more esteem for them. This increased acceptance of others will tend to decrease his and others' defensiveness. This in turn will tend to increase the probability of greater openness, freer use of new ideas, and more tolerance toward new ideas. As these conditions increase, the probability for more effective individual and group decision making increases.

In two cases the laboratory approach has been used at Esso with the entire organization. However, research is needed to develop other strategies for point of entry and staff involvement. One might be to offer the laboratory first to the top executives of the organization. Then the executives can be given all the help that they wish until they develop their own new philosophy of organizational management as well as the competence to carry it out. Once this occurs, the executives might take on more responsibility for planning and conducting laboratories for their subordinates. More important, by embodying the new philosophy in their everyday activities, they could provide for their subordinates living evidence of continual self-development in the organization.

Studies of the effects of laboratory training at several locations have led to a number of positive conclusions:

☐ Most of those who have attended consider the training a significant personal experience. Participating managers are convinced that the program was highly valuable, although it is not easy to measure the effects of these programs in purely quantitative terms.

☐ Desirable effects have been demonstrated in relationships between departments, between peers in the same department, and in the conduct of meetings.

☐ People listen and communicate with each other more effectively.

There is a noticeable increase in the ability to level with others without feeling threatened or disturbed.

☐ Management is better able to diagnose the needs and demands of a group, to move it toward a goal when it seems bogged down.

☐ A new attitude toward human relations seems to be developing among the participants. They are willing to learn how to be subjects of experiments and also to be experimenters in their own groups. They show a readiness to try new ways of behaving, new ways of tackling problems. They realize the need for more specific concrete data as to why people behave as they do.

About seven out of eight participants said they got "a great deal" or "quite a bit" out of the program. They were also asked to describe just what they had derived from the workshops. Here are some typical comments:

> *I will listen more to subordinates, be more vocal in getting management to encourage communication upward, realize colleagues' problems, and listen better.*

> *I will take more time to examine my own position, will set goals jointly with those concerned.*

> *I'll use new approaches. I have a new awareness of behavior.*

> *I'll better recognize the viewpoint of others, listen more to those opinions, and realize other people have problems.*

> *I expect to spend more time soliciting the opinions of subordinates; it will be simpler to discuss our problems together now, and also to talk to superiors.*

> *I asked myself later what I got out of this. I decided I was often stubborn, so I'm more conscious of my acting this way. I could have known this anyway, but I did become more aware of it as a result of the workshops. I'm also more aware now of some behavior of others around me, and better able to analyze what is happening.*

> *One guy who said he got nothing out of it sure acts differently now, whether he knows it or not. He listens better, is more considerate, less dogmatic. I've noted many changes in myself.*

Organization Improvement

The concept of Organization Improvement has been put into practice in many areas of American industry during the past ten years. It involves new methods and strategies intended to change the values, attitudes, and beliefs of the people in organizations, as well as the methods they use. The goals are to improve performance, increase productivity, and add to the quality of life at work.

This new concept has a variety of names. At Esso we prefer Organization Improvement (OI). Most others use the term Organization Development (OD) and a few use Organization Renewal (OR). All are basically the same thing.

What is Organization Improvement? Most simply, it is nothing more than a way of trying to run our organization better by reducing or eliminating blockages on the human side, and expanding its human potential through behavioral science methods.

We are finally beginning to see scientifically derived descriptions of processes which lead to an effective organization, and to see ways of managing organizations to optimize human resources. These models have grown increasingly sophisticated, and, at the same time, more practical. Businessmen no longer look at behavioral science and see isolated bits and pieces of information that need to be applied piecemeal by the organization. Today, we have integrated models.

OI is different from other systems in one important dimension: it deals with organizations *as it finds them.* There is an assumption in OI that there is a substantial amount of potential among our employees for organization improvement, and what we need to do is release that potential. Thus, OI does not demand substantial change in structure or technology or allocation of funds, but does say, "Here is the organization. It has human potential which we have not fully released. Let's work with the organization so that it can learn how to release its own potential and then enable this greater capacity to continue to develop itself and be effective through time."

The organization needs to collect data concerning where it is currently, and then compare itself with where it would like to be. Next, the organization needs to explore alternatives and select the best choice from among those available to improve the situation.

Some of the methods of the OI approach can be used to solve specific problems. For example, during labor negotiations at one refinery, the company had made an offer on economic issues and the union was balking at accepting the package. Executives interrupted bargaining, called the refinery's supervisors together, and presented the financial data on which the company had based its economic package. In effect, the executives said, "Here are the figures; this is what we have to work with as far as our economic situation is concerned. We have to negotiate a new package with the union. What can we offer the union and still remain competitive?" The supervisors were given the opportunity to ask for any facts they wanted and to come up with their own conclusions about what the refinery ought to be offering. Their conclusions were not identical to those the company offered, but matched well in general.

Here people at various levels of the hierarchy had an opportunity to participate with the top management. Because they had worked up the economic factors and knew them to be reliable, the supervisors subsequently exerted tremendous influence on the employees to accept the package.

Another example comes from a refinery that was threatened with being shut down because of its inability to compete. The refinery heads used an OI approach. As a first step they provided data to all their employees on the critical situation. A series of meetings were then held to identify problems, develop options, and come up with proposed solutions. As a result, a number of valuable cost-saving proposals were recommended and the refinery became more profitable, more competitive, and, indeed, a significant contributor to the overall organization.

One problem we constantly face is the shortage of staff members skilled in behavioral science to help line managers initiate an OI program. We prefer to keep this staff small because we think it important that OI specialists make assistance available only on a temporary basis. One of the goals of these specialists should be to minimize the organization's dependence upon them. The OI concept involves maturation not only for the individual but for the organization as well. Thus there should be a self-liquidating relationship. If occasionally there are no inside people available, we turn to outside consultants, though these people usually know too little about our business.

The small group of internal OI consultants at headquarters have been careful to establish their role as consultants and not evaluators. Thus they can work for a manager in the field, gather data from his organization, help improve his problem-solving process, and not be seen as espionage agents from headquarters. The OI staff is kept small because they are always interested in "high leverage" approaches which permit them to get programs started but which do not require substantial time on a continuing basis.

In the past ten years there has been a great deal of research dealing with problems of leadership, motivation, goal setting, job satisfaction, and other kinds of organizational behavior. The studies show that the most lasting effects are gained when organizations raise themselves by their own bootstraps through internal effort. For this reason it is our practice to encourage each operating unit to make its own decision as to whether it wants to engage in an OI project. The decision must have the support of all staff members, particularly the top leaders. We have found that when there is personal commitment by all the supervisory staff, the results are much more impressive than in units where pressure has been exerted on managers to undertake the project.

For example, supervisors and top executives at one refinery have been actively engaged for two years in what they have openly and enthusiastically labeled as their own OI program. They have taken full responsibility. They have revised, modified, and made their own additions to the various tools they had available. They have used all their key management people actively as instructors. They are convinced that this kind of involvement has brought about substantial improvements.

On the other hand, an overseas refinery reluctantly undertook a similar program. Many key executives felt that the project had been imposed upon them. They had no feeling of personal commitment, and although they had spent a considerable amount of money on the program, their behavior conveyed no real support. As might be expected, the results were unsatisfactory. From other similar experiences, it is obvious that an OI program cannot succeed unless managers are genuinely involved.

Our OI approach recognizes that the organization can become more effective only if it can integrate its own resources to work toward an agreed goal.

Broadly stated, the following methods and techniques are part of almost all Jersey's OI programs:

☐ Some type of *analysis*, such as employee-attitude surveys, which bring weaknesses to the surface where they can receive concentrated attention by management.

☐ *Feedback* of survey results to participants for consideration of the question, "What do we want to do about it?"

☐ Some type of laboratory *training* which will get the units to re-examine their present methods in the light of good management theory.

☐ Discussions by all management groups under conditions which facilitate frank *communication* and which stimulate lower levels of supervision to accept more responsibility for bringing about improvements.

☐ The establishment, through *participative methods*, of higher objectives that are both clearly understood and fully accepted by the group members.

The approach, then, is basically a problem-solving one. Troublesome situations are highlighted; data are collected; a goal is set. Its success, however, depends in good measure on the unique contribution of the laboratory training mentioned above.

Laboratory training, in which the participants learn to work as a team, is usually the first phase of our OI programs. Phase two involves the supervisor and his subordinates, or the natural work team, in "family" feedback sessions that are designed to encourage people to talk out their differences and to reach understanding and commitment. The sessions are repeated from time to time and may be used at any level. The topic for discussion always is, "What do we want to do about it?" Not "Why?" or "How can this be?" or "What do you mean by this?"

The concept of Management by Objectives is well entrenched. Annual strategic goal setting by top management, followed by departmental and divisional tactical goals set by each unit in the organization, has proved both profitable and popular. Quarterly reviews of objectives provide a natural follow-up. Personal goal setting and appraisal are used extensively throughout the entire organization and seem to be better accepted than the performance evaluation reviews previously used.

Since it is often difficult to staff an OI program, it is tempting to use fully qualified psychologists. Certainly experience suggests that we need people who are at least knowledgeable in behavioral science. But we do not need a large group of sophisticated experts, since the goal is to integrate an OI program into an ongoing business structure. For this reason we believe that it is best for the OI staff to be made up of people who have both a solid background in business and some knowledge of the behavioral sciences.

The second point to be stressed is the need to avoid being overly ambitious in launching OI projects. Some organizations' initial programs are so far-ranging that they collapse of their own weight. A gradual approach seems more effective as long as the organization is not in a state of crisis. An organization that *is* in crisis may require a massive program, however. If not handled right, this can be an expensive trap; but it may be the only way to achieve the desired change.

With time, managers and behavioral scientists will refine the OI process; it will become faster, cheaper, and more efficient. But the changes will probably be differences of degree rather than of kind.

Jersey is using OI today as a practical way to keep abreast of the latest findings concerning human resources. We have evolved a set of practices that can be handled successfully by line managers and members of small units. The most encouraging sign of OI success is that our units are sustaining the process of their own volition.

ROBERT E. SCHWAB / GREYDON M. WORBOIS
LAWRENCE E. KANOUS

How Detroit Edison
Built a More Effective
Organization

Detroit Edison Company

As a regulated public utility, Detroit Edison has been particularly hard hit by inflation. Almost all business costs have risen substantially in recent years, yet the company has been unable to increase the prices of its services. All our people, both management and nonmanagement, have been feeling the squeeze, and only constant improvements in the efficiency of the organization have enabled us to keep the situation from getting perilously out of hand. Among the chief agents of this organizational change have been the techniques of behavioral science, with which Detroit Edison has had more than a quarter of a century of intimate experience.

We chose not to deal with our cost squeeze by the traditional approach of "methods improvement" imposed from above. Instead, we have made use of behavioral science techniques that have the effect of encouraging employees to analyze their own work, as individuals or as members of teams. Expert advice in such areas as engineering, statistics, and procedures and methods is made available when needed. Since employees themselves are involved in generating new work methods, they tend to be closely familiar with them and to use them regularly. Some 40 percent of all new work methods recommended by the behavioral scientists at Detroit Edison are actually put into practice—an extraordinarily high proportion. The average "adoption rate" among public utilities is 28 percent, and among all industries, 25 percent.

Behavioral science frequently suggests ways of doing things that are quite different from those to which people in the organization are ordinarily inclined. But we have discovered that no basic conflict need exist between the goals of a business organization and the goals of the people who make up that organization. There may be differences in methods or timing, but the goals are largely the same. The reality of this conclusion can be demonstrated by a look at some examples of just how we at Detroit Edison have applied the findings of behavioral science research.

Attitude surveys have become commonplace in industry. Ordinarily they gather information for unilateral management decisions. The quality and appropriateness of these decisions usually depend on how "correctly" the surveys are interpreted. It is our experience that the end results of this decision-making process seldom satisfy the expectations of those who take part in the surveys. Furthermore, the manager who uses surveys unilaterally overlooks an unusual opportunity to improve communication within his organization and to increase participation at all levels.

Beginning in 1948, our company, in cooperation with the Survey Research Center at the University of Michigan, developed a method by which survey results are analyzed by people at several different organizational levels. This method of analyzing "back down the line" greatly increased the participation of company personnel in the problem-solving process.

The results of the first survey conducted by the new method were made available to all company officers, and discussions were started between the president, who had initiated the survey, and each officer. But it was soon clear that a full understanding of the survey, and the remedial actions it suggested, could be obtained only through discussions at a lower level. Officers then talked over the results with their department heads. These conversations indicated a need to seek answers from still lower levels. Consultation filtered down until it reached the first-line or lowest-level supervisors, who gathered their employees together in group sessions to discuss what their survey responses meant and what they would like to see done as a result.

When the supervisors sent in reports of their conclusions, two important things happened. The real problems came to light, and work to remedy the situations began almost immediately. As an example, one work group whose supervisor was highly regarded by his superiors had puzzled top management by responding very negatively to the question, "Is your supervisor the kind of person you like to work for?" When the supervisor discussed these responses with the group he learned that he was rated highly on most of the traits associated with good human relations—fairness, openness, willingness to listen and discuss, keeping his people informed. What upset members of the group was the fact that he had a college degree. He was the first college-educated supervisor they had had, and they saw no reason why that level of education was required. Moreover, they took his appointment as clear evidence that they were forever locked out of a job to which they previously had been able to aspire.

As it happened, the supervisor had been placed in that job as part of a professional development program designed for him, and the company had no intention of restricting the job to college graduates in the future. A discussion arranged by the supervisor between his immediate superior and the members of the work group helped allay the worry. Ultimate reassurance came later, when the supervisor moved on to a different assignment and was replaced by one of the group members.

In that case, the problem was simply a lapse in communication, which was solved when the company's true policy was made clear. But other "down the line" discussions of attitude-survey results led to substantive *changes* in company policies and practices. Among other things, the retirement plan was modified, more equitable means of distributing overtime in work groups were developed, supervisory responsibilities were clarified, and some improvements were made in physical conditions— heating, lighting, rest rooms, and so forth. This was the first time that such frank discussions had been systematically encouraged, and both employees and supervisors declared themselves generally pleased with the discussions and satisfied with their outcome.

Despite its considerable success, however, that first application of the new survey-analysis method did produce considerable anxiety and defensiveness among some employees. To reduce these reactions, the procedure was reversed the next time around. Survey results were first reviewed at the *lowest* level, and reports were then sent upward. This arrangement underlined constructive proposals by employees at the outset and minimized the need for defensiveness. It also gave first-line supervisors an immediate opportunity to understand the situation, leaving them better prepared to present positive suggestions to superiors. People in the upper echelons, although dubious at first, were persuaded by the results that the "bottom up" method was effective.

The Evolution of a Selection System

In times past, a manager selected a supervisor by reviewing the available records and talking about the candidate with his boss and perhaps a few others. It was a fast, direct process. Reference materials on selection of supervisors, including a convenient summary of evaluation methods, were available prior to 1950; but few knew about the literature and even fewer applied it.

Around 1950, a second-line supervisor at Detroit Edison wondered whether there was anything in behavioral science that could help him select a first-line supervisor. He had an unusually difficult job to fill, and several potential problems if he didn't choose wisely. We discussed many courses of action with him, hoping to arouse his interest in finding basic principles from which could follow an appropriate procedure to determine the selection. This turned out well. A good choice was made. Other managers heard about the successful result and asked for similar assistance.

Some scientific principles of selection—for example, "Get reliable and pertinent facts on each candidate"—were easily translated into workable procedures. Others—for example, "Establish conditions in the organization that will permit selection of the best of the candidates"—proved to be a good deal more difficult to put into practice. Nevertheless, we were able, over time, to put together a general plan embodying the procedures that worked out best in practice.

Managers who objected to this systematic approach were at liberty to decide on their own how to select new supervisors. Procedures, methods, and results might be discussed, but what the individual manager wanted to do was always respected. Everyone was encouraged to adjust the plan to suit his particular selection problem. Not until seven or eight years later were the procedures published in a company guidebook. Modifications continue to be made yearly.

Today, however, the "guide" is standard operating procedure. The careful, systematic process is the rule; the hasty decision is a rare exception. Not long ago, a new superintendent short-circuited the participative component of the selection process and named a supervisor without consulting his subordinates. Their objection was so strong that he felt constrained to rescind his arbitrary decision.

Participation as an Operating Principle

We have generally found that participation and high morale go hand in hand. After our original experiments with down-the-line analysis of attitude surveys, members of work groups known for high morale told us: "It does some good to discuss problems." "The boss is interested in my ideas." "He tries to do something about my ideas." "I feel free to discuss job or personal problems." Nevertheless, we knew of studies suggesting that some employees in certain types of work are not motivated by being consulted and may even wish to avoid it.

Anxious to find more conclusive evidence of the value of participation, we designed studies to measure the relationship between an employee's awareness of the degree of participation permitted on the job and his performance level.

A close correlation was found. Work groups in which participation in decision making was encouraged tended to adopt more efficient working methods than those run on authoritarian lines. The pitfalls of authoritarianism were vividly recounted to us during a training session by a former lineman. "You remember Red?" he began. "Well, Red was *the boss*. One time we were trying to put things together after a storm and Red said to me, 'You go and get six of those U-bolt connectors.' I knew when he said it that those weren't the right connectors and that they just wouldn't do the job. But rather than have him give me a hard time, I went and I got them and they didn't work. To Red, he was the brains and we were the hands, and he didn't let us forget it!"

One study also showed that an atmosphere of openness and free-and-easy discussion in a work group—the marks of a participative environment—helped minimize absenteeism, which represents a high cost to our industry. We found further that concern for controlling costs was related to participation. General foremen who were consulted while budgets were being drawn up were much more likely to be concerned about cost than those who felt they had little say about spending money allotted to them.

Three-quarters of the employees surveyed said that a good supervisor shared some or most job problems with them before a decision was made. There was a definite relationship between the frequency with which a supervisor held meetings to talk things over and his employees' comments that he was good at handling people. Their rating of him dropped much lower, however, if they felt the meetings were just so much talk, providing little real opportunity for ideas to get a fair hearing. Indeed, supervisors who never held meetings were commonly judged superior to those who held ineffectual meetings.

Coping with Automation

We have had two opportunities to study the impact of a fundamental change in our organization. In each case, the occasion was a changeover to an automated technical system. In the first instance, the company switched from an essentially manual customer-record system to one based on a large-scale digital computer. The change, spread over a five-year period from 1954 to 1959, required the consolidation of job tasks from two areas of the company—accounting and marketing. This was one of the first major changeovers to electronic data processing in our industry, a very ambitious project at the time.

A study was designed to chronicle the changes and their effects, and to measure them not only quantitatively but also qualitatively. By using trained behavioral scientists as participant observers and by collecting data through survey techniques, we were able to keep managers in close touch with the inevitable transition problems: extensive overtime, weekend work, training and retraining, deadline pressures. We learned a lot about changes in tension levels within individuals and between groups, and also about the nature of anxiety and fear among employees and supervisors, the origins of technical problems, and the reasonableness (or unreasonableness) of schedules. All these processes had been set in motion without our having any real familiarity with them. Awareness led to actions which made for smoother conversion and for more appropriate job assignments.

Our second opportunity to study the impact of major technical change on human and organizational relationships was presented by the opening of a new Detroit Edison power plant, the most modern in the United States at the time. We undertook to compare what went on in the new plant with the situation in an older, less-automated plant having almost the same electrical output. Measurements were made in both plants to determine the effects of differing maintenance concepts, changes in the size of the workforce, changes in organizational structure, centralization of equipment control, changes in job-task structure, and different methods of employee and supervisory training. In addition, differing approaches to scheduling shift-work in the two plants were intensively studied for their effects on the physical, psychological, and social well-being and on the family lives of the employees involved.

Among the important findings was that employees in the modern plant thought of both the new maintenance concept being used there and the more highly automated process as enlarging their jobs. Employees felt they had a greater chance in the new plant to develop skills and to form more satisfying relationships with co-workers and supervisors.

We were surprised to find how much employees in the new plant looked to their supervisors for interpersonal rather than for technical skills. We had expected to find much more weight given to supervisors' technical proficiency in the more automated plant. These results, along with those of a subsequent study, led us to redefine our development programs for supervisors in order to achieve a better balance between these two important abilities—human relations and technical skills.

Introducing Change

Formal training programs have a long history in our company, and over the years the people in charge of the programs developed a strong attachment to their traditional methods. As management became aware of better training methods that were being developed by educational researchers, there arose the problem of how to introduce new training techniques without forcing them on the unenthusiastic instructors. The situation called for special strategies to overcome resistance to change.

Our first step was to conduct a feasibility study identifying those areas of technology appropriate to new and broader training methods. The study team was staffed by an engineer, a training specialist, and a research psychologist. The team was pledged to involve, as deeply as possible, anyone who might profit from or be threatened by the study.

A need for proficiency in applied electrical theory was found in seven different departments, only four of which had training courses to meet it. Two of these had been operating for more than twenty-five years. It was decided that a new programmed instruction system in applied electrical theory should be developed. The people selected to work out the new system were carefully chosen both for their ability to perform the task and for their sensitivity to its social and organizational implications.

The project director was the research psychologist. His staff was recruited from the line departments requiring the training. They were not only competent in the subject matter, but were closely identified with the training already being given in their departments. They remained on the payroll of their own departments and acted as their department's links to the project. Communications were channeled through them, and departmental meetings to gather information were conducted by them. Their approval was required on all objectives, programs, and proficiency measurement methods applying to their department. They also arranged for "laboratory" tests to validate the new materials.

The concept of programmed instruction was introduced, and supervisors and trainers were supplied with appropriate materials for purposes of practice and discussion of techniques. Some studied computer basics, some took up the fundamentals of gas turbine engines, and others studied binary arithmetic and switching theory.

As a result of their involvement in the study, members of the training staff moved toward acceptance of the new techniques, and their attitudes toward the change became favorable and cooperative.

As available methods become increasingly dependable, inspiring growing confidence among people within the company, the applications of behavioral science at Detroit Edison have rapidly expanded from the timid beginnings of several decades ago. Typically, one application has evolved into another, sometimes in an altogether different area. Our underlying assumption is that as people have success with the application of behavioral science, they gain a shirtsleeves understanding of the principles involved and are motivated to try them again. Our evolutionary approach seems validated by the ever-widening array of requests for assistance submitted to us by people at all levels of the organization.

Biographical Notes

CARL H. ALBERS first developed an interest in the psychology of organizations while doing management consulting work in the early 1950s. During those years he concentrated heavily on the improvement of productivity in hotels, hospitals, and other organizations. In 1956, Mr. Albers began a management research and development study for the Hotel Corporation of America (now Sonesta International Hotels), using the Mayflower Hotel in Washington, D.C., as his "experimental laboratory." Three years later he joined the corporate staff of the company. Mr. Albers feels the organization psychologist needs to become more of a generalist, to understand the basic functions and processes of business, and to recognize the interdependencies among the various disciplines.

CHRIS ARGYRIS is the James Bryant Conant Professor of Education and Organizational Behavior at Harvard University. He is the author of 15 books and monographs and about 150 articles. Dr. Argyris reports that his interest in the behavioral sciences stemmed from a commitment he made during World War II to strive to contribute something toward the understanding of man and how the quality of life in organizations could be bettered. He received his Ph.D. in organizational behavior from Cornell University—to our knowledge, the first doctorate in this field. He was Beach Professor of Administrative Sciences at Yale until 1971, when he was appointed Conant Professor at Harvard. Dr. Argyris is convinced that organizations can be made more humane and at the same time more effective, even though there are basic conflicts between the individual and the organization. Dr. Argyris has served as consultant to numerous government agencies and industrial organizations, both in the United States and abroad.

DAVID G. BOWERS reports that he first became interested in industrial psychology when, as a recruit in the Air Force, he was assigned to work in a basic training selection and aptitude testing unit. By the time he was discharged from the Air Force, he had decided to pursue a career in industrial psychology. He received his Ph.D. from the University of Michigan in 1962. Since that time, Dr. Bowers' interest has shifted to "organizational psychology" and, more specifically, to research on how organizations can be enabled to function more effectively.

FABIAN BACHRACH

LELAND P. BRADFORD, early in his career, became deeply concerned with the problem of translating knowledge about individual and group behavior into action. With his training as a psychologist (he took his Ph.D. from the University of Illinois in 1939), this concern led Dr. Bradford into the field of adult education, then into the administration of a complex federal agency. He joined with Kurt Lewin, Ronald Lippitt, and Kenneth Benne in founding the National Training Laboratories in Bethel, Maine, in 1947. NTL became a rallying ground for other theoreticians and scientists to share their knowledge and concerns and to experiment together. He served as director of the National Training Laboratory for nearly twenty-five years.

DOUGLAS W. BRAY, director of manpower action programs for the American Telephone and Telegraph Company, decided on a career in applied psychology while serving as an aviation psychologist during World War II. After the war he earned his Ph.D. at Yale and then became a research associate at Princeton and Columbia. Dr. Bray joined AT&T, the parent company of the Bell System, in 1956 and soon thereafter became director of personnel research. In 1969 he served as assistant vice president of the New York Telephone Company, an AT&T affiliate, before returning to AT&T in his present assignment. Dr. Bray is past president of the Division of Industrial and Organizational Psychology of the American Psychological Association. He has lectured widely in the United States and abroad on management assessment centers.

WILLIAM C. BYHAM, after receiving his Ph.D. in industrial psychology from Purdue, obtained two years of line administrative experience as assistant to the executive vice president of Kenyon & Eckhart, a major New York advertising agency. He left to become the first industrial psychologist ever employed by the J. C. Penney Company. During his seven years at Penney, Dr. Byham was in charge of all selection and appraisal programs and many management development projects. He developed Penney's first assessment center programs. At present, Dr. Byham is director of management development programs at the University of Pittsburgh's Graduate School of Business.

RICHARD J. CAMPBELL received his Ph.D. in psychology from Ohio State University in 1960. During his last year there he worked for the Ohio State University Research Foundation, designing and conducting small-group research. In 1962, after two years with the General Motors Institute in Flint, Michigan, he joined the American Telephone and Telegraph Company as a personnel assistant. In 1967 he was appointed personnel manager–research, with responsibility for research and consulting on the selection and development of managers. In January 1972, he was appointed director of the Manpower Laboratory in AT&T's department of environmental research and development.

ROBERT D. CAPLAN, while attending U.C.L.A., had a summer job in a paint company, which focused his attention on organizational psychology. Specifically, he became interested in gaining systematic knowledge about human behavior in work settings—a knowledge which his supervisor seemed to have developed informally. He received his Ph.D. in organization psychology from the University of Michigan. Dr. Caplan, who is at present involved in program research at the University of Michigan's Institute for Social Research, feels that modern organizations will give increasing consideration to the well-being of employees and of society in general as major factors in decision making. "Recognition of these factors will become more and more important as more people become aware of the long-range interdependence of human organizational goals."

HOWARD C. CARLSON studied at the University of Minnesota and in 1970 won his doctorate in industrial and organizational psychology. He is now assistant director of employee research programs for General Motors and is involved in applications of the behavioral sciences to operating problems. "A vast set of expectations is growing in our society that industry will *do* something about solving its human problems. The same expectations will impel industrial and organizational psychologists to new, exciting, and perhaps even revolutionary breakthroughs in the years ahead."

WILLIAM J. CROCKETT's working career of almost forty years has been about evenly divided between business and government. His government career included service as a member of the U.S. Army during World War II and the Korean War and as a career Foreign Service officer of the State Department. He was appointed by Presidents Kennedy and Johnson to the position of Deputy Under Secretary of State, which is the senior management position in the State Department. While serving in that capacity he inaugurated an extensive organizational development program in the Department. After his retirement from the Foreign Service in 1967, Mr. Crockett joined the IBM World Trade Corporation for a time and then went to the Saga Administrative Corporation to head its organizational development effort as vice president for human relations.

SHELDON A. DAVIS is vice president and director of industrial relations for the Systems Group of TRW Inc. Part of Mr. Davis's motivation for entering the field of organization and industrial psychology came from a variety of jobs he held while attending school, including busboy, hod carrier, and construction laborer. (In each case, he personally experienced significant *de*motivation.) After graduating from Boston University, Mr. Davis earned his M.B.A. from the Harvard School of Business. He is a Fellow of the NTL Institute for Applied Behavioral Science and frequently serves as guest lecturer at universities throughout the country. Mr. Davis is enthusiastic about the growing comprehensiveness of tools and techniques in his field, ranging from individually oriented therapy to job and organization design.

SAM FARRY is a consultant in organizational behavior who has worked in business, government, and education. He received his M.B.A. from the Harvard School of Business. Mr. Farry is primarily interested in finding ways for organizations, as well as individuals, to come closer to achieving their unique potential. His present work with the Saga Administrative Corporation involves the assessment and evaluation of their organization development program.

JOHN R. P. FRENCH, JR., a few years after he had completed his Ph.D. in psychology at Harvard in the early 1940s, was taken on as a psychologist in the Marion, Virginia, factory of the Harwood Manufacturing Corporation and gave him the freedom to investigate anything that might interest a young psychologist. In one of the early investigations in the Marion plant, Dr. French discovered that specific stresses on the job influenced the health of the employees, as measured by minor accidents and frequency of visits to the dispensary. He feels it was this small study which, years later (in 1957), sparked the program research at the University of Michigan's Institute for Social Research on the effects of the social environment on mental and physical health. "Now, after 14 years of research, we have reached the stage where the institute is experimenting with programs for *preventing* coronary heart disease by reducing organizational stress. During the next decade I expect that our research will demonstrate the effectiveness of preventive programs in sharply reducing the appalling death rate from job stress."

ROBERT E. GAERTNER, after receiving his B.A. from Oberlin College in 1958, started his career with Saga Administrative Corporation as a food service manager. Mr. Gaertner has held a number of operating positions with Saga: district manager, regional sales and personnel manager, and director of market services. In 1969 he transferred into the organizational development program.

CARL MYDANS

JUDSON GOODING, now an associate editor of *Fortune* magazine, has been a working journalist in the United States and overseas since 1950. He has become increasingly concerned with the type of lives men and women lead at work. He has reported on the many forms of discontent shown by students, workers, farmers, office employees, and professionals, and has been involved in every kind of response to that discontent, from strikes through street demonstrations and fighting to outright political revolution. Mr. Gooding feels that too many people still regard work as an onerous, almost punitive obligation; this explains the alacrity with which the four-day week is accepted by some—it promises to shorten the misery. He believes work should be made rewarding and stimulating, so that people will make a real contribution of themselves.

DONALD L. GRANT'S career has been entirely concerned with the utilization of human resources. He first worked in the personnel department of Sharp & Dohme (now Merck, Sharp & Dohme). After serving in the military during World War II, Mr. Grant studied at Ohio State University and received his Ph.D. in 1952. In 1956 he joined the personnel research section of the American Telephone and Telegraph Company. He is currently personnel manager–research for AT&T and has prime responsibility for research on employment tests. He has published a number of articles in the professional journals, is a Fellow of the American Psychological Association, a diplomate in industrial and organizational psychology of the American Board of Professional Psychology, and is on its Board of Trustees.

EDWIN R. HENRY, who died in the fall of 1971, had a distinguished career as a university professor and as a consulting psychologist to industry and government. After receiving his Ph.D. from Columbia University in 1931, he served on the faculty of New York University. He resigned to accept a position as coordinator of the Social Science Division of the Standard Oil Company of New Jersey and served the company for more than twenty years. He also served as a consultant to the U.S. Navy and Air Force and as director of selection for the Peace Corps. He was a diplomate in industrial psychology of the American Board of Professional Psychology and held important positions in many scientific societies.

LAWRENCE E. KANOUS received his M.A. from Michigan State University in 1950. He joined the Detroit Edison Company as a research assistant in 1951. He now holds the position of administrator of employee training. Mr. Kanous's special interests include employee selection, placement, and appraisal; industrial social psychology; and the psychology of human engineering. He is a lecturer at the University of Detroit and is associated with the Lawrence Institute of Technology.

DELMAR (DUTCH) L. LANDEN, after receiving his Ph.D. from Ohio State University in 1956, spent three years with the personnel evaluation section of General Motors Institute. In his present capacity as director of employee research for General Motors, Dr. Landen and his associates assist the corporation's operating units by using a broad range of approaches to improve organizational effectiveness. Dr. Landen feels that the most challenging tasks facing the industrial psychologist are: (1) applying scientific knowledge in an environment in which people are attempting to deal with dynamic and at times competing change forces, and (2) applying techniques that assist in overcoming organizational and human inertia. "The ultimate goal is the creation of organizational environments which provide the freedom and stimulation for people to make personally rewarding contributions to organizational goals and objectives."

EDWARD EMMET LAWLER III, a professor in Yale's department of administrative sciences, has published fifty scientific articles. Dr. Lawler's psychology career started in the animal laboratory at Brown University, where for two years he ran experiments using rats in mazes. He felt it was good training but missed working on real-world problems. Thus, he decided to do his work in organizational psychology; he took his Ph.D. from the University of California, Berkeley, in 1964. Dr. Lawler notes the difficulty of doing good research in field settings, but adds that when it is possible to do it, such research is a very rich source of data and hypotheses. He feels that organizational psychology is beginning to acquire the theoretical content it has lacked for a long time and is optimistic that in the future we will be able to solve more of the important problems with which we are confronted.

ALBURTUS
YALE NEWS BUREAU

FABIAN BACHRACH

HARRY LEVINSON, the Thomas Henry Carroll–Ford Foundation Distinguished Visiting Professor at the Harvard Graduate School of Business Administration, is the author of *Executive Stress* and other award-winning books. He received his Ph.D. in clinical psychology from the University of Kansas in 1952. During the late 1940s and early 1950s, Dr. Levinson was involved in reorganizing the Kansas state hospital system. That, together with his work in civil rights and other community activities, whetted his interest in extending clinical psychology concepts to organizational and industrial as well as community problems. "Since social problems are essentially organizational problems (communities are organizations of organizations) and since 90 percent of the people work in organizations, the future for both mental health and community survival lies in organizational effectiveness. I see increasing need for the application of clinical conceptions and insights to organizational and social problems, and, therefore, for more advanced and sophisticated training for those who would be involved in organizational change. It is a major social frontier."

WALTER R. MAHLER is president of Mahler Associates, Inc. He received his Ph.D. from Columbia University in 1950. Dr. Mahler has specialized in management problems created by new technology and automation; he has worked with many of the largest industrial organizations. Dr. Mahler concentrates on problems of organization structure, executive development, and personnel administration.

WILLIAM MC GEHEE received his Ph.D. from George Peabody College in 1939. He continued teaching courses in industrial psychology, and worked on several consulting assignments, until the beginning of World War II. After serving in the U.S. Navy as an aviation psychologist, he returned to teaching and consulting. This led to his joining Fieldcrest Mills as director of personnel research and training. "I have continued in this field because of the inherent challenge of applying behavioral science knowledge to the vital problems of the productivity and satisfaction of industrial workers. I have become more and more convinced that this effort can produce significant data about human behavior and enrich the entire field of psychology."

WILLIAM C. MERCER is president of the New England
Telephone and Telegraph Company, a unit of the
Bell System that provides communication services
for five states and has 47,000 employees. Mr.
Mercer's career with the Bell System started in the
Western Electric Company, where he rose to the
level of superintendent. He then served New England Telephone and Telegraph as personnel vice
president before moving to Indiana Bell as operations vice president and eventually to AT&T, the
parent company of the Bell System, where he was
vice president of both personnel and marketing. He
was named president of New England Telephone
and Telegraph in late 1971. Mr. Mercer earned
his M.A. as a Sloan Fellow at M.I.T. He has recently
served as a member of the Presidential Task Force
on Women's Rights and Responsibilities, the Human
Resources Development Committee of the United
States Chamber of Commerce, and the Advisory
Council on Personnel Administration of the National
Industrial Conference Board.

HERBERT H. MEYER became interested in the ideas
of industrial psychology while serving in World War
II as a flight instructor in the Navy. Upon leaving
the Navy in 1946, he did graduate work in industrial
psychology at the University of Michigan. He received his Ph.D. from the University of Utah in
1949 and shortly thereafter was employed by the
Psychological Corporation in New York as a consultant in the Industrial Division. In 1953 he was
hired by the General Electric Company to start a
personnel research program. Dr. Meyer is now manager of a personnel research component in the GE
Corporate Employee Relations staff, and he holds
adjunct professorships at New York University and
Pace College. He is also the recent past president
of the Division of Industrial and Organizational Psychology of the American Psychological Association.

ROBERT E. SCHWAB is a vice president responsible
for all of Detroit Edison Company's employee and
union relations. He received his B.S. from Miami
University in 1935 and shortly thereafter was hired
by Detroit Edison as a personnel research assistant.
He initiated and directed a long-term human relations
research program linking Detroit Edison and the
University of Michigan's Institute for Social Research.

STANLEY E. SEASHORE's career-long interest in organizations began when he took a job in a steel mill in 1939 and found the work environment rather different from his previous rural and campus surroundings. After some years in personnel management and personnel research he opted for the academic life and received his Ph.D. from the University of Michigan. His formal credentials include Guggenheim and Fulbright Fellowships and a term as president of the Division of Industrial and Organizational Psychology of the American Psychological Association. Dr. Seashore feels that increasingly people are expecting more from their work than pay and economic security; that organizations may expect a handsome return in performance for efforts they make toward the improvement of the quality of work life.

MELVIN SORCHER became interested in organizational psychology while working in a large industrial corporation and studying social psychology. He took his Ph.D. from Syracuse University in 1965 and joined the General Electric Company the same year. During his years at GE, Dr. Sorcher has been engaged in research on motivation and work climate and the application of these findings. He has been involved in adapting clinical therapy to supervisory training programs, conducting research on motivational variables, and doing consulting and research in different parts of the world.

C. PAUL SPARKS began his career as a school psychologist in Mansfield, Ohio, after receiving his M.A. in psychology from Ohio State University in 1938. He entered the Air Corps during World War II and joined the personnel research section of the U.S. Army Adjutant General's Office, where he did research on training, selection, and performance evaluation. He then joined the consulting firm of Richardson, Bellows, Henry & Company. After a career which saw him rise to president of the firm, he joined a major client of the firm—Humble Oil & Refining Company. There he is in charge of personnel research, defined as providing an objective, statistical base for management decisions in all matters involving personnel. "Industrial and organizational psychology is just now entering its golden years. A variety of forces are putting real meaning into the slogan 'People are our most important asset.' "

GREYDON W. WORBOIS spent the early years of his career in the academic community, first as a professor of psychology and education at Greenville College and then as a research assistant at the State University of Iowa. He received his Ph.D. from the State University of Iowa in 1942. He then spent four years in the U.S. Army as a personnel consultant. In 1946 he joined the Detroit Edison Company as an industrial psychologist, where he is involved in the selection and supervision of industrial personnel.

Selected Bibliography

ARGYRIS, CHRIS. *Integrating the Individual and the Organization.* New York: John Wiley & Sons, 1964.

ARGYRIS, CHRIS. *Interpersonal Competence and Organizational Effectiveness.* Homewood, Ill.: Richard D. Irwin, Dorsey Press, 1962.

ARGYRIS, CHRIS. *Intervention Theory and Method: A Behavioral Science View.* Reading, Mass.: Addison-Wesley, 1970.

ARGYRIS, CHRIS. "T-Groups for Organizational Effectiveness." *Harvard Business Review,* March–April 1964, pp. 60–74.

ARGYRIS, CHRIS. *Understanding Organizational Behavior.* Homewood, Ill.: Richard D. Irwin, Dorsey Press, 1960.

BECKHARD, RICHARD. *Organization Development: Strategies and Models.* Reading, Mass.: Addison-Wesley, 1969.

BENNIS, WARREN G. *Changing Organizations.* New York: McGraw-Hill, 1966.

BENNIS, WARREN G. *Organizational Development: Its Nature, Origin and Prospects.* Reading, Mass.: Addison-Wesley, 1969.

BENNIS, WARREN G., KEN D. BENNE, and ROBERT CHIN. *The Planning of Change.* New York: Holt, Rinehart & Winston, 1969.

BENNIS, WARREN G., ED H. SCHEIN, DAVID E. BERLEW, and FRED I. STEELE, eds. *Interpersonal Dynamics.* Rev. ed. Homewood, Ill.: Richard D. Irwin, Dorsey Press, 1968.

BENNIS, WARREN G., and PHILIP E. SLATER. *The Temporary Society.* New York: Harper & Row, 1968.

BLAKE, ROBERT R., and JANE S. MOUTON. *Building a Dynamic Corporation Through Grid Organization Development.* Reading, Mass.: Addison-Wesley, 1969.

BLAKE, ROBERT R., and JANE S. MOUTON. *The Managerial Grid.* Houston: Gulf Publishing Co., 1964.

BLAKE, ROBERT R., HERBERT A. SHEPARD, and JANE S. MOUTON. *Managing Intergroup Conflict in Industry.* Houston: Gulf Publishing Co., 1964.

BRADFORD, LELAND P., JACK R. GIBB, and KEN D. BENNE, eds. *T-Group Theory and Laboratory Method: Innovation in Re-education.* New York: John Wiley & Sons, 1964.

BRAY, DOUGLAS W., and DONALD L. GRANT. "The Assessment Center." *Psychological Monographs,* Vol. 80, No. 17, 1966.

CARTWRIGHT, DORWIN, and ALVIN ZANDER. *Group Dynamics.* New York: Harper & Row, 1960.

COCH, LESTER, and JOHN R. P. FRENCH, JR. "Overcoming Resistance to Change." *Human Relations,* Vol. 1, No. 4, 1948, pp. 512–532.

DALE, ERNEST. *Organization.* New York: American Management Association, 1967.

DRUCKER, PETER. *The Effective Executive.* New York: Harper & Row, 1967.

DRUCKER, PETER. *The Practice of Management.* New York: Harper & Row, 1954.

FESTINGER, LEON. *A Theory of Cognitive Dissonance.* Stanford, Calif.: Stanford University Press, 1957.

FIEDLER, FRED E. *A Theory of Leadership Effectiveness.* New York: McGraw-Hill, 1967.

FORD, ROBERT N. *Motivation Through the Work Itself.* New York: American Management Association, 1969.

FRENCH, JOHN R. P., JR. "Role-Playing as a Method of Training Foremen." *Sociometry,* 1945, pp. 410–425.

FRENCH, JOHN R. P., JR., IAN C. ROSS, SAM KIRBY, JOHN R. NELSON, and PHILIP SMYTH. "Employee Participation in a Problem of Industrial Change." *Personnel,* November–December 1958, pp. 15–29.

GALBRAITH, JOHN K. *The New Industrial State.* Boston: Houghton Mifflin, 1967.

GELLERMAN, SAUL W. *Motivation and Productivity.* New York: American Management Association, 1963.

HAIRE, MASON. *Psychology in Management.* New York: McGraw-Hill, 1964.

HERZBERG, FREDERICK, BERNARD MAUSNER, and BARBARA B. SNYDERMAN. *The Motivation to Work.* New York: John Wiley & Sons, 1959.

HERZBERG, FREDERICK, BERNARD MAUSNER, and BARBARA B. SNYDERMAN. *Work and the Nature of Man.* Cleveland: World, 1966.

KATZ, DAN, and ROBERT L. KAHN. *The Social Psychology of Organizations.* New York: John Wiley & Sons, 1967.

LAWLER, EDWARD E., III. *Pay and Organization Effectiveness: A Psychological View.* New York: McGraw-Hill, 1971.

LAWLER, EDWARD E., III, and JOHN R. HACKMAN. "The Impact of Employee Participation in the Development of Pay Incentive Plans." *Journal of Applied Psychology,* Vol. 3, No. 6, 1969, pp. 467–471.

LEAVITT, HAROLD J. *Managerial Psychology.* Chicago: University of Chicago Press, 1964.

LEVINSON, HARRY. *The Exceptional Executive.* Cambridge, Mass.: Harvard University Press, 1968.

LEVINSON, HARRY. *Executive Stress.* New York: Harper & Row, 1969.

LEVINSON, HARRY. *Emotional Health in the World of Work.* New York, Harper & Row, 1964.

LEVINSON, HARRY. *Organizational Diagnosis.* Cambridge, Mass.: Harvard University Press, 1972.

LIKERT, RENSIS. *The Human Organization: Its Management and Value.* New York: McGraw-Hill, 1967.

LIKERT, RENSIS. *New Patterns of Management.* New York: McGraw-Hill, 1961.

LIPPITT, RONALD, et al. *The Dynamics of Planned Change.* New York: Holt, Rinehart & Winston, 1961.

MC CLELLAND, DAVID. *The Achieving Society.* Princeton, N.J.: Van Nostrand, 1961.

MC GEHEE, WILLIAM, and PAUL W. THAYER. *Training in Business and Industry.* New York: John Wiley & Sons, 1961.

MC GREGOR, DOUGLAS. *The Human Side of Enterprise.* New York: McGraw-Hill, 1960.

MC GREGOR, DOUGLAS. *The Professional Manager.* New York: McGraw-Hill, 1967.

MAIER, NORMAN F. *Psychology in Industry*. Boston: Houghton Mifflin, 1955.

MARROW, ALFRED J. *Behind the Executive Mask*. New York: American Management Association, 1962.

MARROW, ALFRED J. *Making Management Human*. New York: McGraw-Hill, 1958.

MARROW, ALFRED J. *The Practical Theorist: The Life and Works of Kurt Lewin*. New York: Basic Books, 1969.

MARROW, ALFRED J., DAVID G. BOWERS, and STANLEY E. SEASHORE. *Management by Participation*. New York: Harper & Row, 1967.

MARROW, ALFRED J., and JOHN R. P. FRENCH, JR. "Changing a Stereotype in Industry." *Journal of Social Issues*, August 1945.

MASLOW, ABRAHAM. *Motivation and Personality*. New York: Harper & Bros., 1954.

MAYO, ELTON. *Human Problems of an Industrial Civilization*. New York: Macmillan, 1933.

ROETHLISBERGER, F. J., and W. J. DICKSON. *Management and the Worker*. Cambridge, Mass.: Harvard University Press, 1939.

SCHEIN, EDGAR H. *Organizational Psychology*. Englewood Cliffs, N.J.: Prentice-Hall, 1965.

SCHEIN, EDGAR H., and WARREN G. BENNIS. *Personal and Organizational Change Through Group Methods: The Laboratory Approach*. New York: John Wiley & Sons, 1965.

SPENCER, LYLE. "Ten Problems That Worry Presidents." *Harvard Business Review*, November–December 1955, pp. 75–83.

TANNENBAUM, ARNOLD S., ed. *Control in Organizations*. New York: McGraw-Hill, 1968.

TANNENBAUM, ROBERT, IRVING WESCHLER, and FRED MASSARIK. *Leadership and Organization*. New York: McGraw-Hill, 1961.

INDEX

Date Due
